FLINTKNAPPING

FLINTKNAPPING

MAKING AND UNDERSTANDING

STONE TOOLS

JOHN C. WHITTAKER

University of Texas Press • Austin

Requests for permission to reproduce material
from this work should be sent to Permissions,
University of Texas Press
Box 7819, Austin, TX 78713-7819.

⊗ The paper used in this publication meets the
minimum requirements of American National Standard
for Information Sciences—Permanence of Paper for
Printed Library Materials, ANSI Z39.48-1984.

Library of Congress Cataloging-in-Publication Data

Whittaker, John C. (John Charles), date
    Flintknapping : making and understanding stone
tools / by John C. Whittaker.
        p.   cm.
    Includes bibliographical references and index.
    ISBN 0-292-79082-1 (cloth).
    ISBN 0-292-79083-X (paper)
    1. Flintknapping.   2. Stone implements.   I. Title.
GN799.T6W445   1994
930.1'028'5—dc20   93-20729

CONTENTS

ACKNOWLEDGMENTS   ix

1. INTRODUCTION   1
Using This Book   2
Learning to Knap   2

2. FLINTKNAPPING: BASIC PRINCIPLES   11
Flintknapping   11
Conchoidal Fracture   12
Properties of Material   12
Flakes and Cores   14

3. A BRIEF HISTORY OF FLINTKNAPPING   23
Prehistory of Stone Tools   23
Recent "Stone-Age" People   50
Modern Knapping   54
Further Readings   61
Other Resources: Finding Other Knappers   62

4. RAW MATERIALS   65
Stone Quality   65
Stone Materials   67
Heat-Treating   72
Collecting Material: Ethical and Practical Considerations   74

5. SAFETY   79
Proper Technique   80
Eyes   81
Hands   82
Other Body Parts   82
Lungs   82
Waste Disposal   83
Benefits   83

6. HARD-HAMMER PERCUSSION   85
  Material and Equipment   85
  Percussion-Flaking Principles: An Experiment   87
  Percussion Flaking   91
  Platforms   98
  The Face of the Core   105
  Terminations   106
  Curvature   113
  Starting a Core   113
  Summary: Nine Essentials   116
  Examples   116

7. PRESSURE FLAKING   127
  Tools   128
  Raw Material   131
  First Principles   132
  Working Position   134
  Beginning   135
  Platform Preparation   140
  Thinning   147
  Notching   148
  Other Pressure-Flaking Techniques   150
  Summary: Six Essentials   152
  Application: Small Triangular Points from the Southwest   152
  Pressure-Flaking Problems   161
  Patterned Pressure Flaking   166

8. SOFT-HAMMER PERCUSSION AND BIFACES   177
  Definitions   178
  Tools   180
  Beginning   183
  Soft-Hammer Principles and Results   185
  Biface Thinning Flakes   185
  Fracture Theories   188
  The Blow   191
  Platforms   194
  Biface Stages   199
  Knapping Strategy and Other Considerations   206
  Example: A Basic Biface   207
  Biface Problems: Prehistoric Mistakes   212
  Summary   216

9. BLADES AND FLUTING   219
    Blades   219
    Platforms   223
    Holding   225
    Punches   226
    The Blow   228
    Fluting   234
    Example: Fluted Point   237

10. USING STONE TOOLS   243
    Stone vs. Steel   243
    Edges and Cutting   243
    Making a Projectile Foreshaft   248
    Going On   256

11. ARCHAEOLOGICAL ANALYSIS OF STONE TOOLS   259
    Typology   260
    Stone Tool Types and Change through Time   261
    What People Did with Stones   268
    Sources of Variation: Why Stone Tools Are Not All Alike   270
    Analyzing Stone Tool Materials   271
    Technology and What It Tells Us   274
    Figuring Out Function   280
    Questions of Style   289
    Conclusions   298

    APPENDIX: RESOURCES FOR KNAPPERS   301

    REFERENCES   305

    INDEX   337

ACKNOWLEDGMENTS

This book owes so much to so many that I cannot thank them all. Behind my knowledge of stone tools is the accumulated wisdom and skill of those who taught me, and those who went before them, back into the dust of prehistory. François Bordes, Arthur Jelinek, Thomas Lynch, Harold Dibble, and Bruce Huckell are foremost among many knappers and teachers to whom I owe thanks for my lithic training, but ideas have rubbed off on me from dozens of others I have knapped with, watched, or talked to, and I am grateful to them all. Bob Hunt and other knappers at the Fort Osage Knap-ins opened my eyes to the nonacademic side of knapping. Various of my students have served as guinea pigs for my knapping ideas and practical commentators on the manuscript: Rob Feldacker, Jim Harris, Sharon Kramer, Vickie Michener, Alan Miller, Jane Kaufman, Peter McBride, Hans Niehus, and Jay B. Walker. Colleagues who have commented on parts of the manuscript include Phil Chase, Harold Dibble, Kathy Kamp, Ralph Luebben, and Carol Trosset; Thomas Hester and James Woods provided especially useful criticism. I have benefited from all, and where I failed to take their advice, on my own head be it.

Ralph Luebben, who drew most of the diagrams and human figures, was not merely an illustrator, but a collaborator whose help made it possible for me to turn my ideas into a book. Without his help and encouragement I would never have got it done.

Amy Henderson's lithic illustrations added both information and aesthetic quality to the book. Other illustrations and material on which illustrations were based were provided by Errett Callahan, Phil Chase, Harold Dibble, Carl Whittaker, James Woods, the University of Pennsylvania, the Royal Ontario Museum, the Arizona State Museum, and the Western Archaeological and Conservation Center.

Several research grants from Grinnell College between 1984 and 1992 helped support illustrating and other work on this book. Terri Phipps and the other Carnegie secretaries helped with odious tasks like typing bibliographies.

My wife and partner Kathy Kamp has encouraged and inspired me for years, and tolerated chips on the kitchen floor and rocks in the back seat of the car.

1

INTRODUCTION

*If I would study any old, lost art, I must
make myself an artisan of it.*
—F. H. Cushing (1895)

When I was a sophomore in college, I began to fulfill a lifelong ambition to learn how to make stone tools, and even received public recognition for my achievements. Public recognition took the form of being pointed out as the fool who just about cut off his finger trying to make an arrowhead, but that did not discourage me. What was more discouraging was the lack of useful written guides to the subject. Now there are a lot more people making stone tools, and a number of "how to" books that the ordinary reader can find. However, there has never been anything that I consider a really detailed and usable step-by-step guide to learning flintknapping, combined with some basic information on stone tools and how they can be studied. This book attempts to fill that gap.

Why learn such an obscure and obsolete art? I make stone tools first because I am an archaeologist who wants to understand how prehistoric people lived and worked, and second because it is a challenging and enjoyable craft. Making flaked stone tools, or "flintknapping," is the world's oldest documentable craft. It has been continually practiced for almost three million years, by the ancestors of all of us, from australopithecine "ape men" through Neanderthal cave dwellers, American Indians, African tribesmen, Bronze Age farmers of Europe and the Middle East to archaeologists, hobbyists, and a few isolated peoples today. Flaked stone was useful not just to stone-age people everywhere, but well into the industrial age in the form of a few specialized tools, of which gunflints for eighteenth- and nineteenth-century firearms are the best-known example.

I make stone tools partly for entertainment and partly for serious professional purposes of experimentation. I want to know what goes into making a stone knife, how you use it, what it is good for. To most people, arrowheads and the like carry an aura of prehistoric adventure, lost crafts, deadly weapons, and forgotten relationships with nature; stone tools are therefore almost irresistible to anyone with even a passing interest in the past. If you like prehistory, forgotten arts, or developing unusual skills, this is an exotic craft that will not become the overnight fad of everyone in town. At the same time, it requires no unusual strength or abilities to learn the basics. Anyone with normal intelligence and hand-eye coordination can make ordinary stone tools with a little practice. In most stone-age societies, knapping was probably a skill that everyone had.

USING THIS BOOK

This book is intended for that "everyone" who would like to try his or her hand at an ancient skill, for whatever reason. I have tried to write it on a middle level, aimed primarily at the two groups who should find it most useful: students of archaeology and prehistoric technology as well as interested nonarchaeologists. I hope it will be useful both to the serious prehistorian and the weekend hobbyist and everyone in between. I hope that a beginner can use this book to start learning flintknapping, and I have tried to include enough theoretical discussion and advanced material to interest those who have some experience and may want to skip the basics. At the same time, I have tried to avoid being too technical, and to relate everything to the practical problems of making and understanding stone tools.

Despite my efforts to avoid the jargon and stiffness that creeps into much scientific writing, a certain vocabulary is necessary. For words which are essential or in common use by knappers, I give explicit definitions and include these terms in the index so the definition can be found when needed. It is hard to describe actions and motions in words, so I rely heavily on pictures as well. There are a lot of headings so that particular topics can be easily found or skipped. The references in parentheses are authors listed in alphabetical order in the bibliography. Those who want more background, other opinions and techniques, more technical information, or archaeological examples can follow up these sources.

LEARNING TO KNAP

It might be useful to explain how I came to write a book about flintknapping. I almost can't remember not being interested in archaeology. From 1967 to 1969 my family lived in southern California, and in junior high school I found out about the Pacific Coast Archaeological Society, an excellent amateur group. My father, an ecologist, encouraged me to attend some weekend excavations. Sometime in this period my family took a trip to the White Mountains, where I found a very handsome obsidian projectile point. On the way back we stopped at an isolated gas station somewhere in the desert. The owner had a display of arrowheads in a glass case labeled "Some I found, some I made. Guess which." You mean, someone still knows how to make these! Ever since, I have wanted to make stone tools.

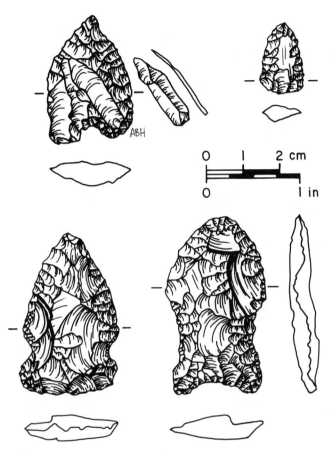

1.1
Four of my first points, made in 1972. The small one is my very first, made of Onondaga chert. The others are bottle glass. The long flake is the one that damaged my finger.

I didn't get anywhere with this for some years, but I continued to do archaeology and became an anthropology student at Cornell University. I found a couple of things in the library there that got me interested again: Mewhinney's *A Manual for Neanderthals* (1957) and Pond's account of the experiments of Halvor Skavlem (Pond 1930). I decided to actually try my hand at making stone tools. I couldn't find any good material around Ithaca, so I broke up some pop bottles. I was very proud of my first crude points (Figure 1.1), but a couple of months into my experiments I managed to drive a pressure flake through my leather glove and into my left index finger. When I pulled off the glove, there was a small cut, less than a quarter of an inch wide, with a glass flake sticking out of it. There was no pain or blood to speak of, but the finger didn't seem to work. The jovial surgeon who worked on my hand kept exclaiming, "I can't believe you severed both the *sublimis* and the *profundis* tendons with that one tiny cut!" The fame I achieved through this did not really make up for the two semesters I spent with my arm in a sling after the surgeon cut me open twice to take a bit of tendon out of my arm and put it in my finger. The accident was my own fault, of course; I was holding the point incorrectly while I flaked it. Now I know better, but my finger still won't completely straighten or clench into a tight fist, which may explain to you why I harp constantly on protecting yourself in the chapters to follow. Once you think you know what you are doing, go ahead and slice yourself if you want, but if you are going to take my advice about flaking, take my advice about safety too.

Anyway, I was back in action by the summer of 1973 and was accepted as a student at Pech de l'Azé IV, a collapsed Mousterian rockshelter in the Dordogne region of France being excavated by François Bordes. François Bordes in Europe and Don Crabtree in the United States are the two men most responsible for the development of flintknapping experimentation as an important part of archaeology. Bordes was a great knapper, but an explosive and temperamental man who was not much interested in teaching beginners. His attitude was encouraging but not actively helpful—when he was in a good mood, you could watch and ask questions as he knapped in the evening, but when things weren't going well, it was best to remain silent. Other knappers also visited Bordes that summer, including Mark Newcomer and Jacques Pelegrin. Between watching and talking to all these people and experimenting on the huge pile of broken flint left by Bordes, I did manage to learn a good deal, and became more interested.

I spent part of the next summer on a dig at Mucking in southern England. Fine flint was easy to find, and for the first time I had as much good material as I could use. I started making bifaces, but hadn't yet figured out how to thin them effectively (Figure 1.2). There followed a period of little progress until I became a graduate student at the University of Arizona.

There I teamed up with Harold Dibble, another new graduate student who was at the same elementary level in learning how to knap. We bought some obsidian from a rock shop, collected more near Flagstaff, and eventually took a trip to Texas, where we rented a U-Haul truck and brought back two tons of good chert. We knapped together a lot, argued and experimented, and with enough time and material at last reached a level of reasonable competence. We experimented with a device that made flakes mechanically so we could observe angles and forces, and in 1979 taught a course in experimental archaeology and knapping. This book actually had its genesis in what I learned from our experiments and attempts to teach knapping, especially a series of handouts that I made for the class.

As I was learning to knap, I was also becoming more involved in using stone tools to solve archaeological problems. The more I saw

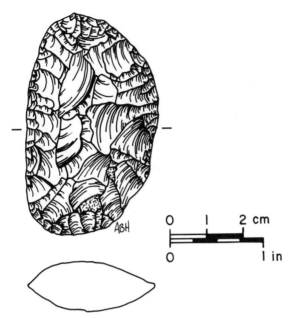

1.2
Small biface of English flint,
1974. It has a metallic sheen
from being carried in my
pocket with coins. I was
proud of it!

stone tools as sources of information about prehistoric people, the more I realized that to understand their place in past lives, I had to know how to make and use them myself.

I would like to point out a couple of morals from this autobiography. First and foremost, there is no substitute for experience, practice, and experimentation. I don't pretend that this book will teach you how to flintknap—you will teach yourself if you learn at all. I can save you some time and some trial-and-error suffering by pointing in the right direction and explaining what I think is important. Reading other books and examining stone tools will help too. Most important, practice and pay attention to what you do. Observe your own work carefully and think about what worked and what did not, and try different things.

Working with other people is also very valuable. At any level of skill, watching another knapper will give you ideas. If you can find someone more advanced to coach you, so much the better. Even two beginners working together will learn faster than either one of them alone.

Finding material to flake and time to flake it are likely to be your biggest obstacles. This brings us back to practice—it takes a lot of time and material to get good. I can't do anything about how busy you are, but I have tried to help with the problem of material by explaining things so that you can begin learning, and may even make fairly showy pieces, without having to go farther than your backyard and hardware store for material and equipment.

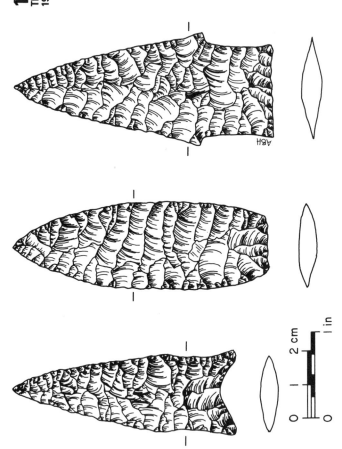

1.3 Three of my recent points, 1992.

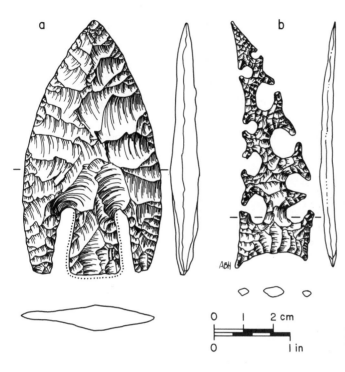

1.4
Representative points by American knappers of the 1970s knapping boom. Points by (a) J. B. Sollberger and (b) Gene Titmus. Redrawn with permission from drawings by Errett Callahan, originally published in *Flintknappers' Exchange,* 1978–1980.

a   b

ABH

0   1   2 cm

0   1 in

In using this book, if you are a relatively inexperienced knapper, I recommend quickly reading as much as possible, even though you will not remember it all. Then, as you begin to work and learn, flip back to relevant sections. More and more of it will make sense, explain what you are beginning to see, or lead you to try something new.

Whenever you can, examine the work of other knappers. The illustrations here and in other books are a start; museum collections, casts, and friends' work are even better. Once you know a little bit, examining a stone tool carefully can teach you almost as much as talking to its maker. This is in fact one of the reasons I enjoy knapping, and my point of view throughout the book. Stone tools are interesting partly because they speak to us of other people, other times.

The difference between my first hideous points (Figure 1.1) and those I make now (Figure 1.3) is striking, but the major development of my skill really took only about a year and was mostly self-taught. However, I continue to learn, and this is also part of the fun. Although I am now familiar with a wider range of techniques and tool forms than most prehistoric knappers would have been, my skills are far below those of many knappers, both past and current.

Figures 1.4 and 1.5 present a few examples of modern stone work,

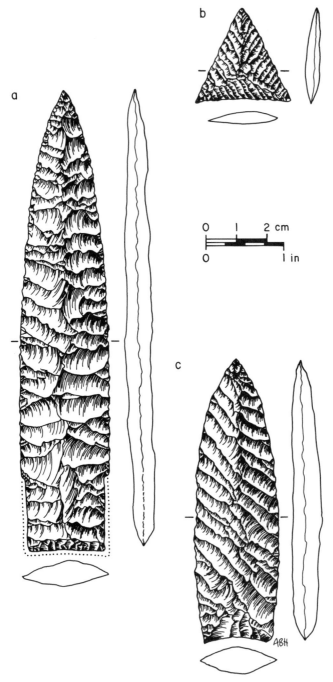

1.5
Representative points by American knappers of the 1970s knapping boom. Points by (a) Jeff Flenniken, (b) Don Crabtree, and (c) Rob Bonnichsen. Redrawn with permission from drawings by Errett Callahan, originally published in *Flintknappers' Exchange*, 1978–1980.

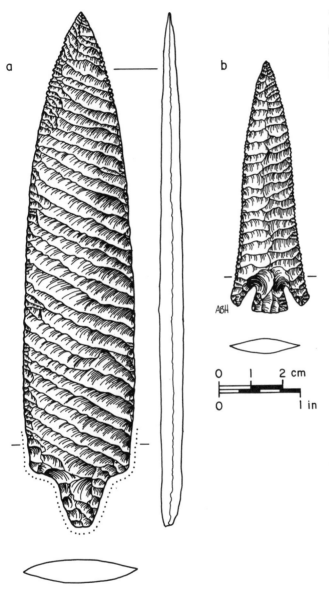

Recent "art" points: (a)
obsidian "Sabertooth" blade
by Errett Callahan, 1988; (b)
pressure-flaked point by Jim
Hopper, 1990.

five pieces by well-known knappers of the great knapping revival of the
1970s. The two points in Figure 1.6 are contemporary pieces representing the attempt of some current knappers to take knapping beyond
replication of prehistoric pieces to new levels of technical perfection
and artistry. Let these inspire you—how far you go is up to you.

2
FLINTKNAPPING: BASIC PRINCIPLES

*But as regards flint fracture there is no excuse
for ignorance on the part of any prehistorians.
Any one can fracture flints in various ways
and take note of the results achieved, and in
the opinion of the author, no one who has not
so fractured flint is in spirit and in truth a
serious student of prehistory.*

—J. Reid Moir (1917:381)

Most knappers learn through experience and flake by feel, and we always have. A Paleolithic hunter knew nothing about shock waves moving through a brittle solid and did not measure the angle of the platform, but with a practiced eye and a calloused hand he could judge what would work and what would fail. However, if we want to discuss stone tools, some understanding of basic principles and terminology is necessary. It is true that you don't have to know all the principles to make the techniques work, but it is a lot easier for me to explain *how* to make things work if you know a little bit about *why* they work. Some other more technical discussions are referenced.

FLINTKNAPPING

Flintknapping is the most common name for the ancient craft of making flaked stone tools. According to the Oxford English Dictionary (Oxford University Press 1971:1544), the word *knap* ("to break into parts or pieces with a sharp cracking sound, to snap or break by a smart blow") came into English from the Germanic or Gaelic languages. By the early 1800s it was being applied to breaking flint for building stone and for gunflints. Specifically, among the British gunflint makers (Skertchly 1879), the knapper was the man or boy who produced finished gunflints by breaking (knapping) long flakes into short sections. This was also the time when archaeology was developing as a science, and stone tools were being recognized as the artifacts of prehistoric humans, so the term was also applied to the prehistoric stone workers.

Modern flintknappers also refer to the craft as knapping, flaking, or chipping. Many archaeological knappers also like to distinguish between *flintknapping,* which can mean making stone tools for any purpose, using a variety of tools and techniques which may or may not have been used prehistorically, and *replication,* which implies not just producing a copy of a prehistoric stone tool, but working with the same tools and techniques that were used in the past (as near as we can tell from available evidence) and producing the same kinds of waste flakes as well (e.g., Crabtree 1973a). It is also important to note that not all stone tools were made by knapping. Some, like axes, grinding stones, and ornaments, were made by pecking or grinding and polishing, technologies that I will not deal with in this book.

CONCHOIDAL FRACTURE

If you have ever seen a window shot with a BB, you have seen the basic principle of stone flaking at work. Stone that can be flaked breaks with a conchoidal fracture more or less like glass, depending on the quality of the material. *Conchoidal fracture* means shell-like—in other words, the fracture surfaces are curved like a cockle shell. In the ideal case of a BB striking a window, a perfect cone is punched out of the opposite side of the window pane (Figure 2.1). This is called a *Hertzian cone.* By changing the forces, the angles, and the shapes of the surfaces involved, the shape and direction of the conical fracture can be controlled, and a piece of rock fractured in desirable ways. The principles of conchoidal fracture are fairly inflexible and must be understood and controlled— my younger brother was not content with a small conical hole in a window and thought he might be able to get a slot instead by shooting a penny at the window with a slingshot. Needless to say, it didn't work, and he produced not just a small conchoidal fracture, but a shattered window and the wrath of God as delivered by my father.

PROPERTIES OF MATERIAL

In Chapter 4 I will talk more about different kinds of stone and their qualities. For the moment, I want to consider only the basic properties of material that are necessary for making flaked stone tools.

Stones that fracture conchoidally and are thus desirable for flaking share several properties: they are homogeneous, brittle, and elastic. *Homogeneous* means that they are the same throughout, lacking differences in texture, cracks, planes, flaws, and irregularities. Stone that is not homogeneous may not fracture conchoidally, and cracks, cleavage planes, and other flaws may make a stone break unpredictably or in undesirable directions. In general, the more homogeneous a stone is, the better it flakes.

Manmade glass is the most homogeneous stone available, although

a

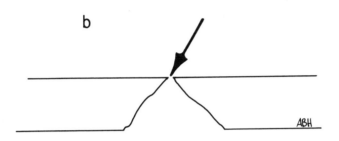

b

c

2.1
Hertzian cone in window glass: (a) detached cone; (b) cross-section showing blow; (c) cone from above.

some obsidians, which are natural volcanic glasses, come close. Other stones vary greatly in texture and composition, and the fact that they are not perfectly homogeneous is one of the obstacles that the knapper must overcome in making a stone tool. Most knappable stones have *amorphous* or *cryptocrystalline* structures. The minerals of which they are formed (mostly silica, SiO_2) either have not formed crystals (amorphous, like glass) or have formed into networks of microscopic crystals not visible to the naked eye (cryptocrystalline or microcrystalline, like flint). Quartz can form into large crystals of relatively pure silica that may be colored by trace elements, as in amethyst, for instance. Large individual quartz crystals can be flaked because they are internally amorphous, but rocks like granite, which are made up of many large crystals of different materials, are usually not flakeable.

Brittle means that the rock breaks relatively easily and cannot be deformed (bent, compressed) very much without breaking. *Elastic* appears to contradict this, but technically elasticity means only that if not deformed too much (to the breaking point) a material will return to its original shape. A rubber ball is elastic—you can squeeze it and it will spring back to shape. Drop a glass marble on a cement floor and watch it bounce—the same thing has happened, although you can't see it. The difference is that, although you can flatten a rubber ball and it will return to its original shape, you cannot deform a glass marble as much because it is brittle as well as elastic. The marble will shatter if it hits the floor hard enough, but it is difficult to break a rubber ball by striking it. Obviously, then, brittleness is necessary if stone is going to be flaked.

With these properties in mind, we can proceed to discuss some of the characteristics of flaked stone tools. Different stones and other materials will be discussed later.

FLAKES AND CORES

The *core* is the piece you strike, and the *flake* is the piece that comes off (Figure 2.2). If you look at the interior or fracture surface of the flake, you will usually see certain features (Figure 2.3). Some people call the interior and exterior surfaces of a flake the *ventral* (belly) and *dorsal* (back) surfaces. These terms are borrowed from biology and bring to mind an image of little scurrying flint animals, so I will avoid them.

The flat surface at the top of the flake, where the blow fell, is called the *platform*. This is the *proximal* end of the flake, while the opposite end is the *distal* end. By convention, flakes and flake tools are usually illustrated with the platform down; I have ignored this convention from time to time since flakes are actually struck with the platform up and are thus easier to visualize in this position.

If the blow was struck with a hard stone hammer, there is often a small crushed area, or *point of percussion,* on the platform. There may also be a small round crack, called a *ring crack,* which is the top of the Hertzian cone (think of the outer hole in the BB-shot window). Beneath this on the interior fracture surface of the flake, you may or may not see an edge of the cone itself, before it spreads out to become the *bulb of percussion,* a "swelling" just below the platform. Farther down, there are often *ripples* which center on the bulb and point of percussion. In some ways, the force of a blow and the crack that results from it move through a piece of material the way waves move through water, and the ripples resemble the ripples around a stone thrown into a pond. Actually, it is more complicated than this, but what actually happens inside a stone in the instant when it is fractured is poorly

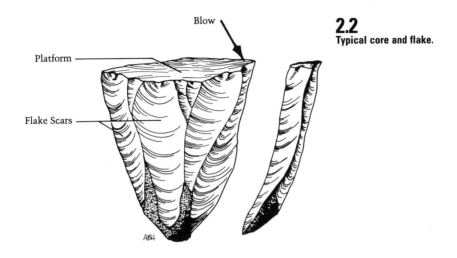

Blow

Platform

Flake Scars

ABH

2.2
Typical core and flake.

understood and not very relevant here. There are a number of useful discussions of fracture mechanics and related topics for those who want to know more (e.g., Cotterell and Kamminga 1979, 1987; Dibble and Whittaker 1981; Faulkner 1972; Luedtke 1992; Moffat 1981; Sollberger 1986; Speth 1972; Tsirk 1979).

In the conventions of lithic illustration, flake scars are often shaded with curved lines that approximate the ripples and indicate the direction from which the flake was removed. There are excellent discussions of lithic illustration by Chase (1985) and Addington (1986).

Other features commonly seen on the interior surface of flakes include radial fissures and parasitic flake scars. *Radial fissures,* also called *hackles,* are tiny cracks that point back toward the point of percussion. *Parasitic flake scars,* or *eraillures,* are left when a small leaf-shaped flake pops off the bulb of percussion when the flake is struck.

There is a lot of variation in the size, shape, and presence of some of these features, which sometimes tell a lot about how a flake was made. In particular, flakes struck from a bifacial tool like a handaxe with a soft hammer of antler or bone often have bulbs and platforms that are a bit different from those of the typical hard-hammer flakes just described. This will be discussed in Chapter 8.

All of these features of a flake's interior surface (except the eraillures) leave an exact negative impression on the core from which the flake was struck. You can tell a lot about the flakes a knapper made by looking at the size, shape, and direction of flake scars on the cores that were left behind. The back, or exterior, surface of a flake often shows

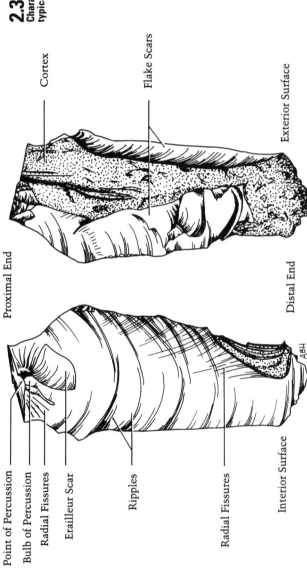

Point of Percussion

Bulb of Percussion

Radial Fissures

Erailleur Scar

Ripples

Radial Fissures

Interior Surface

Proximal End

Distal End

Cortex

Flake Scars

Exterior Surface

2.3
**Characteristic features of a
typical flake.**

the scars of previous flakes. On some flakes the exterior surface may be partly or completely *cortical*, that is, covered with *cortex*. Cortex is the "rind," the rough weathered surface of a nodule of chert or a piece of some other material. The cortex of chert and flint is often calcareous from the chalk or limestone in which the chert formed. The presence of cortex on the exterior of a flake often indicates that the flake was one of the first flakes struck from a core.

Core exteriors and platform surfaces often show signs of blows that did not remove flakes. These can be the result of mistakes by the knapper or the effects of natural forces such as rivers and rock falls that move rocks around and bash them together. Edges become chipped, crushed, worn, and rounded. Blows on a flat surface frequently produce an *incipient cone* that extends down into the material and is visible on the surface as a *ring crack* or, more colloquially, a *peephole*. The surface of a cobble that has been rolled in a river is often roughened by thousands of incipient cones.

Natural forces also produce flakes that look very much like those struck by human knappers. Rivers, coasts, cliffs, talus slopes, mud slides, trampling by animals or vehicles—any situation where the right kinds of rocks are in motion and striking each other or being struck or crushed will produce a small number of random flakes. Although some of these flakes may look manmade, it is usually easy to tell natural flaking from tool making. Natural flaking tends to be random, while human work is regular and patterned. In late archaeological sites with complex and stereotyped tools, there is little chance of mistake—handaxes, arrowheads, and even scrapers are usually unmistakable. However, some of the very early stone tools are so crude that they might be difficult to identify, if not for the fact that they occur in groups and are found with other identifiable remains. In a number of cases, naturally fractured rocks have been mistaken for human tools, as in the case of the eoliths discussed in Chapter 3 and at the Calico site in California (Payen 1982; Simpson 1982).

Flake *terminations* are also important to the knapper. The termination refers to the distal end and edges of a flake, and there are four main types (Figure 2.4; see also Crabtree 1972a; Cotterell et al. 1979). *Feather terminations* are most common and usually most desirable. Here the force and resulting crack that separates the flake from the core exit smoothly from the material, peeling off a flake with a sharp "feathered" edge. In a *hinge termination*, the fracture surface turns sharply upward, forming a rounded "hinge" on the end of the flake. A *step fracture* terminates the flake in a right-angled break. This usually means the flake was broken, and the original force and crack may have continued into the core, with or without completing the removal of

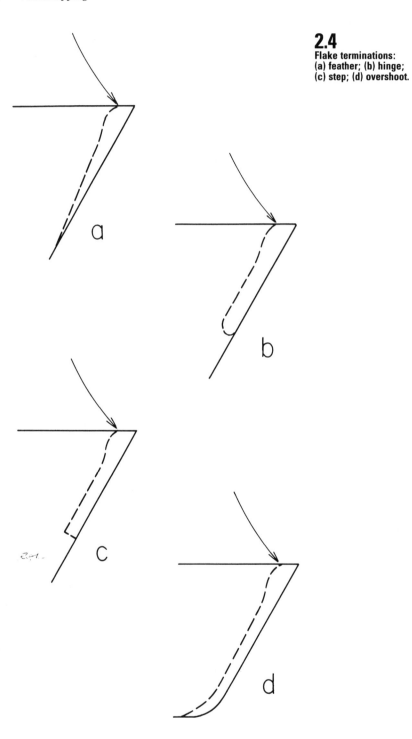

2.4
Flake terminations:
(a) feather; (b) hinge;
(c) step; (d) overshoot.

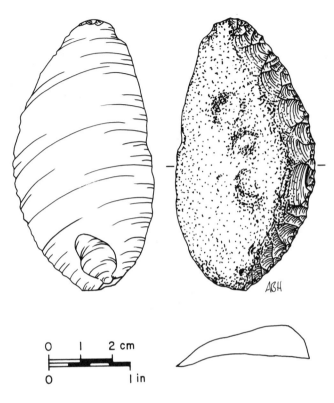

2.5
Unifacial retouch: a side scraper of chert. Most of the exterior surface is cortex, and flakes have been removed only from this face.

O I   2 cm

O   I in

the rest of the flake. In an *overshoot* or *outrepassé* the force and crack continues to the end of the core and then, instead of exiting on the core surface, bends downward and removes part of the end of the core. Reasons for these different terminations will be discussed later.

Both flakes and cores are often modified by *retouching* them. Retouching is a vague term that can cover almost any later modification, but it usually means removing small flakes from the edges and faces. Retouch may be *unifacial*, on only one face or surface of a tool (Figure 2.5), or *bifacial*, on both faces (Figure 2.6). Nothing is so sharp as a fresh, unretouched flake with a good feather termination. The most homogeneous materials like glass and obsidian will flake to edges that are only a few molecules thick, far sharper than a razor. In fact, several archaeologists, including Don Crabtree (Crabtree and Callahan 1979; McIlrath 1984; Buck 1982), have had surgery performed on them by surgeons they convinced to try obsidian tools. The incredibly sharp edges of obsidian blades produce precision cuts which heal with little scarring, and several knappers (Callahan, Flenniken, Sheets; see McIlrath 1984) have been trying to produce and market obsidian blades for medical uses. If you try cutting with stone tools (see Chapter 10), you

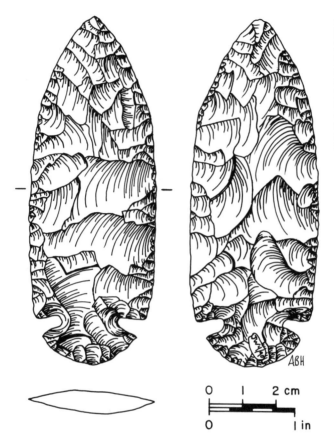

2.6
Bifacial retouch: a large point of black rhyolite, worked on both faces with an antler baton (large flake scars) and finished with pressure retouch (small flake scars) along the edges and for notching. All traces of the original flake's shape and surfaces have been removed.

will find that for many purposes they are just as effective as steel. The major disadvantages of stone tools are that they dull faster and break more easily. Retouching an edge often makes it somewhat duller but usually thicker and stronger as well; it also changes the shape of the tool and the shape of the edge to make a stronger, more useful tool.

Although we are most often interested in the tool itself, making a stone tool produces a lot of byproducts. The waste products of making stone tools can be referred to as *debitage*. As you will see when you try it, making even a simple stone tool produces a surprising amount of debitage (Figure 2.7). Some of it is in the form of flakes, which may be useful as tools, or as blanks to be retouched into tools. Other flakes are too small, too misshapen, or otherwise too flawed to be useful. Many flakes are broken, some so badly that none of the flake features discussed above can be seen. Sometimes flaws in the material or other problems mean that parts of the core break up into angular chunks instead of flakes. Flaking debris that does not show the usual features

2.7
Levallois core and flake and the debitage removed in making them.

of flakes is called *shatter*. Debitage also includes dust and very small flakes and shatter that are so tiny they are not usually found by archaeologists.

The words *chip* and *spall* should be avoided. Both are used carelessly as synonyms of flake. Flakes have special characteristics that are not implied for chips. The older anthropological literature referred to spalls and flakes interchangeably, but spall is now properly confined to a type of specialized flake, the *burin spall*, which will be described later.

Although it may not be of much use to the knapper, debitage is often all the archaeologist finds to work with. Fortunately, as we will see in later chapters, different flaking techniques produce different kinds of debris, and the archaeologist who recovers the debitage can usually say a lot about what prehistoric knappers were making, even if they were so inconsiderate as to take the useful tools with them.

3
A BRIEF HISTORY
OF FLINTKNAPPING

*Implements of flint such as axes, knives,
weapon points, etc., are called by the peas-
antry by the singular name of thunder-
stones . . . ; they believe that these flints,
which are not common in these parts, have
fallen down in thunderstorms.*
—Dean S. Rost (Swedish scholar, in 1808,
quoted in Blinkenberg 1911:73)

Only a few generations ago, stone tools were unknown to most people,
or completely misunderstood. Now we are familiar with a number of
ways in which stone can be flaked and an almost infinite variety of
different stone tools. These were developed over hundreds of thousands
of years to meet the needs of our ancestors. The best way to introduce
the basic techniques of flintknapping, put some of the kinds of stone
tools mentioned later in their places, and squeeze in a bit of archaeology as well is to discuss flintknapping techniques as a sequence of in-
ventions at different stages in the evolution of humans and their culture. This sequence is summarized in Figure 3.1 and described below.
Since I am cramming three million years of prehistory into a few pages,
it is necessary to oversimplify a bit. If you want more details, good
starting points are Oakley's *Man the Tool-maker* (1964) or similar
books by Bordaz (1970) and Watson and Sieveking (1968), which are
now outdated but emphasize stone tools, any recent college text in
physical anthropology or archaeology (e.g., Campbell 1985; Fagan
1983; Jolly and Plog 1979; Jurmain, Nelson, and Turnbaugh 1984; Pfeiffer 1985), or one of the recent popular accounts of human evolution
(Gowlett 1984; Howell 1965; Lewin 1988).

PREHISTORY OF STONE TOOLS
Between two and three million years ago, the first stone tools appear
in African sites (Lewin 1981). They are associated with the fossils of
hominids, of which there are several forms in two major groups, the
Australopithecines and early *Homo*. A robust form of *Australopithe-*

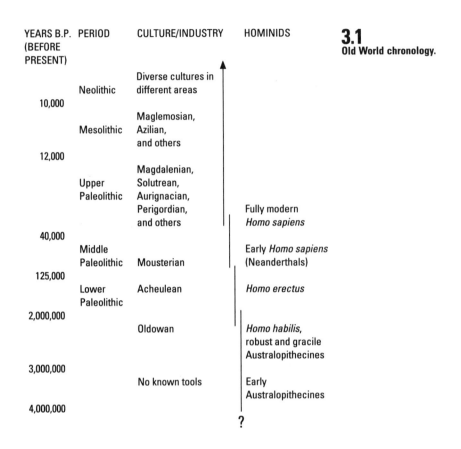

YEARS B.P. (BEFORE PRESENT)	PERIOD	CULTURE/INDUSTRY	HOMINIDS
	Neolithic	Diverse cultures in different areas	
10,000			
	Mesolithic	Maglemosian, Azilian, and others	
12,000			
	Upper Paleolithic	Magdalenian, Solutrean, Aurignacian, Perigordian, and others	Fully modern *Homo sapiens*
40,000			
	Middle Paleolithic	Mousterian	Early *Homo sapiens* (Neanderthals)
125,000			
	Lower Paleolithic	Acheulean	*Homo erectus*
2,000,000			
		Oldowan	*Homo habilis*, robust and gracile Australopithecines
3,000,000			
		No known tools	Early Australopithecines
4,000,000			?

3.1
Old World chronology.

cus, which included at least two variants, *Australopithecus robustus* and *A. boisei*, was the largest, with heavy teeth and jaws that indicate a diet of vegetables and seeds. *Australopithecus africanus* was a smaller species, about the size of a large chimpanzee, and probably had a more omnivorous diet. *Homo habilis* was similar to *Australopithecus africanus*, but with a larger brain and some other differences that have led most scientists to classify it in the genus *Homo*, implying that it is the form most likely to be the ancestor of modern humans. All of these creatures walked upright and had bodies that in many ways were anatomically similar to ours, although their skulls and faces were more apelike and their brains were small compared with ours. They could probably use sticks, stones, and bones as tools, like the modern chimpanzees that stick twigs into termite holes to fish for termites. *Homo habilis* was presumably taking the next step and making more complicated tools by modifying natural materials; the others may have been as well.

The only definite tools that have survived are the stone tools. At this point they are very simple, no more than a pebble which has been struck with another pebble to remove a few flakes and make a sharp edge. These are called *pebble tools, cobble tools,* or *choppers* and are characteristic of the Oldowan industry (Figure 3.2). Archaeologically speaking, an *industry* is a group of different types of tools that commonly occur together at many sites and are characteristic of a particular time or area. They are usually named after a site; thus the name Oldowan comes from Olduvai Gorge in Africa, the site of Louis and Mary Leakey's pioneering finds of Australopithecines. An *assemblage* is the group of tools found at a particular site, or a particular level in a site. Thus we might describe the assemblage from site FLK in Olduvai Gorge as including typical tools of the Oldowan industry.

Choppers and the flakes struck off in making them are not very impressive tools, and they are almost certainly not weapons. If you hit someone with a sharpened stone in your hand, you will do some damage, but a simple club or sharp stick is more effective. In any case, the view of our early ancestors as "killer apes," which was popularized by the prehistorian Raymond Dart (1967) and journalist Robert Ardrey (1961), was based on faulty interpretations. *Homo habilis* and related "ape-men" probably relied mostly on gathering plant foods, catching small animals, and scavenging from the kills of lions and other carnivores rather than hunting big game themselves.

However simple the earliest stone tools are, they are still better than teeth and fingernails, as you can prove to yourself if you care to try any of the experiments discussed in Chapter 10. They gave the early hominids two major advantages. First, they made it possible to work on other materials—in other words, to make other tools. Stones are the beginning point of much primitive technology. With two stones, you can make one into a tool with sharp edges that can be used to work other materials like wood. This technique of course became more and more important as humans evolved. Second, and perhaps more important at the time, stone tools made it easier to collect and process some kinds of food, particularly high-energy and high-protein animal meat and fat. It is not hard to pull apart a rabbit with your bare hands, but even if you are scavenging other creatures' kills, it is difficult to get much out of an antelope if you don't have stone tools to cut the tough hide, disjoint legs to carry off, and crack bones for marrow, which seems to have been what our ancestors were doing (Binford 1981; Blumenschine and Cavallo 1992).

Sometime around 1.9 million years ago, the human ancestors in Africa evolved into a larger-brained form that is different enough to merit a new name, *Homo erectus.* Stone tool technology was developing at

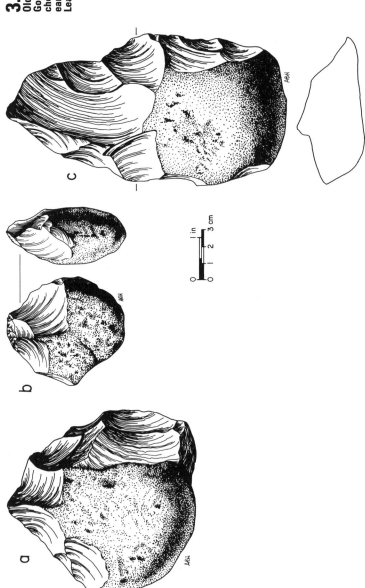

3.2 Oldowan tools from Olduvai Gorge, Beds 1 and 2: two chopping tools (a, b) and an early handaxe (c). After Leakey (1971).

the same time to the point where, instead of making a sharp edge with a few blows, a rock was worked into a definite shape, and most of the edge sharpened. These *handaxes* (Figure 3.3) were the typical tool of the Acheulean industries after about 900,000 years ago in Europe and Africa. Some, especially the earlier ones, were made by *hard-hammer* percussion—that is, striking the tool with another stone to remove flakes. Later, many Acheulean industries relied heavily on *soft-hammer* flaking, using a bone or antler hammer to strike off flakes. Flakes struck with a soft hammer tend to be wider and flatter, with smaller bulbs of percussion. This makes it possible to produce a thinner, flatter handaxe with straighter, sharper edges.

At this point I may as well say something about the way archaeologists name stone tools. Many stone tool types (e.g., handaxe, scraper, arrowhead) are given names that imply a use. Most often this is pure speculation by some early archaeologist. Calling something a handaxe does not really mean that a particular tool was used like an axe, or even that a particular type of tool was usually used for chopping. In the case of handaxes, we can be quite sure that they were not used to cut down trees, because we can try it and see that they are just not useful as hand-held felling axes. Handaxes were more likely general-purpose tools used for butchering, but also suitable for digging, shaping wood, and a variety of other tasks (e.g., Keeley 1980). I will return to the question of how the archaeologist decides what a stone tool was used for in the last chapter. For the moment, remember that the name given to a type of stone tool implies a certain shape, techniques of manufacture, and so forth, but it should not be taken to mean that we have a clear understanding of its use.

In any case, Acheulean industries include handaxes and the large flakes removed from them, which make very good sharp tools, plus flakes struck from other cores. The flakes may be *retouched* or modified by flaking into a number of other tool types. The most common of these are *scrapers*, which are unifacially retouched tools with a steep, wide-angled edge that is suitable for a number of tasks, including scraping hides, planing wood or bone, and cutting like a knife.

While the Acheulean industries emphasized handaxes, other industries associated with human ancestors at this time emphasized heavy flake tools (the Clactonian in England) or simpler chopping tools (some of the Asian industries). We also have definite evidence of wooden tools that were worked with stone, including what is probably a spear from the site of Clacton (Oakley et al. 1977). Such finds are extremely rare, since wood and other organic remains usually decay rapidly. *Homo erectus* built simple brush structures or tents for shelter and may have made and controlled fire (de Lumley 1969; Eiseley 1954; James 1989; Straus 1989).

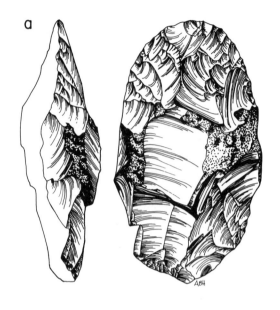

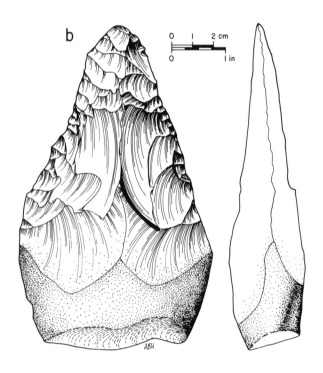

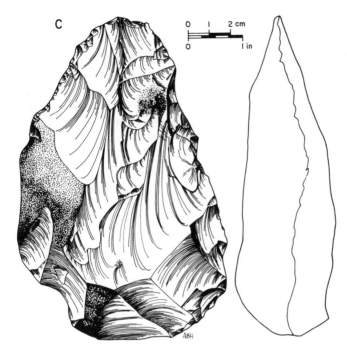

c

0 1 2 cm

0   1 in

3.3
Four Acheulean handaxes:
(a) Stoke Newington,
London, England;
(b) France; (c) Amiens,
France—rather crude,
probably made by hard-
hammer percussion; (d)
Galley Hill, Swanscombe,
England—heavily patinated
and water-worn. University
of Pennsylvania (a, c) and
Royal Ontario Museum (b, d)
specimens.

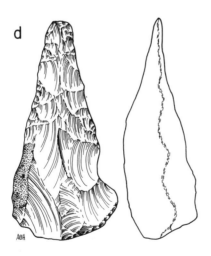

d

The stone tools themselves are also evidence of increasing intelligence. Handaxes are far more complex than Oldowan choppers and require complex hand-eye coordination, a controlled sequence of flaking, and some ability to think abstractly, visualizing the possibility of turning a rock into a complicated, consistent, and not-yet-existing tool. These tools embody some abstract geometrical relationships producing symmetry in shape and cross-section (Wynn 1985; Gowlett 1984). This cannot be taken to mean that early human ancestors discussed Euclidian geometry, or even that they had very much of our ability to use language and symbols, but their behavior was complexly patterned and involved some degree of forethought.

Some 100,000 years ago or so, our ancestors evolved into what is popularly known as *Neanderthal* man. Neanderthals and other humans of their time are usually classified as *Homo sapiens*—that is, the same species as all modern people. Their bodies and physical abilities seem to have been essentially the same as ours, and we no longer see them as bent-legged ape-men (Trinkhaus and Howells 1979). There are some physical differences, including heavy brow ridges over the eyes, and large, strong bones that indicate stocky, muscular people. Their brains averaged a bit larger than ours, and there is evidence that they cared for old and crippled members of their groups and occasionally buried their dead with care (Solecki 1971), suggesting some degree of self-awareness and social order. Nevertheless, their intelligence may have been of a different kind than ours—there is no art, no use of pictorial symbols, and very little change in Neanderthal cultures over more than 50,000 years. Whatever the nature of their intelligence, they succeeded in surviving for 50,000 years in a very rugged world, enduring several major climatic changes, and spreading all over the parts of the Old World that were not under glaciers.

The Neanderthals are usually associated with a group of industries called *Mousterian*. Mousterian industries all emphasize flake tools, especially scrapers, although handaxes survive in some. Different Mousterian industries, sometimes in the same site, have consistent differences in the number of scrapers and other kinds of tools. The differences may reflect some change through time, different tribes or social groups living at the same time (Bordes 1972), or sites where different activities were being performed, each using a particular set of tools (Binford and Binford 1969). Probably all of these explanations are partly true, but this remains one of the longest-running arguments in archaeology today (Binford 1983) and will be discussed further in the last chapter.

Mousterian tool kits emphasize a variety of scrapers, usually made on large flakes (Figures 3.4, 3.5). Some with serrated or toothed edges are called *denticulates*. The *Levallois* technique, aimed at striking a

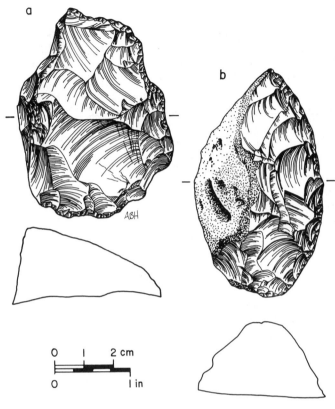

3.4
Two French Mousterian scrapers on thick flakes: (a) denticulate, La Quina; (b) side scraper of Quina type, Pech de Bourre. University of Pennsylvania specimens.

single large flake from a carefully prepared core, is also common in some Mousterian sites (Figure 3.5c, d). It is described in detail in Chapter 6 (Figures 6.41–6.47). The importance of the Levallois technique is that the preparation of the core allows a flake to be made with a predetermined shape. Most ordinary hard-hammer flakes have some blunt or irregular edges. A properly made Levallois flake has sharp, useful edges all the way around it except at the platform. It is an ideal cutting tool as it stands, or it can be modified to make a scraper or other retouched tool. Some of the triangular flakes called Levallois points (Figure 3.5d) could have been hafted as spear points, although the evidence that any Mousterian tools were hafted is controversial (Holdaway 1989; Shea 1988).

About 40,000 years ago, the last Neanderthals gave way to humans who were fully modern physically, and probably mentally. At least, the new cultures at this time are vastly more varied and innovative, and change much more rapidly. The cave paintings of this Upper Paleolithic period are amazing works of art and show the capacity to communicate and think symbolically. Bone tools such as needles, awls, and

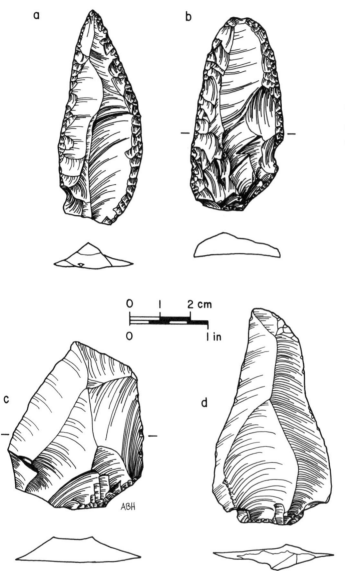

3.5
Mousterian tools:
(a) convergent scraper or
Mousterian point, Warwasi,
Iran; (b) convergent scraper,
Pech de Bourre, France;
(c) Levallois flake, Castel
Merle, France; (d) Levallois
flake or point, Bisitun, Iran.
Note the similarity of tools
from Europe and Western
Asia. University of
Pennsylvania specimens.

0   1   2 cm

0   1 in

harpoon heads are made for the first time, and there is evidence for increasing variety in the kinds of foods hunted and collected.

Upper Paleolithic stone tools change rapidly through time, compared with earlier industries, and there are more different local traditions, but most Upper Paleolithic industries include a large number of tools made on blades. A *blade* is technically defined as any flake that is more than twice as long as it is wide, with more or less parallel edges (Bordes 1961; Crabtree 1972a). Most archaeologists use the term to imply flakes that are intentionally made this way, and are relatively consistent and even. Long, straight flakes that are not typical of an industry and may be pretty much accidental are often called *blade-flakes*.

Blade making will be discussed in Chapter 9. A number of techniques can be used to make blades, but in the Upper Paleolithic many blades seem to represent the invention of a new technique, indirect percussion. In *indirect percussion* a punch of antler or wood or other hard material is placed on the platform and struck with a hammer, instead of striking the stone directly with the hammer. This allows the force to be directed very precisely, an important factor in making blades, which require a carefully prepared core with an even platform and regular ridges for the blades to follow.

Upper Paleolithic blades with long, straight cutting edges (Figures 3.6, 3.7) are excellent tools, even without retouch, and ideal blanks for making other tools, such as end-scrapers, spear points, and burins. *Burins* are tools made by striking off a retouch flake that runs along the edge of the flake and removes the edge, leaving a steep or even right-angled edge. The strong, steep edges and sharp points of burins are good for scraping and engraving hard materials such as bone, antler, and wood (Movius 1968; Semenov 1973; Crabtree 1973b; see also Chapter 6).

Soft-hammer percussion work on bifaces was very refined in some Upper Paleolithic cultures and lacking in others. The most famous examples are the "laurel leaf" points found in some Solutrean sites in France. These were apparently spear points and knives, but some are so large and fragile that they were probably more art, ceremonial, or prestige pieces than working tools (see Figure 8.15). Only expert knappers could have made such pieces, but most are more ordinary (Figure 3.8).

Some Upper Paleolithic projectile points and other tools were finished by pressure flaking (Figure 3.7c). *Pressure flaking* (Chapter 7) involves removing flakes from the edge of a tool by pressing against it, usually with an antler or bone tool, instead of striking it. Pressure flaking is generally used for the final retouch on tools that were begun by other techniques.

After the Upper Paleolithic, different kinds of blades continued to be

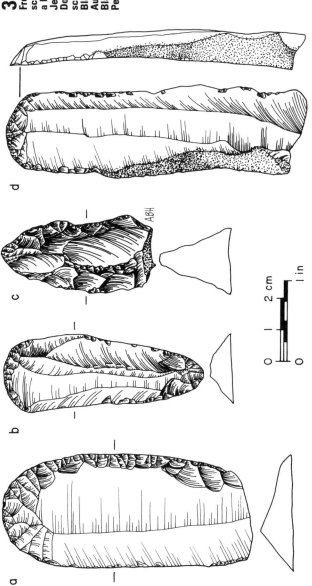

3.6
French Upper Paleolithic scrapers: (a) end scraper on a backed blade, Solutrean at Jean-Blanc; (b) end scraper, Dordogne area; (c) keeled scraper, Aurignacian at Abri Blanchard; (d) end scraper, Aurignacian at Abri Blanchard. University of Pennsylvania specimens.

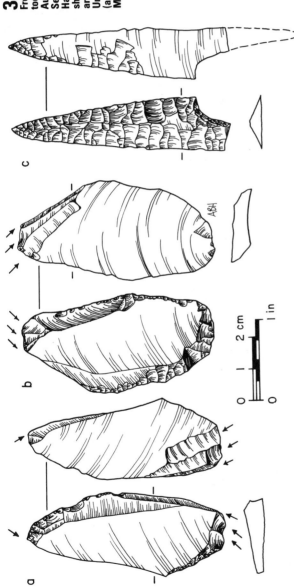

3.7
French Upper Paleolithic tools: (a) burin, Upper Aurignacian at Roches de Sergeau; (b) burin, Laugerie Haute; (c) Solutrean shouldered point. Small arrows indicate burin blows. University of Pennsylvania (a, b) and Royal Ontario Museum (c) specimens.

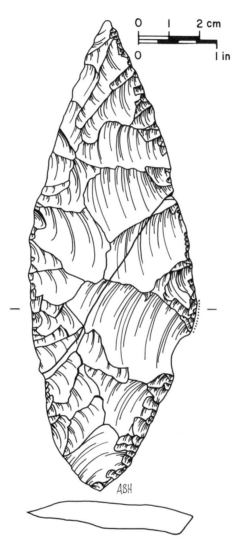

0 — 1 — 2 cm

0 — 1 in

3.8
Solutrean "Laurel Leaf" from
Le Ruth, France, ca.
20,000–16,000 B.C., made of
white flint. The notch is a
knapping error. The remnant
of ground platform (indicated
by dots) and the fracture
(heavy diagonal line)
suggest that this specimen
was never quite finished.
Drawn from Lithic Casting
Lab Cast SL-1, original
in American Museum of
Natural History.

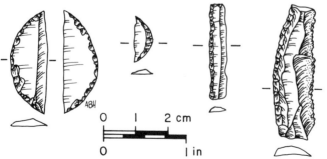

3.9
Four microliths made from
small blade segments, from
the Natufian site of El Wad,
Palestine, ca. 10,000 B.C. The
large toothed specimen is
stippled to indicate polish
from use as a sickle blade.
Royal Ontario Museum
specimens.

0 — 1 — 2 cm

0 — 1 in

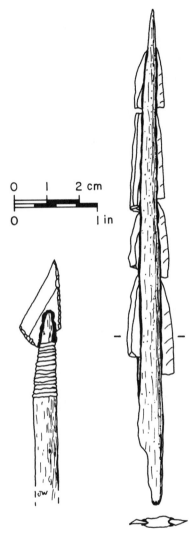

3.10
Hafted microliths: an arrow point (after Tringham 1971) and a reconstructed Mesolithic projectile point from a Scandinavian bog (after Montelius 1888; Clark 1975).

the most important flaked stone tools. During the Mesolithic, after the last of the major glaciers had retreated from Europe, a number of cultures in Europe and the Middle East made microlithic tools. *Microliths* are very small stone artifacts usually made from sections of small blades (Figure 3.9). They were too small to be used by themselves and would have been set into wooden or bone handles to make *composite tools*, some of which have been found (Figure 3.10). This way, a single long, straight edge could be made of many small pieces, or individual microliths could serve as the barbs and tips on weapons.

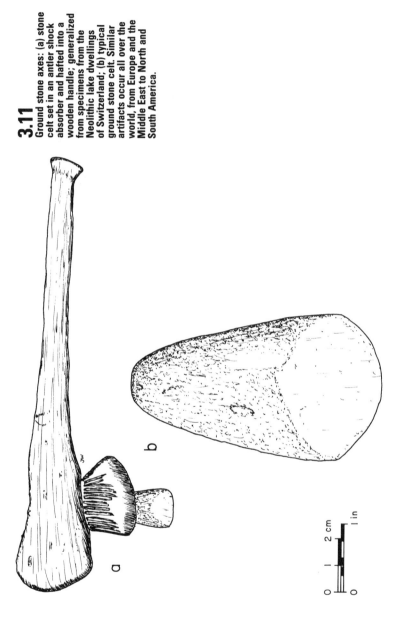

3.11
Ground stone axes: (a) stone celt set in an antler shock absorber and hafted into a wooden handle; generalized from specimens from the Neolithic lake dwellings of Switzerland; (b) typical ground stone celt. Similar artifacts occur all over the world, from Europe and the Middle East to North and South America.

a

b

2 cm

1 in

0   1

0

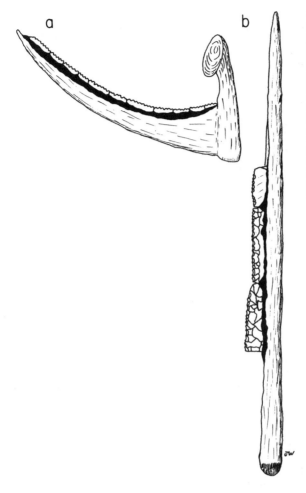

3.12
Stone-edged sickles (not to scale): (a) First Dynasty, Egypt, from the royal tombs excavated by Petrie (after deMorgan 1926); (b) Neolithic Fayum, Egypt (after Caton-Thompson and Gardner 1934; Cole 1970). Note that the flints in this sickle are bifacial, while the other sickle blades shown are blades. This sickle was 51 centimeters (20.4 in.) long, made of tamarisk wood with a plant resin holding the flints.

The Neolithic period, or New Stone Age, was originally defined by the use of ground rather than flaked stone for axes and other heavy tools (Figure 3.11). Now the beginnings of the domestication of plants and animals and the establishment of the first agricultural villages are considered more important. Ground stone tools are often shaped by *pecking* with another stone to crush and crumble off little bits to reach the desired shape, and then sometimes finished by grinding against an abrasive stone. This allows some tough crystalline rocks like granite and basalt that usually don't flake well to be shaped into cutting edges for heavy tools like axes and gouges. Flaked stone does not stand up to heavy chopping and repeated blows as well as ground stone, which often uses tougher, less brittle materials, although flint was occasionally

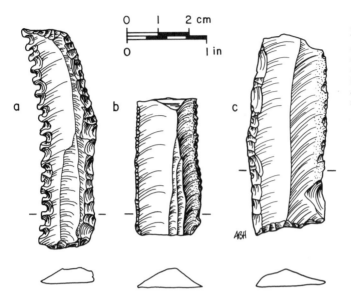

3.13
Three stone sickle blades:
(a) Egyptian Neolithic
(after deMorgan 1926);
(b, c) Bronze Age sickle
blades from Tell el Hayyat,
Jordan. Stipple indicates
sickle sheen.

flaked and then ground for axes and adzes. Ground stone tools also include the various kinds of grinding stones, such as manos and metates, mortars and pestles, that are necessary to process grains and other plant foods. While new ground stone tools and techniques were introduced, the older flaked-stone technologies continued to provide Neolithic people with sharp edges for basic cutting tasks. In the Old World the flints from stone-edged sickles for harvesting grains are common archaeological finds (Figures 3.12, 3.13).

Even after the development of metal technologies in the Chalcolithic Age (Copper-Stone Age) and the Bronze Age, stone tools remained extremely important. Metal was scarce and expensive, mostly used for weapons and ornaments owned by the elite, and sickles and other household and farm implements continued to be made of wood, bone, and stone.

In the New World things happened later and a bit differently. Humans arrived sometime during the Pleistocene ice ages as fully modern *Homo sapiens*. Just when this happened is a major source of controversy. At various times during the Pleistocene, a colder worldwide climate trapped water in the ice of enormous glaciers, and as glaciers grew, the sea level went down. Large land areas that are now under water were exposed and inhabited, including a "bridge" between Asia and Alaska across what is now the Bering Strait. The ancestors of the modern American Indians crossed the Bering land bridge, and even today the native populations of Asia and North America show some ge-

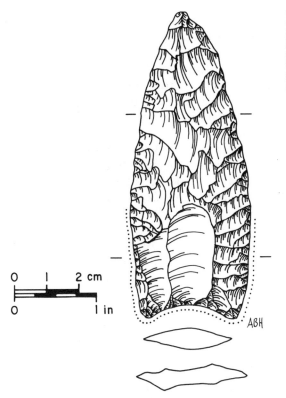

3.14
Clovis point, Dent Site, Colorado. Two fluting flakes were removed from this face, and dots indicate ground edges. Drawn from Denver Cast No. 4.

0 | 2 cm

0 | in

ABH

netic similarities. The earliest immigrants to the New World would have been Upper Paleolithic hunters following the herds of big game— mammoths, bison, horses, camels—across wide, grassy plains that are now under the waters of the Bering Sea.

The earliest North American culture of which we are absolutely certain is the Clovis culture. Radiocarbon dates for Clovis fall between 11,500 and 11,000 years ago—that is, 9500–9000 B.C. The Clovis people made large spear heads, *fluted* with a single large flake scar forming a channel up each face (Figure 3.14; see also Chapter 9). At a number of sites, Clovis points have been found with the butchered bones of mammoths, and it is clear that Clovis hunters successfully killed even this largest of big game. They also hunted extinct bison, horses, camels, mastodons, and other large animals that are now extinct in North America. Probably they also hunted small game and used a variety of plant foods, but there is less evidence for these resources. We expect that they lived much like recent hunter-gatherer peoples, in small mobile bands. Some of the Clovis points from mammoth kills are made of stone only found miles away, showing that they either traveled considerable distances or had trade connections to other groups.

At present, it is hard to connect the Clovis culture to its likely ancestors in Asia, partly because appropriate studies in northern Asia are only beginning (Bonnichsen and Turnmire 1991). Still, what we know of the Clovis way of life is similar to what we see for the Upper Paleolithic in the Old World.

While everyone agrees about the Clovis culture and its dates, not everyone believes it represents the first humans in North America. There is a reasonable body of evidence suggesting that humans arrived as early as 40,000 years ago (Ericson, Taylor, and Berger 1982), and there are some extremely dubious claims for even earlier sites. However, all of the proposed pre-Clovis sites and artifacts so far have some kind of problem with them. Either the dates are being disputed or the artifacts are very crude and may be stones and bones shaped by natural forces rather than man-made tools. These very crude artifacts are also not what we should expect 40,000 years ago or even earlier, when people all over the Old World were making fairly complex stone tools. Those who believe in pre-Clovis humans in the New World usually feel that there is so much arguable evidence that we can expect to find the clincher that everyone accepts at any time. Others, myself included, prefer the more conservative view that if there had been a pre-Clovis occupation of the New World, we would have proven it by now, just as we have many early sites from the Old World. Either of these positions is respectable, and we conservatives remain willing to be convinced by some really good evidence.

Sometime around 11,000 years ago, most of the Pleistocene megafauna—the mammoths, camels, horses, ground sloths, and the like—became extinct. It is very possible that the Clovis hunters helped or even caused this wave of extinctions, but that is another subject that is hotly argued (Martin and Klein 1984), partly because the Pleistocene was also drawing to an end at this time, with major climatic changes that caused the retreat of the glaciers and certainly affected the plant and animal populations.

In any case, bison and other modern herbivores replaced the extinct species as the primary game of the later Paleo-Indian cultures. These later Paleo-Indians also concentrated on big-game hunting, using a variety of different *lanceolate* (lance-shaped) spear points, some very finely flaked (Figures 3.15, 3.16). The earliest ones, the Folsom points, are clearly derived from the Clovis points. Folsom points among the ribs of extinct bison at the Folsom site in New Mexico were the indisputable evidence that convinced American archaeologists of the

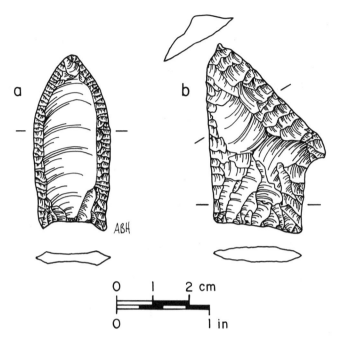

3.15
Later Paleo-Indian points:
(a) Folsom point from
Lindenmeier site,
Colorado—the classic
example of its type; (b) Cody
knife from Mathieson site,
New Mexico. Drawn from
Denver Casts Nos. 6, 15.

1920s that humans had coexisted with Pleistocene animals in the New World.

Some groups also began to shift their subsistence to emphasize small game and especially plant foods, as do most recent hunter-gatherers. They exploited a wider range of resources to occupy deciduous woodlands as well as the drier plains and deserts that developed as the climate warmed up. These are referred to as Archaic cultures, and after 6000 B.C. people at an Archaic hunter-gatherer level of culture occupied the whole of the New World. In many parts of the New World, Archaic cultures lasted until they were destroyed by the coming of the Europeans in historic times. In terms of technological development, the diversity of resources used by Archaic cultures is reflected in the increasing diversity of their tool kits. In particular, ground stone tools for processing seeds and other plant foods are common, and some groups made ground axes, adzes, and gouges that indicate the importance of woodworking and the beginnings of more permanent settlement. Mostly groups were still small and mobile, and without powerful leaders. In some areas, however, fancy ornaments, often made of materials that had to be acquired by trade at some distance, are found in graves and suggest that these societies were becoming less egalitarian, developing leaders who received special treatment at death.

The typical projectile point of the New World Archaic was relatively

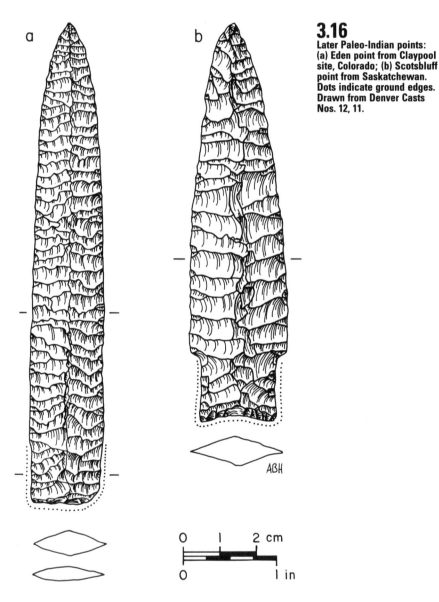

3.16
Later Paleo-Indian points:
(a) Eden point from Claypool
site, Colorado; (b) Scotsbluff
point from Saskatchewan.
Dots indicate ground edges.
Drawn from Denver Casts
Nos. 12, 11.

large, with notches or a stem for hafting (Figure 3.17). They would have been mounted on darts, light spears for use with an atlatl, or spear thrower. *Atlatls* serve to extend the arm and greatly increase the distance a spear can be thrown (Figure 3.18). Atlatls were used in Upper Paleolithic Europe and perhaps as early as Clovis times in the New World, where they also survived in some cultures until quite late. The word *atlatl* is from the Aztecs, who fought the Spanish with atlatls and darts, and wooden swords edged with obsidian blades. By the

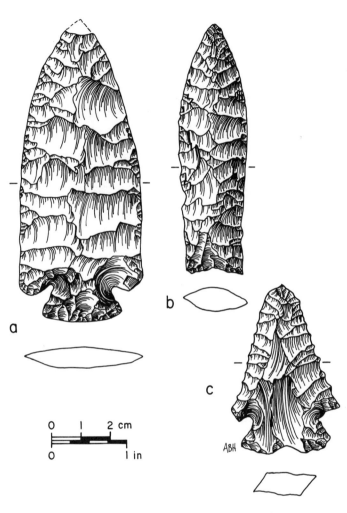

3.17
Archaic projectile points from Iowa (C. French collection): (a) St. Charles point; (b) Nebo Hill point; (c) Thebes point. Note beveled resharpening typical of some knives.

a

b

c

0   2 cm

0   1 in

ABH

Archaic we find definite atlatl parts in archaeological sites, mostly weights that apparently improved balance (Raymond 1986) and the hooks that fit a socket on the end of the spear much like the nock on an arrow.

Perhaps as early as 5000 B.C. Archaic peoples in the dry highlands of central Mexico began to cultivate some of the native plants. These were the wild ancestors of corn, beans, and squash, the great triad of native American crops, plus some others, such as avocado, chile pepper, cotton, and tobacco. Agriculture was apparently invented separately in South America as well, with a different set of native crops, including the potato. For a long time the basic Archaic lifestyle of seminomadic hunting and gathering was not much changed by the addition of a few unreliable and not too productive cultivated plants.

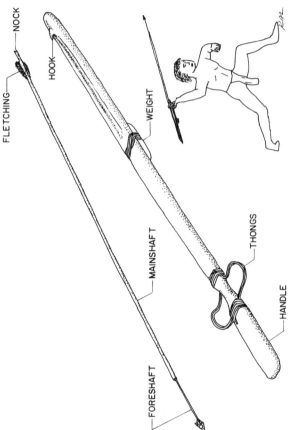

3.18
Atlatl and dart (not to same scale) and manner of use.

NOCK

FLETCHING

HOOK

WEIGHT

MAINSHAFT

THONGS

FORESHAFT

HANDLE

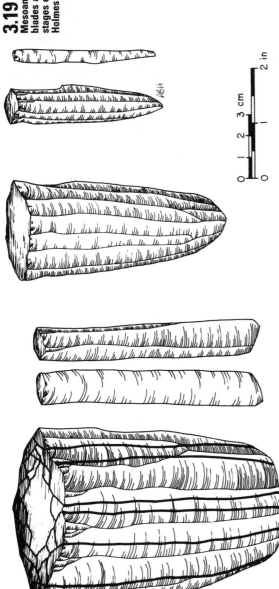

3.19
Mesoamerican obsidian blades and cores at three stages of reduction (after Holmes 1900).

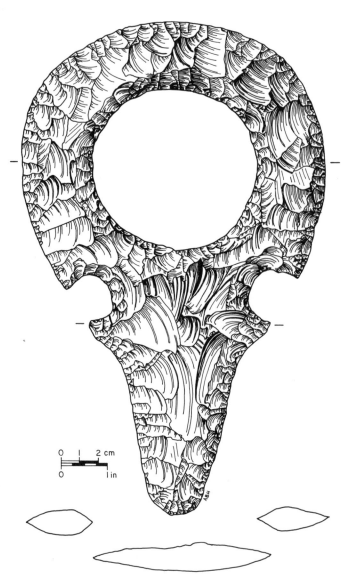

3.20
Maya chert eccentric, Altun Ha, Belize. Eccentrics are ritual artifacts usually found in caches of offerings buried under temples. Some may have been heads of staves, carried as badges of office or symbols of ritual power. This large, flat biface was knapped around a natural hole or drilled to start the hole. The steep retouch enlarging the hole and the notches was probably done by indirect percussion. Drawn from Lithic Casting Lab cast.

0   2 cm
0   1 in

Eventually the important crops that could serve as staples became more productive and reliable enough that larger populations could depend on them, and new, more complex cultures began to emerge.

These early horticultural societies are often referred to as the Formative stage in American prehistory. People began to form more permanent communities, located near arable land and other important resources. Populations expanded, and social organization became more complex, with some development of craft specialization and chiefs or other central authorities.

Sometime after about 2000 B.C. corn and the idea of domesticated plants spread into North America. Again, it took a while for the effects to be felt, but by the birth of Christ there were communities in the Southwest that relied at least partly on corn growing, and although corn may not have reached the Midwest and Southeast that early, squash and the idea of cultivation had. From the point of view of the flintknapper, the major development in this period was the bow and arrow, whose origins are hard to trace, but which resulted in more effective hunting technology and is often evidenced by smaller projectile points than those of the earlier atlatl and dart hunters.

In Mesoamerica and South America the Formative agricultural villages eventually developed into the great American Classic and Post-classic civilizations: Teotihuacan, the Olmec, the Maya, the Aztecs, and the Incas, to name only the most familiar. All of these groups are known for their sophisticated art, monumental architecture, the beginnings of writing systems, complex calendars, and mathematical and astronomical knowledge. Cities developed, even empires that controlled large areas under the leadership of an authoritative upper class. There were extensive trade networks, and specialist craftsmen produced many of the goods. Among these goods were stone tools. Some were basic agricultural tools such as axes and hoes, mass-produced in the Maya area at sites like Colha as early as 250 B.C. (Hester et al. 1983; Shafer and Hester 1983, 1991). The workshops at Colha produced vast mounds of flaking waste and millions of tools that were traded to consumer sites (McSwain 1991). The most important lithic industry throughout prehistoric Mesoamerica was the production of obsidian blades, whose razor-sharp edges were used for all manner of tasks (Figure 3.19). Control of the sources and trade in obsidian may have been a major factor in the rise and collapse of cities like Teotihuacan (Charlton 1978; Nelson et al. 1977; Spence 1967, 1981; see Clark 1986 for negative view). Some of the fancier Mesoamerican stone work was for ritual or status use (Willey 1972; Iannone 1992), and knappers of tremendous skill were involved (Figure 3.20).

While the Mesoamerican civilizations were developing, some parts of North America followed suit on a much smaller scale. In the Southeast and Southwest there were relatively large centers supported by agriculture. There was some monumental public architecture, important trade networks, and differences in social status, but the level of political organization was less complex than in Mesoamerica, and writing systems and large cities never developed. How much the North American cultures were influenced by the Mesoamericans is still debated, but it is quite clear, despite a lot of nonsense to the contrary, that the civilizations of the New World were not established by Egyptians, Chinese, imaginary Atlanteans, or any other Old World group. If we put all the folk who sell books about Atlantis, Mu, space gods, and the like in the spot where Atlantis was supposed to have been and let them sink, the world would be a better place.

So much for an outline of prehistory; let us end with a word about the recent historic past of stone-age technology. Well into the nineteenth century there were groups who had little or no contact with metal, and who maintained their old stone-age technology. There are even a few remnants today, and these survivors are one of the most important sources of information we have.

RECENT "STONE-AGE" PEOPLE

During the era of colonial expansion European explorers, colonists, and eventually scientists encountered the aboriginal occupants of the rest of the world, some of whom were still using stone tools. The early accounts of the use and manufacture of stone tools were important in the development of archaeology and especially lithic studies, and today are important because they are all we know about some cultures and technologies that became extinct soon after contact. For our purposes as knappers, these reports are usually not very good, because they lack the detail necessary to accurately reconstruct and replicate the exact techniques used. A good example is the rather vague Spanish description of making obsidian blades, which has led to at least a dozen articles arguing the exact meaning of the description and trying by experiment and analyses of the blades themselves to decide exactly how they were made (e.g., Clark 1982; Crabtree 1968; see Chapter 9).

Unfortunately, the nineteenth century was truly "the vesper hours of the Stone Age" (Bourke 1890), about the last chance to actually see a complete stone tool technology in use in a culture that depended upon it. Metal tools were quickly adopted by most people as soon as they became available. However, new technologies and imported goods were often scarce and expensive, and some native technologies such as basketry, pottery, and even stone continued to see some use long after their makers were receiving some European replacements. For instance, Indian converts at Spanish missions in Mexico and the western United States, who were being taught blacksmithing and other new crafts and even had some metal arrow points and knives, continued to use stone as well, although in some cases the quality of the stone tools declined (Fox 1979; Hester 1989; Whittaker and Fratt 1984).

Today there are still a few people who use stone tools, but no cultures that have the wide range of tools and techniques that most of the North American Indians had, for instance. Soft-hammer percussion bifaces, the Mesoamerican obsidian blades, and Levallois flakes are only a few of the things that no one at all makes now, except us nonaboriginal revivalists. Most stone tools survive in isolation as specialties in a metal-using culture. Some groups of Australian aborigines have the most complete stone tool industries left, in terms of importance to some of the population, usefulness for many functions, and continuity with the past. Some important studies have been done (e.g., Binford 1986; Gould 1980; Gould, Koster, and Sontz 1971; Hayden 1981; White 1968), but Australian lithic technology is and has mostly been extremely simple, lacking most complex tools and relying on very simple percussion techniques, although some fine pressure flaking was done in a few areas (Balfour 1903; Crabtree 1970; Elkin 1948; Tindale 1985).

Perhaps the most important aspect of some of the studies of Australian stone use is the recognition that stone tools, like all artifacts, are part of complex symbol systems. Their users assign values and meanings to them that may have little to do with their functions or material properties, and some tools or materials are important because they are associated with the spiritual power of the ancestors or with qualities like "maleness" (Jones 1990; Jones and White 1988; Sharp 1952; Taçon 1991). Too often archaeologists, who work with material remains, forget that artifacts have meanings in the minds of their users as well as functions in their hands.

Iron technology put an end to the stone age in most of Africa well before the Europeans got there, but again a few things survive. A typical example is the use of obsidian by some Ethiopian tribesmen, who make scrapers for working hides but who use no other stone tools (Gallagher 1977; Clark and Kurashina 1981).

In South America there are a few groups who have only recently been contacted and still use some stone tools, or at least remember how to make them. In Mesoamerica another good example of the kind of changes that come over stone tool industries can be seen among the Lacandon Maya (Clark 1989, 1991; Nations 1989; Nations and Clark 1983). The Lacandon still make traditional stone-tipped arrows, using indirect percussion to get a blank and shaping it by pressure flaking, usually with a piece of a broken machete blade. However, they do all their hunting with shotguns and rifles. The bows and arrows are made in large numbers for the tourist trade, and there are bundles of them for sale in Merida and other Mexican cities. In 1985 I bought one of the

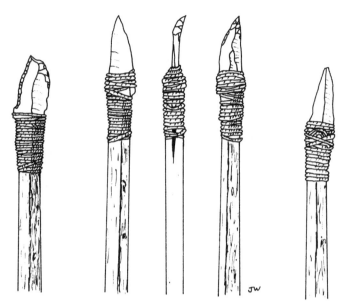

3.21
Lacandon Maya flint arrow points. The one in the center is shown in three views. Each is a small retouched blade set in a slotted square shaft and bound with commercial cordage.

standard sets in Merida for about three dollars. The set included a hardwood bow and six arrows, four with stone tips (Figure 3.21). The stone arrowheads were minimally flaked and quite crude, and the bow was weak—all too obviously not intended for use.

A few stone tools also survived into industrial Europe, in the rare cases where they could do something cheaply and as effectively as metal, or even performed a task metal could not. Around the Mediterranean short flint blades are inserted in the bottom of a wooden sledge that is driven over piles of mown wheat to separate the grain from the chaff (Bordaz 1965, 1969; Fox 1984).

The most important survival was the gunflint (Figure 3.22). Fire making with flint and steel is an ancient tradition, and even before metal was made, sparks could be struck with flint and iron pyrites, also known as "fool's gold." Flintlock firearms (Figure 3.23) use the same principle: pulling the trigger releases the hammer, which holds a piece of flint; it falls against a piece of steel called the frizzen, producing a shower of sparks that ignites a priming charge, which sets off the main charge of gunpowder. Flintlock muskets and rifles were the major arm of all European nations from the late 1600s until the early 1800s. Until the middle 1800s, there were major gunflint industries in France and England (Skertchly 1879; Clarke 1935). Fred Avery, the last knapper at the old center of Brandon in southern England, still makes flints in 1993 for outdated guns in remote parts of the world and for collectors and black-powder enthusiasts in the United States and elsewhere (Gould 1981).

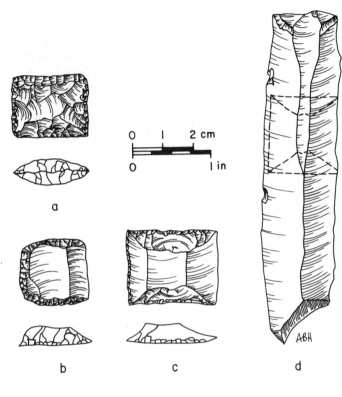

3.22
Gunflints: (a) Native American bifacial gunflint of local chert, New York, 1600s (after Witthoft 1966); (b) French gunflint made on a blade of yellow Presigny flint, 1700s; (c) British gunflint knapped from blade of black Brandon flint, 1800s; (d) British gunflint blade (called a "flake" by the knappers) with outline of one of the several flints that would be knapped from it (after Skertchly 1879).

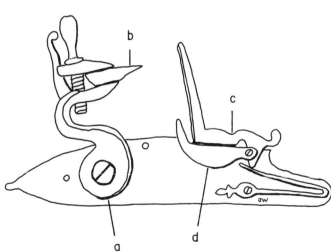

3.23
Flintlock mechanism. When the trigger is pulled, the cock or hammer (a), which holds the flint (b), snaps forward, striking sparks on the battery, or frizzen (c), which is knocked forward, uncovering a small charge of powder in the pan (d). The sparks fall on the priming powder and ignite it, which in turn sets off the main charge in the barrel of the gun.

Our ancestors began making stone tools before there were creatures we would recognize as fellow humans, and so the early archaeological record presents a unique case of a technology that developed along with humans and influenced their evolution. In recent times, stone tool industries present an unusual opportunity to see how technologies eventually become extinct. Stone tool technology could usually not compete with more efficient, versatile, and durable metal tools and was rapidly abandoned. The exceptions above illustrate some important principles about the survival of obsolete technologies. Stone tools continued in use where they were effective enough, and much cheaper than metal alternatives, as among the western mission Indians and Ethiopian hide-workers. Lacandon lithic skills are no longer useful in hunting technology, but survive because they can be used to produce salable folk craft. In the case of gunflints, lithic technology survived first because it produced a very specialized product that could not immediately be replaced by new technology. Gunflints and modern knapping currently represent a technology that has been kept alive and is even expanding because it is symbolically valuable—people are interested in their past, identify with it, and practice ancient crafts for personal reasons. Without modern experimenters who revive and preserve some practical knowledge of how stone tools are made and used, it would be difficult to understand any stone tools and the lessons we can learn from them.

MODERN KNAPPING

Before the 1700s, educated people generally considered stone tools to be freaks of nature or the products of lightning and thunder (Blinkenberg 1911). The common folk often called them "elf stones" or other names implying supernatural origins. By this time, however, explorations in the New World had encountered people using stone tools, and it is a little surprising that this knowledge did not spread to the scholars interested in antiquities sooner than it did. One reason of course was the general belief that the world was only a few thousand years old, as calculated from the Bible, and the lack of any good idea of what ancient people were like, other than the picture of metal-using barbarians presented by the Bible and classical writers. It is also only fair to add that while arrowheads are pretty obviously man-made tools, many of the older European stone tools are not obvious at all.

In any case, by 1800 John Frere, an eccentric English scholar, described what we now recognize as Acheulean handaxes from the site of Hoxne. He noted that they occurred with "extraordinary bones . . . of enormous size," and suggested that "the situation in which these weapons were found may tempt us to refer them to a very remote period indeed; even beyond that of the present world" (Frere 1800:204).

Evidence of the antiquity of the world and the long prehistory of humanity continued to mount; by the time Darwin published *On the Origin of Species* in 1859 and *The Descent of Man* in 1871, it was already obvious that humanity had existed long before the date given by biblical scholars for the mythical Garden of Eden. In the late 1800s prehistory became an accepted branch of science, and systematic archaeological studies were begun. It was in this environment that the interest in stone tools led to the beginnings of experimental flintknapping.

There were really three main thrusts. First, stone masons and gunflint makers had known and applied the principles of knapping for a long time. There were also a number of people such as England's Edward Simpson, alias "Flint Jack," who was producing forgeries of stone tools by 1850 (Blacking 1953; Marsden 1983:71–76). However, as Blacking (1953:207) puts it, the motives of Victorian prehistorians were largely "acquisitive rather than truly scientific." In other words, they were quite content to collect flint artifacts but showed little interest in men like Simpson whose skills could have taught them a great deal about their antiquities. They bought his artifacts, occasionally watched him demonstrate knapping, and eventually reviled him for the forgeries with which he eked out a precarious existence.

One outstanding exception was Sydney Skertchly, who published a study of the gunflint industry at Brandon, England, in 1879. He incorrectly believed that he could trace the making of gunflints from the stone-age scrapers of prehistoric times, but in other respects his work was excellent and far ahead of his times. He discussed the economic and social structure of the industry as well as the technology involved, and not only observed but learned how to make gunflints. Nevertheless, the practical knowledge of people who worked stone outside of the scholarly circles was rarely used by the early prehistorians.

In Europe, especially Britain, the main impetus behind knapping experiments eventually developed from the controversy over *eoliths*. These were crudely flaked stones, from very early geological contexts, that some people felt were artifacts. Most are now considered to be stones flaked by natural forces, but at the time the controversy raged hot and heavy, and a number of people both learned some knapping and experimented with mechanical fracturing of stone to duplicate natural processes (e.g., Moir 1917, 1919; Warren 1914; see also Johnson 1978).

In the United States the situation was a bit different. Archaeology was greatly stimulated by the westward expansion of the country; as the Native Americans were encountered and rapidly destroyed, a few anthropologists made heroic efforts to record some of the vanishing cultures. A number of Indian groups were still making and using stone tools in the nineteenth century, especially in California, and there are quite a few accounts of "how they make arrowheads" (e.g., Avery 1873; Bourke 1890, 1891; Gifford 1936; Goddard 1903–1904; Goldschmidt 1951; Lyon 1859; Ray 1886; Redding 1879; Schumacher 1877; Sellers 1886; Waite 1874; see also Ellis 1939 and Holmes 1919).

Most of the early observations of arrowhead making were not very detailed and reflect the lack of understanding of knapping that might be expected of observers who had no practical experience. Even the relatively detailed demonstrations and reporting on one skilled native knapper, Ishi, had little effect on mainstream archaeology (Kroeber 1961; Nelson 1916; Pope 1918, 1974). Ishi represents, on a very personal level, the tragedy of the American Indians (Kroeber 1961). He was the last survivor of a small band of Yana people who led a fugitive existence in the mountains of central northern California, where for a time they escaped the slaughter perpetrated on most of their tribe in the 1800s. Through the late 1800s the small band of survivors hid and dwindled. Finally Ishi, having watched the last of his friends and relatives die of hardship and age, slipped into an Anglo settlement to steal food. Exhausted, starved, and hopeless, he was cornered by dogs, and the last "wild" Indian in California was put into jail, more because no one knew what to do with him than out of any malice. When the newspapers printed the story, Alfred Kroeber and T. T. Waterman, a couple of prominent California anthropologists, rescued Ishi and made a place for him at the University of California's Museum of Anthropology in San Francisco. Here he spent the last years of his life (1911–1916) before dying of tuberculosis, one of the imported diseases that had already decimated the native population of America. Some folk who are hostile to anthropologists these days use this story as an example of how we can turn anyone into a specimen to be studied, but the motives of Kroeber and his colleagues were not merely scientific. They did the best they could for a fellow human who was truly lost in time, and when Ishi died, the quiet, patient, cheerful man was mourned by his friends in the museum and by a public that had learned to see him not just as an exhibit, but as a person.

Ishi was a skillful knapper in the tradition of his people—that is, making pressure-flaked arrowheads (Figure 3.24). While he lived at the museum, he frequently demonstrated his skills to anthropologists and museum visitors. Ishi was the most closely observed and probably the last of the North American Indians who relied on a stone-age technology. He inspired Saxton Pope to study native archery and embark on a series of experiments with different bows and arrows (Pope 1923), but Pope never developed much interest in stone flaking. Nels C. Nelson (1916), who also worked with Ishi, did, and some of the other early anthropologists and archaeologists (most of them worked with both

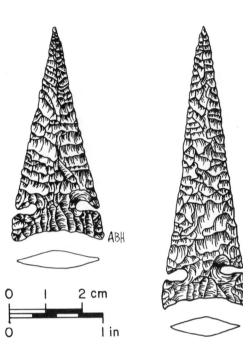

3.24
Obsidian points by Ishi.
Drawn from Lithic Casting
Lab Casts H-3, H-1. Originals
in Charley Shewey
collection.

living and prehistoric people) figured out the basics of flaking on their own or from observing native knappers and applied this knowledge to interpreting prehistoric material (Cushing 1895; Holmes 1891, 1919; McGuire 1896).

Nevertheless, knapping remained a rare skill and a very small part of archaeology through most of the first half of the twentieth century. This was a period when archaeology was primarily interested in recording basic information about prehistoric cultures—cataloguing their artifacts, classifying them, and sorting the cultures into time and space units, producing descriptions of the sequence of cultures and artifacts in different regions. A number of individual prehistorians developed knapping skills, and there were a few important works on knapping, but they made no great impact. Two of these works, which in retrospect are very good, are Pond's (1930) lengthy account of stone working based on the work of an amateur, an old Norwegian immigrant named Halvor Skavlem, and an exhaustive study in 1939 by Holmes Ellis (Ellis 1939). Ellis was director of the Ohio Historical Society Lithic Laboratory, and he and his associates collected and attempted to duplicate all of the knapping techniques reported in the ethnographic literature at the time. An early attempt to apply flintknapping skills to the interpretation of a specific archaeological assemblage was Barbieri's (1937) analysis of implements from Lake Mohave. As a knapper, Barbieri was

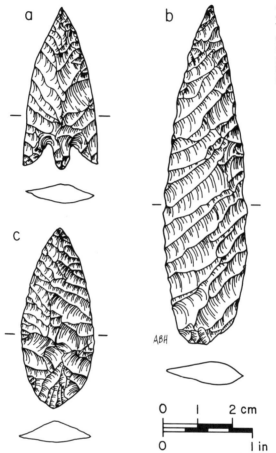

3.25
Two pressure-flaked obsidian points by Don Crabtree, ca. 1974 (a, b); a pressure-flaked point of heat-treated chert by François Bordes, 1973 (c).

ahead of his time in that he discussed some of the important variables in knapping, such as platform angles, platform preparation, and the angle of the blow.

It wasn't until the late 1960s that flintknapping came into its own in archaeology. Scientific archaeology was undergoing a period of soul-searching and change, shifting its emphasis from description and chronology to finer-grained attempts to understand people and their cultures as well as the processes of change and adaptation that affect them. It was increasingly important to recognize the functions of tools, how they were used and made, in order to understand what people were doing and how they made a living in their environment. Experiments in making and using all sorts of artifacts, which had always been a minor part of archaeology, increased and achieved a new respectability (Coles 1973, 1979).

Two men, Don Crabtree and François Bordes (Figure 3.25), were

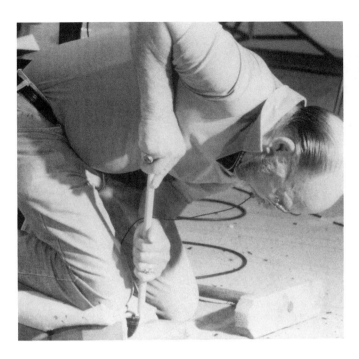

3.26
Don Crabtree making
pressure microblades,
University of Lethbridge,
1979. Photo courtesy of
James Woods.

primarily responsible for sparking a vastly enlarged interest in flint-knapping. Don Crabtree (Figure 3.26) was an American knapper who began making stone tools as a youth (Crabtree and Callahan 1979; Johnson 1978; Knudson 1982). He never finished a college education, but worked for several institutions as a paleontologist and lithic technician. The most important of these was Ellis's laboratory at the Ohio Historical Society. After World War II Crabtree was diverted into business pursuits, but he continued his own lithic studies as a hobby. Eventually Earl Swanson of Idaho State University recognized the potential value of his skill and drew him into mainstream archaeology. Crabtree eventually produced a whole string of classic articles, many published in the journal *Tebiwa* (Crabtree 1966, 1967a, 1967b, 1968, 1970, 1972a, 1972b, 1973a, 1973b, 1974; Crabtree and Butler 1964; Crabtree and Swanson 1968).

François Bordes (Figure 3.27) was a French prehistorian who also had worked with stone for years (see Bordes 1947, 1961). These two men, and Jacques Tixier, another important French knapper, came together at a conference in Les Eyzies, France, where they demonstrated knapping to a number of other prehistorians who studied stone tools (Jelinek 1965, 1982). This not only began a long and fruitful interchange (Bordes and Crabtree 1969), but impressed a number of influential archaeologists with the value of this kind of experiment.

3.27
François Bordes making
blades at his summer house
in Carsac, France, 1973.

It is probably fair to say that even without Crabtree and Bordes, others would have eventually popularized flintknapping; the intellectual climate in archaeology was right. Nevertheless, the influence of these men went beyond their published works, both in establishing knapping as a useful facet of archaeology and in training others. Crabtree in particular eventually taught a summer field school in knapping, from which came many of the American knappers cited in this book. In the 1970s stone tool experiments of all kinds became frequent, even commonplace. The number of skillful knappers has multiplied geometrically, and even many archaeologists whose main interests are not in stone tools know some of the basics.

Amateur knappers and nonacademic professionals who make and sell replicas to museums and collectors have always existed, usually ignored by the academics. In the last ten years they have become much more common, more visible, and more in contact with each other and with archaeologists. There are probably more nonacademic knappers than archaeologists at the highest levels of knapping skill, but their goals are somewhat different. The archaeologist is usually interested in stone tools as one way of interpreting the past, while most of the modern nonacademic knappers are more interested in efficiently producing fine stone work. As a result, many of them use modern tools such as copper billets and modern shortcuts like saw-cut blanks in their knapping. My approach to flintknapping reflects my academic bias, but no matter how you approach knapping, you can learn a lot from the modern nonacademic knapping community.

FURTHER READINGS

Those interested in more detail on the history of flintknapping should look up Johnson's (1978) "A History of Flint-Knapping Experimentation, 1838–1976" (see also Flenniken 1984). Willey and Sabloff's (1974) *A History of American Archaeology* and Glynn Daniel's (1981) *A Short History of Archaeology* are both good accounts of archaeological history in general.

A number of other books are, or try to be, useful to someone who wants to learn to knap. Crabtree's classic *An Introduction to Flintworking* (1972a) is mostly an illustrated glossary. It is not very useful in teaching the beginner and is marred by some mistakes and eccentricities, but is still commonly cited as a source of generally agreed-on definitions. Mewhinney's *A Manual for Neanderthals* (1957) is the oldest how-to still in print. It is amusing and generally accurate, but doesn't have enough illustrations, and the how-to descriptions are sometimes hard to follow or downright misleading. Hellweg's *Flintknapping: The Art of Making Stone Tools* (1984) is more detailed and explicit and can be bought at some museum shops and elsewhere. There are a number of inaccuracies and bad usages of terms, but overall it is fairly good. *The Art of Flint Knapping,* by D. C. Waldorf (1984), is published privately by its author. It too is generally good and well illustrated, although it suffers from a lack of attention to basic hard-hammer percussion and some misuse of standard terminology. It has been the starting point for many good knappers. Errett Callahan's important study, "The Basics of Biface Knapping in the Eastern Fluted Point Tradition" (1979a), is not the place for a beginner to start, but contains some extremely useful information, some of which I have borrowed. Some basic knapping is briefly covered in *Outdoor Survival Skills* by Larry Olsen (1990) and *Primitive Tools: Making and Using Them* by John and Geri McPherson (1991).

Two useful bibliographies of works on stone tool manufacture and analysis are those by Hester and Heizer (1973) and Honea (1983). The techniques and conventions of lithic illustrations are ably covered by Chase (1985) and Addington (1986).

Many of the professional journals of archaeology and some of the amateur society journals carry articles on knapping experiments and analyses of stone tools from prehistoric sites. Once you have some background, these can be useful sources of ideas and inspiration. *American Antiquity, Plains Anthropologist,* and *Tebiwa* are professional journals that deal mostly with other things but have frequent articles on stone tools. *Lithic Technology* was a more specialized journal for professional accounts of experiment and analysis, mostly fairly technical. It has been defunct for several years, but is expected to be revived in 1993.

In the last few years knapping has expanded enormously, not just as an archaeological tool, but also as a craft and even a commercial art. It is mostly the nonacademic knappers, both amateur and professional, who are responsible, and their expanding interest and influence has resulted in several small newsletter-type journals. The best of these, *Flintknappers' Exchange,* has unfortunately ceased printing, but you may be able to find a knapper who has it. *Bulletin of Primitive Technology* is the best current successor, with articles on a wide range of other prehistoric technologies as well as knapping. *Chips, The Flint Knapper's Exchange,* and *The Platform* are current publications as I write (see Appendix). These publications run articles and correspondence by knappers of all kinds, mostly dealing with details of knapping techniques, experiments, and results. The quality varies from excellent to grotesque, with a distressing tendency among some knappers toward boasting and backslapping. Nevertheless, such publications produce a steady stream of valuable information and, more important, promote communication among knappers both within archaeology and in other circles.

OTHER RESOURCES: FINDING OTHER KNAPPERS

Even twenty years ago, when I was beginning to learn knapping, there were very few other knappers around. Fortunately this has changed as many more archaeologists learn how to knap and as professionals and amateurs who already knew how have become more common and visible. If you are a student or live in a city with a university that has an archaeology program of any size, there is probably someone who at least analyzes stone tools and very likely someone with at least a little knapping skill. Most of them should be willing to talk to interested people, even if you have no connection with their institution.

There are also amateur archaeological societies in all states, usually with chapters in many towns and cities. A few of these groups are just looters and buy-and-swap artifact collectors, but many are excellent, and most of them have at least a core of serious and knowledgeable people, including a surprising number of knappers.

In the last few years enough people, professional and amateur, have become interested in knapping and related primitive crafts to support a number of small enterprises. The newsletters in the Appendix carry advertising for many of these. It is now possible to purchase some raw materials, antler and knapping tools, primitive bows and arrows, atlatls and knives, kits for making these, some of the instructional material cited in the bibliography, casts and replications of stone tools, and lithic creations by modern knappers. Some of these outlets occasionally print announcements of various informal meetings, from atlatl contests to "knap-ins," and directories of knappers or other information that can help you get in touch with other knappers.

"Knap-ins" are now held once or twice a year in several states. The Appendix lists those current in the last couple of years. These events bring together all sorts of knappers and others interested in primitive crafts. They can be small, but the most popular may draw over one hundred knappers, mostly professional, semiprofessional, and amateur rather than academic. There is no better way to see large numbers of skilled knappers in action and to become aware of the variety of ways the same artifacts can be made. For many people knap-ins are probably the easiest way to find knappers to learn from and work with.

4

RAW MATERIALS

*To prehistoric man flint, obsidian, jasper, and
chert represented the highest values. Without
some hard stone having a conchoidal fracture, they were powerless against their ene-
mies and almost impotent in the chase. With
implements made from these stones . . . they
do numberless things which civilized man
now does with iron and steel.*
— B. B. Redding (1880, in Heizer 1976)

In Chapter 2 I discussed some of the necessary qualities of flakeable
stone and defined the major techniques of working it. Here I would like
to describe the raw material of stone tools more explicitly and provide
some ideas on where to get raw materials. Flaking tools will be discussed as needed for each technique.

One of the first and most severe problems that the would-be knapper
encounters is finding material to flake. In some areas, there simply are
no good sources, and even the prehistoric inhabitants had to import
stone or use ground slate, bone, bamboo, or other materials instead.
Modern American knappers may find they have the same problem, at
least as far as finding good-quality natural materials in reasonable
quantities. Fortunately, the vast amounts of waste produced by our industrial society include an excellent flaking material which can be obtained for little or no cost in virtually infinite quantities—glass. In the
following section I will define and describe the most common natural
and man-made materials and try to provide some ideas on finding sup-
plies of material to work.

STONE QUALITY

As I explained in Chapter 2, the materials for flaked stone tools must
fracture conchoidally. Furthermore, they should be elastic but brittle,
and homogeneous both in crystalline structure (amorphous or cryptocrystalline) and in lacking cracks, inclusions, and other flaws. The ho-
mogeneity of the crystalline structure is visible in the texture of a
freshly flaked surface. The crystalline structure is also the most im-

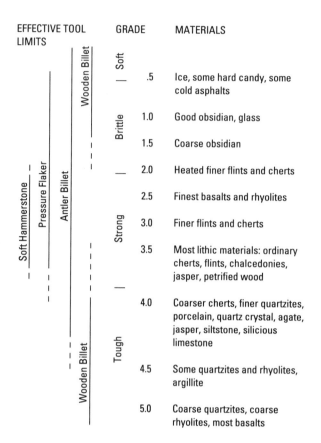

EFFECTIVE TOOL LIMITS   GRADE   MATERIALS

4.1
Lithic Grade Scale ranking material types by ease of working (after Callahan 1979a).

	GRADE	MATERIALS
Soft	.5	Ice, some hard candy, some cold asphalts
Brittle	1.0	Good obsidian, glass
	1.5	Coarse obsidian
	2.0	Heated finer flints and cherts
	2.5	Finest basalts and rhyolites
Strong	3.0	Finer flints and cherts
	3.5	Most lithic materials: ordinary cherts, flints, chalcedonies, jasper, petrified wood
	4.0	Coarser cherts, finer quartzites, porcelain, quartz crystal, agate, jasper, siltstone, silicious limestone
Tough	4.5	Some quartzites and rhyolites, argillite
	5.0	Coarse quartzites, coarse rhyolites, most basalts

(Effective tool limits labeled: Soft Hammerstone, Pressure Flaker, Antler Billet, Wooden Billet, Wooden Billet)

portant factor in how easily a material works. The most homogeneous materials with amorphous crystalline structures, like glass and obsidian, fracture very easily, with extremely sharp edges and smooth fracture surfaces. Cryptocrystalline materials like flint and chert are harder (they will scratch glass), more difficult to fracture, and do not form such sharp edges. The fracture surfaces are smooth to slightly rough, although in most cases the crystal structure is invisible to the naked eye. The toughest and least amorphous materials like basalt or quartzite are hard to work, and the fracture surfaces are usually rough, with a grainy or sugary texture; you can see that these rocks are composed of small crystals.

Errett Callahan (1979a:16) has proposed a Lithic Grade Scale to classify raw materials. Figure 4.1 follows his point system and ranks some common materials according to how easily they are worked. It is not a true scale because the points are not a real measurement, only a rough subjective ranking. Most materials vary a good deal over the grades as given, and the ranks are by no means discrete.

STONE MATERIALS

The knappable rocks are all composed largely of silica. Silica is silicon dioxide (SiO_2), and silicon is a nonmetallic element that bonds easily and is the most common element in the world other than oxygen. Silicon dioxide occurs in two forms that are of importance here, quartz and opal. Quartz is essentially pure SiO_2 and forms crystals that are hexagonal prisms with pyramidal ends. When pure, quartz is glassy and clear, as in rock crystal, or it may be colored by trace elements, as in the case of amethyst. Quartz is extremely hard, 7.0 on Moh's scale of hardness (diamond = 10, steel file = 6.5, glass = 5.5).

Opal is an amorphous or noncrystalline form of silica bonded colloidally with about 10 percent water (Shepherd 1972). It is the most soluble of the forms of silica, and the silica that forms the structures of some living organisms, such as plants, sponges, and diatoms, is opal.

In most of the materials used by knappers, the important form of silica is quartz. Some materials like flint and chert are made of essentially pure quartz in the form of microscopic, needlelike crystals with pores that hold water amounting to several percent of their weight. In other materials, like rhyolite and basalt, the quartz crystals are mixed with crystals of other minerals, and crystal size is generally larger.

Glass and Other Man-made Materials

Glass is largely made from quartz sand—you can consider it a man-made silicious rock. Because of its purity and relatively rapid cooling, it is amorphous, without a crystalline structure. It therefore flakes extremely well.

Most of my earliest flaking was done on bottle glass, and although there are many things you can't do with bottle glass, it is a good material for learning the basics. It is even authentic for some projectile points from Australia and the New World. The story goes that the first telegraph lines across Australia ran into trouble because the native people discovered that glass insulators flaked well. A good many telegraph lines went suddenly dead when someone shinnied up the poles and removed the insulators. The problem was ultimately solved by leaving extra insulators at the base of poles (Tindale 1985:24; Flood 1983:188).

Most bottle glass and window glass is only good for small items, usually pressure flaked. You can get pieces that are large enough to percussion flake from really big bottles like office water cooler bottles, or glass bricks, or heavy plate glass. I have heard stories about drunken archaeologists at a convention making bifaces out of the hotel's ashtrays. The convention was asked not to return.

Almost every town has a glass dealer, and I have several times been given fairly large pieces of scrap plate glass for free. One disadvantage of plate and window glass is that it usually has right-angled edges all around. This can be overcome, as described in Chapter 6. Another disadvantage is the flat surfaces, which may be difficult to remove entirely, leaving flat shiny spots and a flattened cross-section. On the other hand, glass is likely to be the cheapest, most readily available material around for many beginning knappers, and it flakes beautifully and with little effort, which is also helpful. If you have exotic tastes, you can find bright colors and you can do very delicate work with glass.

Another man-made material that is easy to find is porcelain. Toilet bowls and tanks, electric insulators, and cafeteria plates come to mind. Try your local landfill before you remove your plumbing or get expelled for taking more than food from the dining hall. Porcelain is much more difficult to work than glass. It is a bit grainy and a lot tougher, so it requires more force to flake, and it is harder to get long flakes. This of course makes it more like most natural materials. It is better for soft-hammer percussion than for pressure flaking.

There are various exotic things around if you look. When I taught the class in knapping at Arizona, we used slag from molybdenum smelting. We found this by chance as we were looking for material to set up the course. Southern Arizona does not have much in the way of good stone that is easily collected in large amounts. Having learned that some of the local copper mining and smelting operations used limestone as a flux and ran limestone mines, we inquired whether any chert came out of the limestone. The chert we found when we looked was useless, but when we explained what we wanted it for, the engineer who showed us around suggested trying the "moly" operations. Molybdenum is a rare metal used in some alloys and is produced by some of the southern Arizona copper mines. We finally found a smelter that produced a glassy slag, and were told to help ourselves. Some of it was too bubbly, but we filled a pickup with solid pieces. It varied from an opaque sea-green to a very dark translucent green that looked almost exactly like some of the obsidian from the Valley of Mexico. It all worked very well and came in large chunks suitable for percussion flaking. We were told at the time that the particular process that produced the green slag was becoming obsolete, so I don't know if that material is still available or not. Anyway, it goes to show what you can find if you look, and there must be other industrial processes and materials that could be useful.

Obsidian

Obsidian is a natural glass produced by volcanic action. It is related chemically to rhyolite and granite, and therefore includes large amounts of nonsilica minerals such as potassium feldspar as well as quartz. Extremely rapid cooling of the molten rock prevented the formation of distinct crystals, which is what distinguishes obsidian from its chemical relatives. Usually the color is dark, most often black, but there are also red, brown, striped (red/brown/black), green, gray, silver, and clear obsidians, and probably others I have not seen. Textures range from perfectly homogeneous and glassy to rather crystalline with a grainy, sugary texture. Some obsidians have crystals, bits of tuff, or other inclusions, or strange cracks and stress lines from uneven cooling. Others have "bruises" or incipient cones from rolling down slopes.

Obsidian occurs in large massive flows in some places and as lumps or beds in rhyolite flows. Often it is difficult to extract pieces from the original deposits, and prehistoric knappers collected material from secondary deposits like talus slopes and streambeds where it ended up in the form of chunks or nodules after eroding out of the original deposits.

Obsidian was prized by many prehistoric groups. The Hopewell mounds in Ohio contained several hundred pounds of obsidian from the Yellowstone area, and obsidian from the various sources in California was carried across the Sierra Nevada mountains and spread far and wide across the region. In the more advanced cultures of Mesoamerica, specialist knappers made millions of blades and other artifacts on an industrial scale, and trade and control of the obsidian sources was a factor in the rise and fall of cities.

Many of today's knappers prefer obsidian to any other material because it can be worked with great control. The ease with which obsidian can be flaked makes it a good material for the beginner as well as the virtuoso. However, because it is brittle and easy to flake, it is also easy to break in manufacturing, and it has a tendency to spray fine bits of shattered material around when worked by percussion. Obsidian flakes to extremely sharp edges, which makes it easy to get nicks and even serious cuts if you are not careful.

Basalt and Rhyolite

Basalt and rhyolite are also igneous or volcanic rocks. Rhyolite includes up to about 50 percent quartz, but basalt has very little and is mostly composed of plagioclase feldspar and ferromagnesian minerals. The slower they cooled, the more the different minerals sorted out into crystalline formations. For this reason, the flaking qualities are variable, ranging from fairly homogeneous, to coarsely grainy, to completely unflakeable. Some basalts in particular are often porous or vesicular. Although there are a few basalts and rhyolites that are similar to coarse obsidian, and some very silicious chertlike rhyolites, both basalts and rhyolites are usually quite tough, and not a good material for the beginner or for making fine tools.

Chert and Flint

Chert and flint are very similar materials, and different people define them differently in a confusing variety of ways (Luedtke 1992). Some say chert is light-colored while flint is dark, but others say the opposite. Others call only the finest-quality materials flint and coarser stone chert, but the amount of texture variation in any single nodule of either makes this nonsense. Some call only a few European stones flint and feel that there is only chert in the United States. The most common definition limits flint to material formed in chalk deposits, while chert can come from limestones or other materials. I tend to follow this definition, but only loosely, and do not worry much about the distinction. Chemically and structurally chert and flint are essentially the same.

Cherts and flints are usually found as nodules or beds that form as secondary deposits in rocks that are mostly composed of calcium carbonate—that is, limestones and chalks. The exact process by which this happens is disputed (Shepherd 1972; Luedtke 1992), but it involves the concentration of silica and often a chemical replacement of parts of the limestone by silica. The parts replaced often begin with or include fossils and other irregularities, some of which can be seen in the resulting chert or flint. Most nodules have a rough and often calcareous surface called *cortex*, like a crust on bread. Nodules range in size from microscopic to several hundred pounds.

The finest flints and cherts have smooth, almost glassy fracture surfaces, but are still a good deal tougher than glass or obsidian. The quality ranges on down from this through fine material that is cryptocrystalline but not glassy, to rather tough grainy stuff, to extremely coarse material with visible crystals. It is not uncommon for the chert to grade into the limestone around it when the process of replacement is still continuing. Many cherts and flints will *patinate,* developing a weathered surface as water and sometimes chemical stains work their way into the flint and as silica and other materials are leached out, producing a thin patina or rind of a different color. Weathering, especially extremes of heat or cold, can also crack or fracture exposed nodules, leaving them useless for flaking.

In some areas it is possible to extract chert or flint from its primary deposit in limestone or chalk. There were extensive flint mines during the Neolithic in southern England and parts of Europe, where literally miles of tunnels and shafts were dug to extract this important raw material (Bosch 1979; Rudebeck 1987; Schild 1987). At Grimes Graves in southern England, according to Mercer and Saville, "Enormous efforts were undertaken by the prehistoric miners to reach the layer of 'floor-stone,' the only flint of interest to them . . . After the evacuation of 800–1000 tonnes of chalk and sand, 8 tonnes of flint would have been produced—all at the very termination of the exercise" (Mercer and Saville 1981 : vi–viii). When we remember that the digging and earthmoving was all done with antler picks and baskets, we have to agree with their British understatement: "That the flint was much desired can remain in little doubt."

Probably most of the flints and cherts used throughout the world in prehistory came from secondary deposits, as these were and are usually easier to exploit. As chert nodules are usually more durable than the material around them, they are often eroded out of the parent bedrock and incorporated in sedimentary deposits such as river gravels or even exposed on the surface. In some areas, glacial deposits carry material far from its bedrock source. Streambed gravels and modern road cuts are good places both to spot material as you travel and to collect it. If you live in limestone country, see if there is a limestone quarry near you that produces chert as a waste product, like the one near George-town, Texas, that has been a favorite of American knappers in recent years.

Other Cryptocrystalline Silicates
Beside chert and flint, cryptocrystalline silicates include jasper, chalcedony, agate, and onyx. Geologists, archaeologists, and rock hounds often have confusing and contradictory definitions for these different rocks.

Chalcedony appears amorphous but is actually made up of micro-crystals of quartz, as is flint. It seems that chalcedony differs from flint and chert either because it has smaller intercrystalline pores and thus less water content (Shepherd 1972), or because its crystals grow in bundles of radiating fibers rather than forming grains (Luedtke 1992). Chalcedony is often dissolved and deposited in crevices in other rocks, often igneous rocks and geodes. It frequently has concentric rings and smooth surfaces with little mammillary or breast-shaped lumps.

Jasper is used for any red, reddish, yellow, or orange cryptocrystalline silicate. How red chert has to be before you start calling it jasper is up to you. Agate is supposed to be banded, but so are some rocks that everyone would call cherts. Some petrified woods are composed of silica and will flake, but often tend to have odd angular fracture patterns.

These different rocks do not normally occur as large pieces and often are too irregular or too flawed for good knapping. However, all were exploited where suitable, and some have particularly attractive colors and patterning.

Quartzite and Related Metamorphic Rocks

Metamorphic rocks have gone through a change by heat and pressure, usually having been originally formed as sedimentary rocks deposited by water as sand and mud. Quartzite began life (so to speak) as sandstone, but the individual quartz sand grains were welded together by later heat and pressure, so that instead of breaking between grains, which prevents conchoidal fracture, it now can be knapped across grains. Although it does occur in beds, most of the quartzite used by prehistoric knappers was found in the form of cobbles in riverbeds. Most quartzite is very tough stuff and usually produces rather crude-looking tools, even in the hands of skilled knappers. However, there are some fine quartzites, including what some archaeologists call Hixton Silicified Sandstone, from a source at Silver Mound, Wisconsin. This distinctive material was intensively exploited throughout prehistory, and artifacts made of it were widely distributed in the Midwest.

Quartzite pebbles also make very good hammerstones. Being hard and tough, they are best for working cherts and other hard materials.

Argillite, silicified shale, silicified mudstone, silicified limestone, and the Arkansas novaculite sold as whetstones are examples of other sedimentary materials that either began with a lot of silica in them and were welded by metamorphosis, or had the silica added after deposition. The flaking quality of these materials is quite variable, and they are usually common only in restricted local areas.

HEAT-TREATING

Many of the cryptocrystalline silicates can be improved by heat-treatment. This may in fact be the source of that absurd old story about making arrowheads by heating the stone and dripping cold water on it to crack off flakes (Eames 1915; Fraser 1908; Nagle 1914). Enough serious knappers have tried this (e.g., Ellis 1939) to show that it does not work, never did work, and could not work, but you will still hear it. Courtesy inhibits us from calling people liars, but if someone claims to have seen arrowheads made by fire and water or to have done it themselves, don't invest in any real estate with them.

Nevertheless, heat can be used in stone working, although not for flaking. Some stones, if heated slowly to a high enough temperature, change their texture and color. When heat-treatment works, the stone usually becomes less grainy and smoother in texture, and more brittle and thus easier to flake. What actually happens during heat-treatment is not entirely clear. Some suggest that silica crystals or fibers melt and fuse on a microscopic scale, making the material more homogeneous, while others argue that microscopic cracks are formed that weaken the material and make it fracture more readily and more evenly. Luedtke (1992) provides an extensive discussion. The knapper notices that heat-treated material flakes more easily and with smoother fracture surfaces, sharper edges, and fewer step and hinge terminations (e.g., Mandeville and Flenniken 1974; Patterson 1979b, 1981a). Many mediocre cherts can be made into top-notch material by heat-treatment, and some materials like novaculite are virtually unworkable without it. One disadvantage of heat-treatment for practical stone tool users is that treated materials are weaker and more likely to fracture.

Prehistoric and ethnographic knappers in some areas routinely heat-treated their stone (Harkness 1986; Hester 1972; Keyser and Fagan 1987; Mandeville 1973; Shippee 1963; Tindale 1985). It is often possible to recognize heat-treated stone tools. Heat-treatment of a good chert gives it a very smooth, glossy fracture, with almost a "soapy" feel. This texture change is visible only on a fresh fracture or flake scar. If there are older surfaces with grainier, duller textures that contrast to the rest of the flake scars, it is likely that the tool was heat-treated. Colors often change too, becoming brighter and redder (as iron is oxidized). This may be obvious only when you can compare treated and raw samples of the same material.

All that is necessary for successful heat-treatment of the right stone is a high enough temperature and slow heating and cooling. Modern archaeologists and knappers have experimented extensively with different materials and techniques in recent years (e.g., Ahler 1983; Collins and Fenwick 1974; Crabtree and Butler 1964; Geyer 1988; Griffiths et al. 1987; Imel 1988; Joyce 1985; Luedtke 1992; Patterson 1978; Purdy 1974). Prehistoric knappers did quite well by burying flakes and building a fire over them. It is better to heat-treat flakes or partly finished tools rather than large nodules or cores, and the pattern of treated and raw scars on prehistoric tools shows that many were treated as rough blanks before final flaking. A bed of clean sand helps spread the heat slowly and evenly. Pieces of material should be buried shallowly, from a couple of centimeters (1 in.) to no more than about 10 centimeters (4 in.), unless you want to build a really big fire. A good hot campfire-sized fire will usually do. Build it up slowly and let it burn well for a couple of hours, then leave the coals to burn out and let the hearth cool down until you can dig with your hands. If the heat increases too fast, or if the hot flakes are exposed suddenly to cold air, they will crack, shatter, or develop potlid fractures. *Potlids* are little round flakes that pop off the surface and leave an irregular pitted scar. Potlids often indicate deeper flaws and mean that the material is ruined. The potlids themselves sometimes look like flakes, but can be distinguished because they have no platforms. The tendency of stone to fracture unpredictably under heat stress is why it is impossible to flake an arrowhead by dripping water on hot stone.

If you live in an area where outdoor fires are discouraged, you can improvise a heat-treating hearth in a charcoal grill or the like. Even simpler (but not available to prehistoric folk) is the modern gas or electric oven (Patterson 1978). Many cherts can be heat-treated at around 450–500 degrees Fahrenheit. I bury flakes in a baking pan filled with sand and heat them in the oven, raising the temperature 100 degrees Fahrenheit every hour and leaving them at 500 degrees for two to five hours before turning the oven off and letting it cool. This makes a very noticeable difference in the quality and ease of flaking of most cherts, but it will not be sufficient for novaculite and some tougher cherts. These tougher materials require temperatures of 600 to 800 degrees Fahrenheit. A number of knappers use electric kilns, and if you intend to heat-treat on a large scale or process big pieces of material, a kiln may be worth the expense. Obsidian, basalt, rhyolite, quartzite, and so on cannot be heat-treated at all. For the beginner with mediocre materials, heat-treating will be a considerable help.

COLLECTING MATERIAL: ETHICAL AND PRACTICAL CONSIDERATIONS

I have not tried to give specific information on where to find flakeable stone, but I will make a few suggestions about how to go about it. You can buy material at rock shops, knap-ins, or commercial suppliers advertising in the knapping newsletters (Appendix), but if you want a lot of material to learn on, this is probably too expensive an option. If you just want to experiment with some unusual or particularly colorful stones, it may be worth it.

Your best approach is to start by finding out what is in your area. State Geological Survey offices, geology departments in local colleges, museums, and rock hounds are a few possible sources of information to begin with. You should be able to find out at least where to find the right kinds of rock formations that might have knappable material so that you can go poke around in the area, looking in exposures such as road cuts and streambeds. Other knappers can give more detailed information on specific sources than you can find in most other ways.

The best and most common materials, obsidian, cherts, and flints, can sometimes be found in large flows, beds, or other deposits. Some of these are spectacular enough that they are protected as national or state parks, like the Obsidian Cliffs in Oregon or Petrified Forest National Monument in Arizona. Even if they are not, you should take care not to damage a natural wonder, even a minor one. Geological processes do not replace them fast enough.

Ownership is another problem. If you want to collect material from private land, the usual rules of courtesy apply and you should get permission. When Harold Dibble and I began to knap, we decided we needed a large supply of good material. We had heard of good sources in the area of Austin, Texas. Unfortunately, they were not well known to us or our Arizona friends and connections, so we drove 1,000 miles with only vague directions. As it turned out, we did well, but at first we were inhibited by rumors of Texan hostility to strangers on their land, and the numerous "Keep Out, NO Trespassing" signs suggested that Southern hospitality had suffered a decline. We found a dry river-bed where large chert nodules were visible from the highway, across a fence bedecked with "Trespassers Will Be Prosecuted" signs. A back-hoe was loading gravel into a truck, so we asked the driver if we could collect some chert. He pointed to a large house on the hill above, so we sent Harold, our best negotiator, to parley with the landowner. Harold asked him if he minded if we collected some chert. "Waall, Ah usually git five dollahs for a load of gravel," he said. We were not planning to use backhoes and trucks, Harold explained, just pick up some rocks. "Waall, Ah usually git five dollahs" was the reply. Harold got the same refrain to each song he tried, so he shelled out five dollars. As it turned out, that was the best source we found, and having paid the price of a dump-truck load, we ultimately came back with a U-Haul and back-packs and lugged almost two tons of nodules up out of the riverbed. Only a few scoops for a backhoe, but we felt we got our money's worth. We also avoided making another landowner hostile to trespass-ing knappers.

Rock is often so worthless to the people who own it that they will simply tell you to go ahead, but you should always ask. Sometimes it is possible to find public areas where no one minds, like road cuts. Similarly, material from many of the large sources that are protected on public land can be collected nearby. I favor road cuts and streambeds for several reasons. Material is easy to spot in them without intensive searching, sometimes even from a car. Both occasionally turn up fresh unweathered material that has not been picked over by other knappers, modern or prehistoric. And both are disturbed areas, where your col-lecting and flaking activities are unlikely to disrupt either other people or the archaeological record.

Never, ever, disturb any archaeological site! Our archaeological sites, and thus our chances of learning about prehistoric people, are vanishing at a horrible rate, destroyed by development and looting. Many people collect arrowheads and other artifacts. A lot of them are sincerely interested in archaeology, quite knowledgeable, and some-times helpful to the science of archaeology. The better collectors col-lect only surface material from sites that are disturbed by plowing, construction, erosion, or other forces, and they record the location of finds and report important sites so their work can be useful to archaeologists. Collectors who disturb sites by digging for artifacts rather than for information are inexcusable. An artifact means very little unless we know where it came from and what was with it (see Chapter 11 on interpreting stone tools). People who are only interested in artifacts to put in their display case and are willing to destroy sites to get them, or buy from those who do, are thieves who are stealing the heritage of all people. If you like handsome artifacts (and who doesn't?), replicating prehistoric tools or buying the work of modern knappers are much better ways to collect them.

Under no circumstances should your stone collecting disturb an archaeological site. Some of the source areas that are of interest to the knapper looking for material were also used by prehistoric knappers. The quarries and workshops that they left behind are important archaeological sites, all too often little known. After some early reports of important quarry sites (Holmes 1890, 1900, 1919), serious attention has only recently returned to quarries and workshops (e.g., Banks 1990; Butler and May 1984; Ericson and Purdy 1984; Ives 1975; Kamp and Whittaker 1986; Singer and Ericson 1977; Torrence 1986). Do not remove or displace the worked material on these sites.

Some of the early books on knapping (e.g., Mewhinney 1957) suggest using flakes from Indian sites to make your stone tools. As has been mentioned, even waste flakes can tell the archaeologist a lot about what was being made, so removing any artifacts from sites for your own flaking is not acceptable. Besides, if you are too lazy or inexperienced to make your own flakes, you should be using glass or other simple blanks.

You should also avoid confusing the archaeological record by dropping your own flakes on prehistoric sites. It is frequently impossible to tell the difference between a flake that is thousands of years old and one made yesterday. Some knappers consider it okay to flake in source areas like talus slopes, which were used prehistorically but are still sliding down slope and are all jumbled up. However, even here you are damaging a potential source of information. I take my material home before flaking unless I am collecting from a truly disturbed area like a road cut or a riverbed or a beach. Sometimes this means carrying a lot of waste weight, but the archaeological record is irreplaceable and should come before a bit of inconvenience.

Stones are not produced very fast, and the number of knappers is increasing. A couple of areas where I used to get material are now so picked over that it is hardly worth the time to visit them. Don't take more material than you will use, and don't waste it. As a beginner, you will ruin a lot of material in learning—that is unavoidable. But try to use it thoroughly. You can practice on pieces that won't make a nice finished product, or get small flakes from a broken handaxe, and so forth. It really pains me to see someone who just wants to make big bifaces throw away lovely flakes that would make a fine point. A good craftsman respects his or her material, understands it, and uses it with reverence.

One way to conserve material is to saw large nodules into slabs with a diamond rock saw. This requires expensive equipment, and slabs have some of the same problems as plate glass, but you can learn to overcome these. Most knappers only bother to saw fine, scarce materials, but you can make a lot more bifaces from a nodule by slabbing it than by knapping, so in the interests of conservation, this is a good idea.

If you have space, you can just keep a pile of flakes growing in your knapping area, and then all the waste is available to be picked over when you need a sharp edge for cutting or a blank to make an arrow point. A large pile of flakes is, however, messy and a menace to bare feet and small children. At the moment I have no place to keep a pile of flakes, and I knap on a tarp and pick up everything. Unless I am collecting debitage for research purposes, unusable waste goes into the garbage and ultimately the city dump, while the good waste flakes are saved for later use in labeled boxes so I know where the material came from. Stuff that is not so good but still usable I keep in another box for my students to practice on.

Returning to the subject of ethics, many knappers today sign or permanently mark their work. In many cases, it is virtually impossible to tell a well-made replication from a prehistoric artifact, so marking replications prevents anyone from later selling them fraudulently as antiquities. More important, it makes sure that a future archaeologist will not mistakenly analyze them as ancient artifacts. Our knowledge of the range of variation of some point types and their geographical distribution is probably already distorted by fakes that have been published as prehistoric specimens. This problem is especially severe where much of our knowledge of some point types comes from collections made without proper archaeological documentation. This problem will only become worse as more and more skillful knappers arrive on the scene, as more people make undocumented artifact collections, and as the original owners and finders of old collections die or sell their finds.

Many knappers, especially those who sell or trade their work, correctly point out that they are artists who deserve credit for their work. As knapping expands as a hobby, a craft, and a part of archaeology, knappers should want to distance themselves from the old reputation that many knappers had as "fakers." Signing stone work and exchanging pieces that are proudly modern for their value as craft and art is one way to do this.

I usually mark points the way I mark artifacts from my excavations, using black India ink and a dab of clear nail polish to protect it. A better and more permanent marking can be made using inexpensive engravers available in any hardware store. I use my initials, a date, and sometimes abbreviations indicating the material source or technique used. For example, "JW 4/88 Mono wood" is a biface made in April of 1988 from Mono Basin obsidian using a wooden baton. I do not sell or trade my work much, so I mark it mostly because in a few years I may want to remember when I made it or where the material came from. I also keep records of tools used, time spent, and other information on some pieces, and occasionally collect the debitage for future analysis. I usually do this only when I have a specific problem in mind, but some other knappers do it routinely and are already providing some useful insights on the development of knapping skills, the differences between individuals, and other problems. For a beginner, it is very useful to sit and examine an artifact and its debitage carefully, sketch it, and write notes about making it, remembering problems and how you solved them, or what went wrong and what you should have done.

5
SAFETY

To make arrows properly one should smear
his face with mud and sit out in the hot sun
in a quiet secluded spot. The mud is a precau-
tion against harm from flying chips of glass,
possibly also a good luck ritual.
      —Ishi's opinion (according to Pope 1974)

I have already told you how sharp stone tools can be, and described how I severed the tendons in my finger, so it should be obvious that stone tools are potentially dangerous. When you are experienced, you will be able to judge the risks more accurately and do what you wish about protecting yourself. As you begin, if you are willing to take my advice about how to knap, I hope you will take my advice about safety. I guarantee that if you knap for long, you will cut yourself, but if you pay attention to the basic safety rules, you should be able to escape with nicks instead of stitches.

My own injury is one of the worst I have heard of, although I have met several other knappers who also severed tendons or came near to removing fingers. Scars from cuts that just required a few stitches are so common that no one even shows them off. Let me tell you a couple of stories with morals from the class I taught in 1979.

On the first lab day, our ten students, who had been told to bring gloves, all showed up bare-handed. A couple who had some experience or had worked with other knappers protested that bare hands gave you a better "feel"; others just weren't impressed by our warnings. Harold Dibble and I gave our demonstration and set the students to work, using chunks of glassy green molybdenum slag. It worked just like obsidian—that is, it flaked easily and was extremely homogeneous and very, very sharp. There were a number of interruptions as people stopped working to swear and go get a bandage. By the end of the session every single student had cut his or her hand, and one had gone to the clinic for a couple of stitches. There was a distinct trail of little red spots from the work area to the bathrooms inside the anthropology building. It took a long time for the rains to wash them off the sidewalk, but at the next lab everyone wore gloves. Nowadays I'm older and wiser, and the courts are so utterly irresponsible about awarding huge sums to people who deserved what happened to them but sued anyway that I refuse to teach anyone unless they are properly protected.

The students didn't really know any better and mostly learned their lesson, but even experienced knappers make mistakes, or get careless, and pay for it. Later in the course, as we were sitting down to work one day, a student asked Harold to remove a large flake for him from a troublesome core. Harold hadn't yet put on his glove, but he picked up the core and struck a flake, which was a little bigger than expected. The sharp end of the flake sliced a quarter-inch of skin and flesh off the tip of one of the fingers of the hand he was using to hold the core. After we bandaged him and sent him to the clinic, I picked up the flake, which I still have. It still has a patch of skin with recognizable fingerprints stuck to it with blood. A picture doesn't do it justice; if I could pass it around and really shock you, maybe you would be a careful knapper.

Anyway, you get the point. I have seen some knappers who refuse to wear protective gear. They mostly claim it is because gloves and the like get in the way and make them less sensitive to the feel of the stone. Sometimes this is true, but in many cases I suspect a strong streak of *machismo*—the sense of danger pleases them and a bit of blood really impresses the spectators. Believe me, it is not worth the pain and inconvenience of the real injury you risk. Now you have been amply warned, so if you still want to knap, on your head be it.

PROPER TECHNIQUE

As I have said, everyone gets cut, and even leather gloves are not foolproof or indestructible. With a healthy respect for sharp flakes, some basic rules, and simple equipment, you can minimize the chance of accident and avoid serious injury. I will detail both safe techniques and protective equipment in the chapters on specific flaking techniques, but there are some general rules which should be observed always.

I hurt myself in spite of a good leather glove because I was not using my tools correctly. You do not want a flake to be going *toward* any part of you when it comes off. When a flake is removed, there is usually some force left over, and the flake tends to be pushed in the direction of the blow that removed it. If there is a sharp end or edge on the flake and flesh is in the way, you will regret it. You should hold a core or a pressure-flaked piece so that any flake you remove either falls free or is caught between your hand and the core, running parallel to the core and your hand rather than into your hand.

While it is sometimes okay to let a flake fall free, it is usually best to catch it somehow. If you can't do it with your hand, a pad or wrapping may work. There are two reasons for not letting flakes fly around.

First, you may damage the flake, chipping or shattering it if it hits something hard. Second, flying flakes are dangerous to you and anyone within a few feet of you. Eventually you will be able to predict and control your flaking enough to know where and how hard a given flake will come off. Most of the time, that is. Everyone makes mistakes, so be protected even when you think you are safe. This is doubly true if you are working with other knappers. You can't watch everyone and pay attention to your own work, so sit far enough away to be safe from flying debris and wear your glasses. Small pieces that splatter unpredictably can do a lot of damage if they hit your eye, even if anywhere else you would hardly notice them.

While I am on the subject of proper technique, I might as well add something about mental technique. Your mind is as important as your hands in knapping. To do good work, to avoid injury, and to learn from what you are doing, you must concentrate. Ishi worked in a secluded spot and maintained silence (Pope 1918, 1974). It is pleasant to work with others and you will learn from it, but you will probably do your best work when alone. I find that pleasant, familiar surroundings and an orderly arrangement of my tools and materials helps too.

Each knapper develops his or her own pace and rhythm. For instance, I work quite slowly compared with some friends. I find that if I try consciously to work very fast, I can occasionally force myself to a state of extra alertness and concentrated effort that works very well for a short while. More often, when I rush, I ruin my work, and I have worked with knappers who I think will never be very good because they are always working faster than they can think. I also know knappers who work faster than I can think and can produce a good point almost before I have decided where to strike the first blow.

Everyone has good days when for no apparent reason everything works, and also bad days when each attempt produces a worse result and the only thing to do is to take a rest. Even on good days, you may get tired, lose concentration or grip, and start making avoidable mistakes. I usually begin a knapping session by warming up on a piece of scrap. When I become tired of what I am doing or too fearful of spoiling a good piece, I work on something else (pressure flaking instead of percussion, for instance). If I get bored, tired, or cross, I quit altogether rather than waste time, energy, and material.

EYES

Your eyes are hard to replace and easily hurt. If you do not ordinarily wear glasses, spend a few bucks for some safety glasses sold in many hardware stores. Any knapping produces a lot of powder and tiny sharp fragments that fly around at random. This is especially a problem with glass and obsidian, which have a tendency to shatter and crush. Even pressure flaking produces dust and small flakes that can get flicked into your face. I admit to being a bit lax about wearing glasses, but I am especially careful to wear them when flaking obsidian or working with other knappers. If you do get something in your eye, do not rub it. Go to the sink immediately and wash it out with running water.

HANDS

Your hands are the part you are most likely to hurt in knapping. For percussion flaking I wear a leather glove on my holding hand (left for me), but usually not on my striking (right) hand. This is because the holding hand is where the sharp edges are being produced, and knocked around and against the hand. The striking hand is at less risk, although I have seen some damage from bashing it against a rock, or slashing it on a sharp edge in the follow-through motion of removing a flake. If you have to move large, sharp chunks of material or dig through a pile of debitage to find a flake, gloves on both hands are a good idea. Pressure flaking can be done into a glove, but a smaller pad that protects the palm but leaves the fingers free works better (see Chapter 7).

You can also injure yourself by repeated strenuous use of particular muscles, joints, and tendons. A number of knappers have complained of tendonitis in wrists and shoulders; a few have had to stop knapping. When you begin to get sore, rest or do something else. Repeatedly overworking joints can do permanent damage and lead to arthritic conditions.

OTHER BODY PARTS

Most modern knappers work sitting, and use their laps and legs to hold and stabilize cores. A large piece of soft leather provides good protection. You also want to avoid striking flakes off and letting them go zinging down at your calves and feet. Long pants and shoes instead of sandals are best. I have knapped in shorts, and while I don't let flakes fly free, I have usually collected an assortment of small nicks on my legs from the tiny bits of shattered material that fly off at every blow. I also find it more comfortable if my pants leg covers my shoe tops, so small, sharp objects don't fall into my shoes and work their way down between my toes. You will develop your own preferences about details like this as you go along.

LUNGS

Many of the nineteenth-century British gunflint knappers died of "consumption"—that is, lung diseases such as silicosis, cancer, and pneumonia (Kalin 1981). Skertchly (1879) unkindly commented that consumption of drink was even deadlier to them than consumption of the lungs, but that's beside the point. The British knappers spent ten to twelve hours a day flaking in small enclosed rooms, breathing the silica dust they produced. Knap in a sunbeam sometime, and you can see the dust that rises from your blows. You presumably will not be exposed to knapping dust as long or as intensively as were the British knappers, but it is best not to breathe any more of it than you can avoid. Cigarette smokers are at a greatly increased risk from other pollutants in the lungs, but if the obvious health hazards of stink-sticks have not convinced you to stop smoking, the added risk of knapping probably will not impress you either.

I don't worry too much about knapping dust because I don't flake very much and I don't smoke, but I do always try to work in well-ventilated areas. Outdoors is best if possible; if I work indoors, I make sure there is good air circulation and try to blow dust away from me after each blow rather than bending over the piece and snuffling it in. I have seen some modern knappers, such as Gene Stapleton, who work their pieces wet, dipping them in water to keep the dust down.

WASTE DISPOSAL

Disposal of waste is also a safety problem. Either knap in a limited area that can be closed off to children and barefooted visitors, or clean up very thoroughly. Even a small flake lost in the lawn can spoil your Sunday picnic. Keep untrained children away from stone tools—they may know a knife is sharp and not to be played with, but a flake can do unexpected damage.

Debitage from your quarrying and material collecting should also be properly disposed of. Do not leave it on prehistoric sites where it will muddle the archaeological record, and do not leave sharp bits of stone in public places where innocent feet may suffer.

BENEFITS

Having warned you at great length about the dangers of flintknapping, it is only fair to put in an encouraging word here. Flintknapping is probably less dangerous than home carpentry with power tools, downhill skiing, or many other things that perfectly normal people do for fun. Like many crafts, it can be relaxing, even a form of meditation if you like, or an opportunity to relieve your stresses upon a defenseless rock. If you knap a lot, it will improve your hand-eye coordination and the strength of your grip. On a more intellectual plane, it should increase your awareness of the natural world and your respect for our prehistoric ancestors, some of whom were superb craftsmen and all of whom coped with a world that we would find hard to imagine, let alone live in.

6

HARD-HAMMER PERCUSSION

*One old fellow, with energy surprising for his
years, dashed one stone upon another, mean-
while leaping high into the air to avoid the
flying splinters.*

—Hambly (1931:91, describing
Tasmanian knapping)

Hard-hammer direct percussion, in which flakes are produced by striking one stone with another, is the first and most basic knapping technique. The Tasmanians described above were using the simplest form.
If you throw one rock at another hard enough, it may shatter, and some
of the pieces may be useful, but the results are unpredictable and even
dangerous. Most people want better-shaped pieces and fewer flying
splinters and prefer to strike a core with a hammerstone held in the
hand. Hard-hammer percussion can be used to produce flakes, retouch
them into tools such as scrapers, and manufacture simple, heavy core
tools such as the earlier types of handaxes. Hard-hammer percussion is
also the starting point for many more refined tools, used to produce
flake blanks and to rough out forms that can be finished by other
techniques.

Hard-hammer flaking is a good way to understand many of the basic
principles of knapping, but it requires fairly large pieces of material. If
you are just beginning to knap and have not yet found a good source of
material, you should read this, try as much of it as possible on glass,
and then concentrate on pressure flaking at first.

MATERIAL AND EQUIPMENT

You will need something to flake, preferably in fairly large pieces—fist-
sized to head-sized. If nothing else is available, you can make do with
thicker pieces of man-made materials such as the bottoms of large
bottles, glass or porcelain insulators, or toilet bowl porcelain, as described in Chapter 4. Some other desirable characteristics of the cores
will become obvious as we go on.

Tools are simple. First, you need basic safety equipment: glasses,
leather gloves, and a piece of leather to cover your leg for padding and
protection. An assortment of hammerstones (Figure 6.1) is next. As a

6.1
Assorted hammerstones.
Bottom row, three
hammerstones from my tool
kit. *Top row,* three typical
hammerstones from Lizard
Man Village, Arizona. Most
heavily used ends are up.

10 cm.

general rule, the hammer should be lighter than the core it is striking, and the size of the hammer will also affect the size of the flake you can strike off. Hammerstones wear out and break, so you will want to have several, of different sizes, before you begin. My kit usually contains about five: a couple of small ones, 100–200 grams (3.5–7 oz.), which I use a lot for working small cores and in the early stages of bifaces; a couple of medium to large ones, 250–500 grams (about 8 oz. to 1 lb.), which are mostly for striking larger flakes to be worked into points and for making blades; and one large hammer, 600–1,000 grams (about 20 oz. to 2 lb.), which I only use when I need to remove very large flakes from really big cores.

Stream-rounded pebbles and cobbles of less brittle stone make the best flaking hammers. A rounded egg or oval shape fits the hand well, balances nicely, and has a definite end to strike with. On a flatter, rounded stone, you can use the edges. Different knappers prefer different shapes; all that really matters is the size and a convenient but definite point or spot on the hammerstone with which to strike.

Hammerstones should ordinarily be of tougher, less brittle material than the core they are used on. Quartzite, basalt, and similar tough, dense stones are best for most purposes, but softer stones like limestone and even hard chalk can be used on obsidian, and are also used by some skillful knappers to thin bifaces.

Stones that flake easily, like chert and obsidian, do not make the best hammerstones for knapping because each blow produces an incipient cone of percussion in the hammer as well as in the core, reducing the useful force of the blow, producing a rough irregular surface on the hammer, and occasionally flaking or shattering the hammer. Rocks that have cracks, flaws, or fracture planes or that are brittle and easily broken are no good. Although I have a couple of hammerstones that I have used for years, most hammers eventually break from the repeated blows. When you are beginning, you will strike many inaccurate blows that fail to remove a flake and stress the hammer even more, so you will break a lot of hammerstones.

Hammerstones quickly develop distinctive wear patterns, as each blow crushes a bit of the stone. If you use a hammer long enough, it will also become polished where your fingers grip it. The wear on hammerstones makes it possible for an archaeologist to recognize them as tools in an archaeological site rather than just random rocks (Figure 6.2).

PERCUSSION-FLAKING PRINCIPLES: AN EXPERIMENT

Although direct hard-hammer percussion flaking is the simplest knapping technique and the easiest to describe and understand, even here the knapper is simultaneously observing and controlling many inter-

6.2
Close-up of two hammerstones showing typical wear patterns. *Left,* a chert specimen from Lizard Man Village, Arizona. *Right,* a quartzite pebble hammer from my tool kit.

related variables. "Orgo" (Figure 6.3) was drawn to make fun of this, but a good knapper really is observing and controlling the force of the blow, the direction, the point on which it strikes, the shape of the core, the angles of the edges, and other things, all of which work together to affect the size and shape of the flake. Each time you strike a blow, the conditions are slightly different, but a good knapper can produce the flake he or she wants each time. The gunflint knappers of England could turn out thousands of gunflints a day, all so similar they look machine-made.

When you are actually knapping, it is hard to tell exactly what you are doing. Some of it is pretty much unconscious by the time you have some experience, and some of it is just hard to see, like the exact angle at which your blow meets the stone. In order to understand exactly what a knapper controls and how these variables affect the flake, Harold Dibble and I set up a controlled experiment using a mechanical knapper (Whittaker and Dibble 1979; Dibble and Whittaker 1981; see also Speth 1972, 1974, 1975, 1981). This experiment helped explain a lot of my own knapping to me, so I will describe it in some detail.

Not all our friends shared our interest, and we took a lot of guff (Figure 6.4) for the "flake-breaker," which was a gun sight and electromagnet mounted on a stand to release a steel ball bearing to drop and strike a precise point on a plate-glass core (Figure 6.5). We experimented with several variables that we considered important to a knapper. As I will discuss all of these from time to time, we may as well define them here (Figure 6.6).

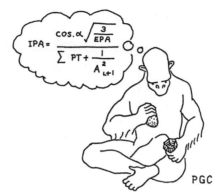

6.3
Orgo considers the variables in making an Oldowan chopper. Cartoon by Phil Chase.

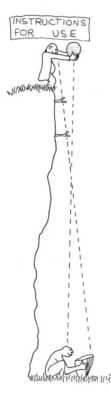

6.4
Mechanical knapping experiment as it appeared to our friends. Cartoon by Phil Chase.

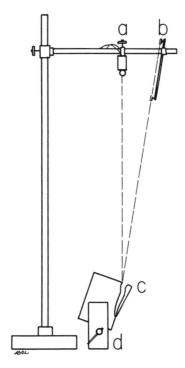

6.5
Mechanical knapping
apparatus as published:
(a) electromagnet holding
ball bearing, (b) gunsight,
(c) core and flake, (d) vise.

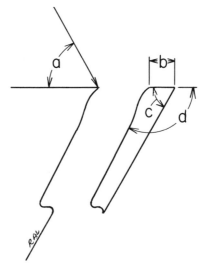

6.6
Variables defined on
experimental flakes:
(a) angle of blow,
(b) platform depth,
(c) exterior platform angle,
(d) interior platform angle.

Independent variables—that is, those controlled by the knapper—included:

1. *Platform depth:* how far back from the edge the steel ball struck the platform or, on a flake, the distance between the point of percussion and the edge of the platform.
2. *Angle of the blow:* the angle at which the hammer contacts the platform. We varied this by tilting the core.
3. *Exterior platform angle* (abbreviated EPA or *platform angle*): the angle formed by the platform and the surface of the core where the flake will be removed.
4. *Force of the blow:* varied by using three different sizes of steel balls, dropped from the same height.

The cores we used were all cut from plate glass and struck along an edge, so all the flakes had the same width. Dependent variables of the flakes are affected by what the knapper does (the independent variables above) and included:

1. *Interior platform angle:* the angle formed by the platform and the interior surface of the flake.
2. *Flake length.*
3. *Flake thickness.*

Our conclusions can be summarized in a few words, and their application to real knapping situations will follow. As might be expected, more forceful blows produce larger flakes, and greater platform depth also produces both longer and especially thicker flakes. A less obvious discovery was that the exterior platform angle strongly affected length. The closer the EPA came to 90 degrees, with everything else held constant, the longer the flakes, until at 90 degrees no flakes could be removed. The angle of the blow had little effect on flake size, but we experimented only with angles of 75, 65, and 50 degrees. The interior platform angle, which has been considered an indication of the angle of blow (Crabtree 1972b), did not actually respond measurably and was in fact so useless that we feel it can be ignored in archaeological studies. Henceforth, when I speak of the platform angle, I mean the *exterior* platform angle.

PERCUSSION FLAKING

Actual knapping is quite different from the artificial experiment described above, although analyses of archaeological flakes show the same trends (Dibble 1981, 1985). The most important things to keep in mind when beginning are the exterior platform angle, the angle of

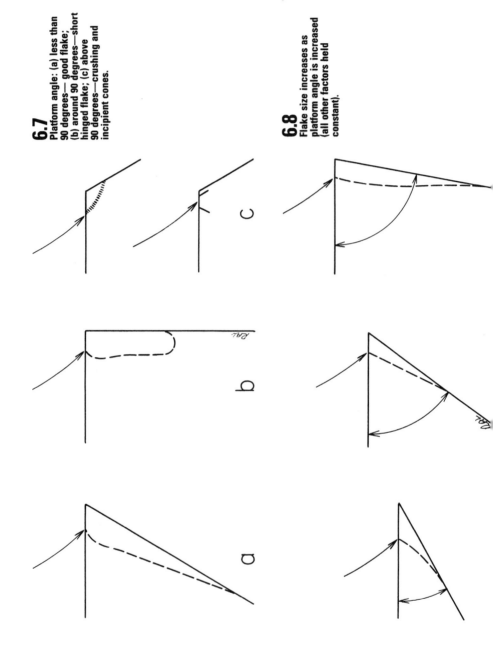

6.7
Platform angle: (a) less than 90 degrees— good flake; (b) around 90 degrees—short hinged flake; (c) above 90 degrees—crushing and incipient cones.

6.8
Flake size increases as platform angle is increased (all other factors held constant).

a

b

c

the blow, and the shape of the exterior surface from which the flake is to come.

1. *Select a suitable piece of material.* To begin with, pieces about the size of your hand or fist are best. Flat is better than spherical—somewhere along the edges you need to find a spot where a smooth surface for a platform makes an angle of less than 90 degrees with the surface from which the flake will come (Figure 6.7). If the exterior platform angle is around 90 degrees, you are likely to get short, thick flakes with pronounced hinge terminations unless you take steps to prevent it. If the exterior platform angle is much more than 90 degrees, no flake at all will be detached, and a blow will often produce a crushed area or an incipient cone, either of which may cause you trouble during later work.

As mentioned earlier, the angle of the platform also affects flake length. If we ignore other factors, any increase in platform angle will increase flake size (Figure 6.8), but in ordinary knapping, other factors must also be controlled to allow large flakes. Start with exterior platform angles well below 90 degrees, and don't try to strike huge flakes until you know what you are doing.

2. *Choose a suitable hammerstone.* It should be lighter than the core you are going to strike. Otherwise, the weight of the hammer's slow, heavy blow will overcome the inertia of the core and knock it aside so that a flake is prevented or accuracy is ruined.

3. *Seat yourself comfortably.* I like a chair or stool that is about knee height so that my thighs are almost level. I do most of my flaking with the core either held in my left hand with the left wrist steadied on my left leg, or resting against the outside of my left leg.

When the core is held in your hand (Figures 6.9, 6.10), you can let the flakes fall between your feet at first. However, they will frequently fly and splatter rather than falling gently, so beware. Once you can produce consistent flakes and predict where they will terminate and come off the core, you can wrap your fingers around the core, keeping the surface from which the flake will come flat against (parallel to) your flesh, and let the flake come off and be pinned between hand and core.

With the core against the outside of my left leg, as in Figure 6.11, the flake comes off between my leg and the core and is caught. This position is good for large cores that are too big to hold comfortably or steadily in the hand, but requires a little care to avoid bashing the leg or cutting it with a flake. The leather pad helps a lot, but you also need to make sure that the flake does not come off above your leg and go down into it. Again, the surface to be flaked must be flat against your flesh. I recommend flaking against the leg with a good leather pad at

6.9
Basic sitting percussion
position, with core held
in the hand, wrist supported
on leg.

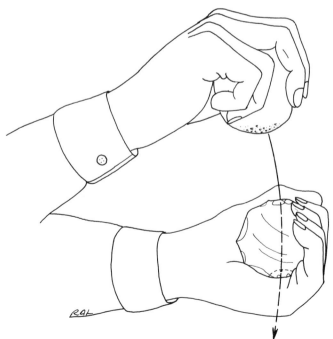

6.10
Freehand percussion flaking.
This works best sitting, with
the holding hand steadied on
the knee. The intended flake
is indicated by the dotted
line on the core. The left
hand is shown without a
glove for clarity, but you
should wear one.

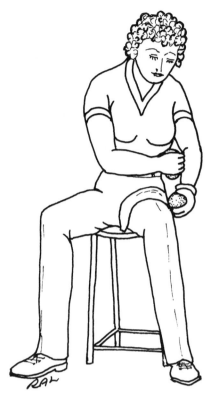

6.11
Hard-hammer percussion,
sitting with core steadied on
outer thigh.

first as the all-around safest method. It also allows you to hold the core very steady and see and adjust the angle of the blow easily by tilting the core.

4. *Position the core and aim the blow.* Aiming requires control of several factors: the point of impact, the angle of the blow, and the force of the blow. The point of impact, or point of percussion, should be about 3–6 millimeters (⅛–¼ in.) in from the edge at a spot where the exterior platform angle is less than 90 degrees. The distance of the point of percussion from the edge of the platform will partly decide how big a flake you remove. If you strike too close to the edge, you will get only tiny chips; if you strike too far in, you will probably not remove a flake at all (Figure 6.12). Accuracy is something you develop with practice.

5. *Try to make the angle of the blow less than 90 degrees* (Figure 6.13). One of the most common problems I have seen in giving new knappers their first lesson has been a tendency to hit straight down on the platform, or even into it at an angle greater than 90 degrees. This crushes platforms and produces steps and incipient cones that spoil a platform. When you swing a hammerstone, it moves in an arc, which

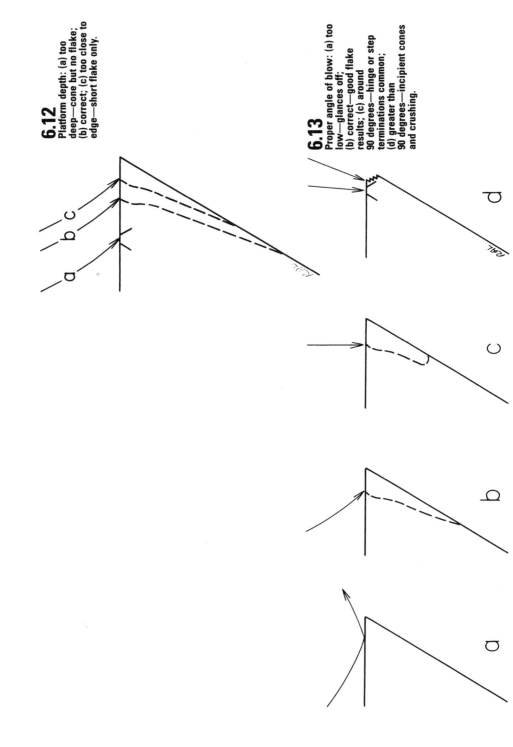

6.12
Platform depth: (a) too deep—cone but no flake; (b) correct; (c) too close to edge—short flake only.

6.13
Proper angle of blow: (a) too low—glances off; (b) correct—good flake results; (c) around 90 degrees—hinge or step terminations common; (d) greater than 90 degrees—incipient cones and crushing.

a

b

c

d

is one reason why experimenters use mechanical flakers—a dropped ball bearing strikes a straight blow, and the angle of the blow can be controlled and measured. In real knapping, if you keep a consistent swing, you can adjust the angle of the blow to the platform by tilting the platform. Bracing the core against your leg also helps prevent you from moving the core or tipping it the wrong way just as the blow reaches it. You want the core to remain absolutely still; only the striking hand should be in motion. If you move the core, you will lose accuracy and probably spoil the angle of the blow. When you actually strike the core, the force of the blow will cause it to move, but you want to keep the motion of the core as small as possible.

Another way to visualize and calculate the correct angle of blow is to picture the fracture you want as one side of a cone spreading out from the point of impact (Figure 6.14; see also Crabtree 1972b; Hellweg 1984). I offer this only as a mental aid, since the angle of the blow does *not* actually work this way. This was one of the surprising conclusions of our mechanical flaking experiment (Dibble and Whittaker 1981). As I have already noted, the interior platform angle, which is supposed to reflect the angle of blow (Crabtree 1972b), did not change significantly as the angle of the blow was changed. There are two reasons. First, it is sometimes assumed that the upper part of the interior surface of a flake is largely the edge of a cone of percussion. This is a gross oversimplification. The fracture may begin in a cone shape, but in most flakes it is almost immediately distorted to a relatively flat fracture plane. Second, the Hertzian cone itself responds only a little to the angle of the blow. You can test this yourself on a flat piece of thick glass.

Nevertheless, most knappers, myself included, find that changing the angle of the blow will change the flake produced. I think this results mostly from some other, unrecognized variables, especially a tendency to strike closer to the edge of the platform as the angle of blow decreases. Also, a blow that is an arc exerts force down and force out, and as the angle of blow increases, more of the force of the blow is applied down (into the core) and less outward (see discussion of terminations below). This is a problem that needs further study, and points out the usefulness of artificial experiments like our mechanical knapper that allow some control of variables that are very hard to see when you are knapping.

In any case, however you visualize your angle of blow, the essentials to remember are that it *must* be less than 90 degrees and greater than about 35–45 degrees. Above 90 degrees a blow will crush the platform or produce only an incipient cone; below about 35–45 degrees it will often glance off. By far the greatest problem for beginners is keeping the angle less than 90 degrees.

6. *Control the force of the blow.* Nonknappers expect flaking to re-

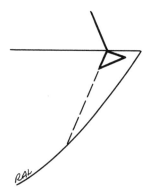

6.14
Using a cone model to visualize angle of blow. This socalled "cone angle principle" is only a model—this is not really how cones behave.

quire a lot of strength, because they figure you have to hit a stone pretty hard to break it. Actually, unless you are flaking a really tough stone, you don't need much more force in the blow than you get from the weight of the hammerstone. You can think of it almost as guiding a falling stone rather than *hitting* with it. Your arm and wrist should be relaxed, with a smooth easy swing. You should hold the hammerstone with a precision grip (see Figure 6.10), pinched between your thumb and first two fingers, rather than a power grip with the stone in your palm and fingers wrapped around it. Accuracy is more important than force. The blow should follow through if the flake comes off, or bounce back slightly if it does not. Don't smother it dead against the core, or pull it and reduce the force and accuracy. Using a pecking motion is a common fault in beginners. Also, on most stone, if the flake does not come off, it is probably not because you didn't hit hard enough, so don't rear back and wallop the next try. Stop and look at the core and platform. Did you hit it where you wanted to? Was the point of percussion close enough to the platform edge to allow a flake? Was the exterior platform angle less than 90 degrees? Was your angle of blow less than 90 degrees? All of these things are more likely to be the problem than the amount of force. Striking harder usually decreases your accuracy and is likely to make you move the core, forget to maintain the right angle, and bring out other bad habits you are trying to avoid.

PLATFORMS
Platforms are the key to successful knapping. You cannot get beyond the most basic levels of knapping without understanding and knowing how to control and use platforms. In teaching knapping, platforms are the most difficult thing to explain, and in flaking they are the hardest thing to remember and prepare. Always pay attention to your platforms. As you begin knapping, it is very helpful to stop and think about each one, look closely at it before you strike, then pick up the flake

and put it back on the core to see whether you struck where you intended to and how the flake responded. Time spent thinking about platforms is never wasted and will be well repaid by producing successful flakes and avoiding crushed edges and hinge scars. The way someone knaps tells you something about his or her personality. I have worked with several impatient types who will never be good knappers, simply because all they want to do is hammer away without thinking about what they are doing.

As I will explain, there are a number of ways to modify and prepare platforms. If a platform does not look good, don't strike it. If you strike a platform that is too weak, or the wrong angle, or in the wrong place, you will crush it, get a bad flake, or break the piece, and you have made your problems worse or spoiled your piece completely when a moment's preparation work would have given you the flake you wanted. As we discuss platform preparation, there are a few more basics to explain.

The platform surface should be clean. If it has ridges, or steps left by previous flakes, or small prominent irregularities, or soft cortex, a blow will fall "dead," crushing these and dispersing the force without removing a flake. Low ridges or facets left by the feather edges of previous flakes are usually no problem.

If you have an edge with a good platform angle of less than 90 degrees but the platform surface is unacceptable, you can often clean it up by turning the core over and detaching a flake using the other face of the edge as a platform. If done correctly, this removes the problems on the platform you want, and you can then turn the core back and strike your flake (Figure 6.15). This makes your core bifacial.

I have already said several times that the exterior platform angle must be less than 90 degrees, but I will emphasize it again for beginners. If the exterior platform angle is equal to or greater than 90 degrees, a couple of outcomes are likely. Around 90 degrees, short, thick flakes with pronounced hinge terminations are common. If you strike a hard blow to overcome the tendency to hinge, the flake is likely to overshoot and carry away the end of your core. If the exterior platform angle is much more than 90 degrees, no flake at all will be detached, and a blow will often produce a crushed area or an incipient cone, either of which means trouble during later work on the piece.

In our mechanical knapping experiment, we found that increasing the exterior platform angle increased flake length. In some prehistoric industries, especially blade industries where long flakes were especially desired, exterior platform angles close to 90 degrees are common. However, this need not be the case, because in real knapping situations several other things can be more important than exterior platform angle in determining flake size.

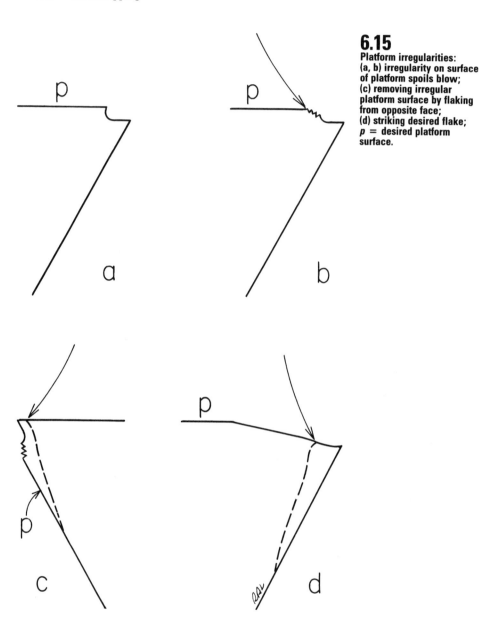

6.15
Platform irregularities:
(a, b) irregularity on surface
of platform spoils blow;
(c) removing irregular
platform surface by flaking
from opposite face;
(d) striking desired flake;
p = desired platform
surface.

Nevertheless, control of the platform cannot be emphasized enough, and one of the most important aspects that can be easily controlled is the exterior platform angle. I distinguish three basic techniques, used separately or in combination, to control the exterior platform angle and prepare the platform for a blow. These are facetting, trimming, and rubbing.

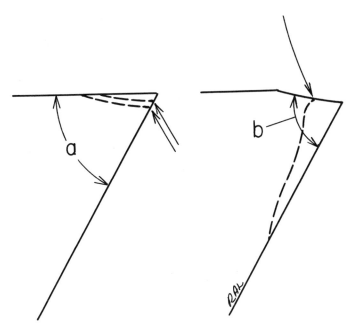

6.16
Facetting used to increase exterior platform angle: (a) original platform angle (blows are actually struck in usual position); (b) increased platform angle and desired flake.

In *facetting* flakes are removed from the platform surface. I have already mentioned this as a useful way to remove irregularities on the platform surface. Facetting also changes the exterior platform angle, usually increasing it (Figure 6.16). This tends to increase flake length and is a common feature of some techniques—for instance, the Levallois technique, which will be described later. However, if a large flake with a deep bulb of percussion is removed from the platform surface, the effect is to lower the platform angle close to the edge of the platform (Figure 6.17). In some situations this can be done to overcome an exterior platform angle that is too close to 90 degrees.

Trimming removes small flakes from the exterior surface of the core, in the same direction as the large flake you intend to remove. Trimming can also change the platform angle if the trimming flakes are relatively long and run down the face of the core; in effect they increase the exterior platform angle (Figure 6.18).

Much trimming is on a smaller scale, removing only very small flakes. This changes the exterior platform angle at the very edge of the core, but if the blow is struck far enough in, the effective platform angle for the removal of the objective flake is the same as for the untrimmed platform (Figure 6.19). This sort of trimming is useful because it removes thin platform edges that cannot withstand a blow. This improves the accuracy of your blow and reduces the chances of accidentally striking an edge that would crush, leaving an impaired platform. Trimming, for instance, is usually the best way to remove the small

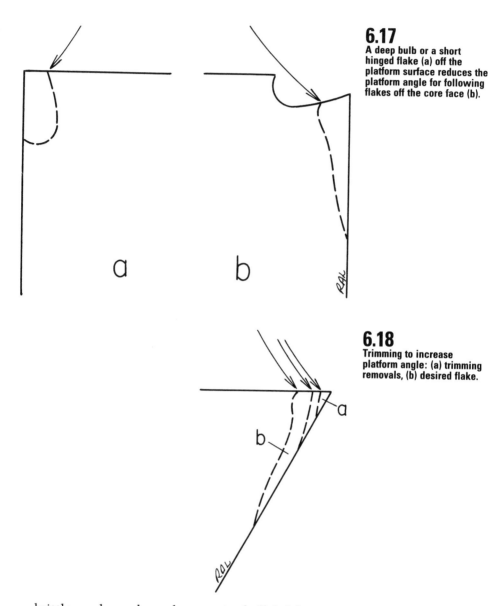

6.17
A deep bulb or a short hinged flake (a) off the platform surface reduces the platform angle for following flakes off the core face (b).

6.18
Trimming to increase platform angle: (a) trimming removals, (b) desired flake.

brittle overhang above the negative bulb left by a previous flake detachment from the same platform.

Rubbing is usually done with the hammerstone, or another abrasive stone, rubbing it across or along the edge of the platform. If the rubbing motion is up and down across the platform, flakes may be caught and pulled off, usually very small flakes. The effect can be either trimming or facetting or both (Figure 6.20). This is a useful way to remove thin, crushable edges and overhangs. Trimming by rubbing across a platform

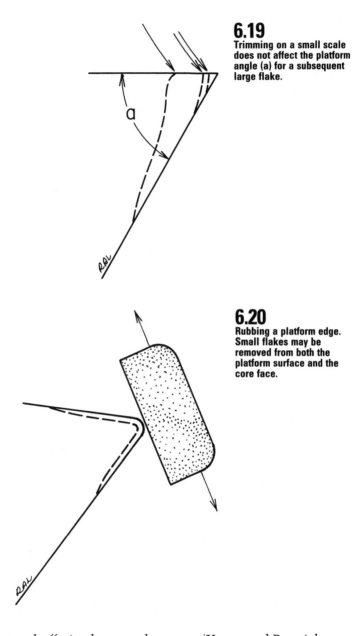

6.19
Trimming on a small scale
does not affect the platform
angle (a) for a subsequent
large flake.

6.20
Rubbing a platform edge.
Small flakes may be
removed from both the
platform surface and the
core face.

is also referred to as *buffeting* by some knappers (Young and Bonnichsen 1984:101). Rubbing with an abrasive stone, either across the platform or along it, rounds and dulls the sharp edge of the platform. We will discuss this more in the sections on soft-hammer and pressure flaking.

Rubbing the surface of the platform with an abrader can also be use-

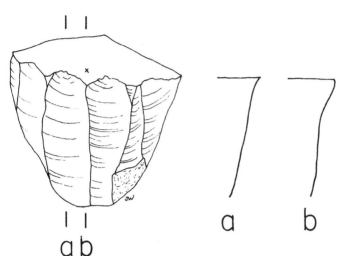

6.21
Core with irregular platform edge left by previous flake removals. *X* marks next point of percussion. Views of edge (a, b) show overhang at negative bulbs of previous flake scars.

ful. The scratches left on the surface help keep tools from slipping off when the blow is struck, and they weaken the surface, making it easier to begin a flake fracture (Patterson 1979a).

I have described the effects of facetting, trimming, and rubbing as seen on the platform cross-section and exterior platform angle. These techniques also help to regularize the platform in its other dimensions. Just as there should be no weak, easily crushed irregularities on the platform surface, the platform edge too should be fairly straight. Seen from above, the platform in Figure 6.21 is wavy and ragged, the result of previous blows. The point of percussion for the desired flake is marked by an *x* above a good ridge on the core face. Trimming small flakes from the core face removes the thin edge overhanging a bulb at *a* and the platform remnant jutting out between flake scars at *b*, making the edge straighter, easier to aim at, and more predictable in its behavior as well as improving platform angles (Figure 6.22).

A specific target platform can also be *isolated* (Figure 6.23). The platform can be slightly notched on either side of the target point. Trimming is usually the best way to do this, but facetting may also be appropriate. Isolating a target platform has three effects. First, it gives you a better, more specific point to aim at. Second, it reduces the distance the initial crack on the platform surface has to travel, and thus the force required to detach the flake. Third, it increases and straightens the ridge on the core face directly under the platform, which guides and shapes the flake, as will become clear in a moment.

To summarize my own use of these techniques, I can say that I routinely trim platforms, especially to remove overhangs left by previous flakes. I don't ordinarily facet or isolate platforms except to solve specific problems.

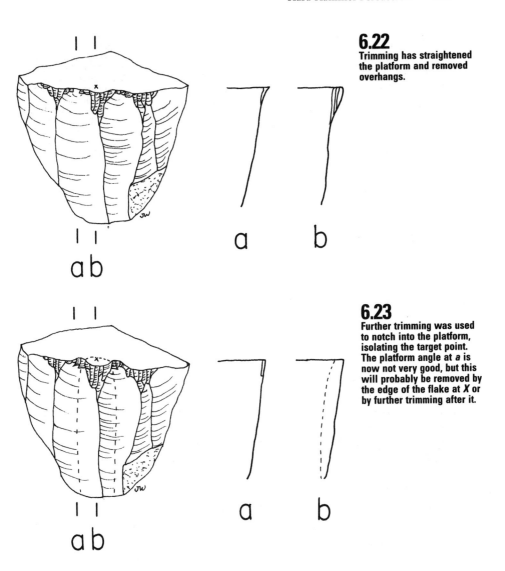

6.22
Trimming has straightened the platform and removed overhangs.

6.23
Further trimming was used to notch into the platform, isolating the target point. The platform angle at *a* is now not very good, but this will probably be removed by the edge of the flake at *X* or by further trimming after it.

THE FACE OF THE CORE

The characteristics of the platform are one set of attributes that influence the form of a flake and that must be controlled by the knapper. The second major group of influences comes from the shape of the core face from which the flake is removed.

As a general rule, the fracture plane for any flake tends to pass under the greatest mass. In other words, flakes tend to follow ridges on core faces (Figure 6.24). The extreme case of this is seen in making blades, where the establishment of a regular set of parallel flake scars forming ridges on the core face is what allows a series of long, straight flakes,

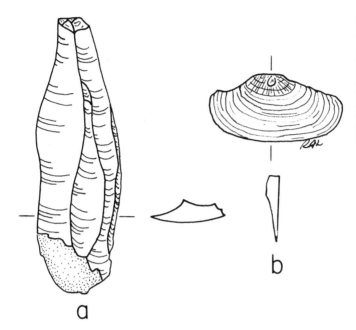

6.24
The shape of the core face affects the shape of the flake: (a) flake tends to follow any ridge, such as the intersection of two flake scars on the exterior of this blade; (b) flake tends to expand on flat surface, as did this one on plate glass (interior surface).

as the subsequent blades follow these ridges. Observation of ridges, usually the scars of previous flakes, allows you to predict and control flake length, shape, and termination. Eventually the ability to set up ridge systems where you want them will become a crucial part of your knapping skill. For now, note that a platform established over an existing ridge will produce a long flake; a platform above the hollow of a negative bulb or a flat surface will produce a short expanding flake.

TERMINATIONS

Flake terminations have been previously defined (Chapter 2). In most cases, sharp feather terminations are desirable because they produce a sharp edge on the flake and a smooth surface on the core. If you are flaking correctly, most terminations will be feathered, or close to it.

Step and hinge terminations are usually undesirable. They are common errors that result from several kinds of mistakes. One common cause of step and hinge terminations is in the way the core is struck. A blow with a hammerstone follows an arc, but when it strikes the core, you can think of it as applying force in two directions (Figure 6.25). There is a downward force that compresses the material and drives the fracture into the core in the direction of the flake's length. There is also an outward force that is pulling the flake away from the core, as the crack between core and flake lengthens and widens. This outward tensile stress not only helps to open the crack, but actually flexes the flake a little bit, as can be shown with photographs (Crabtree

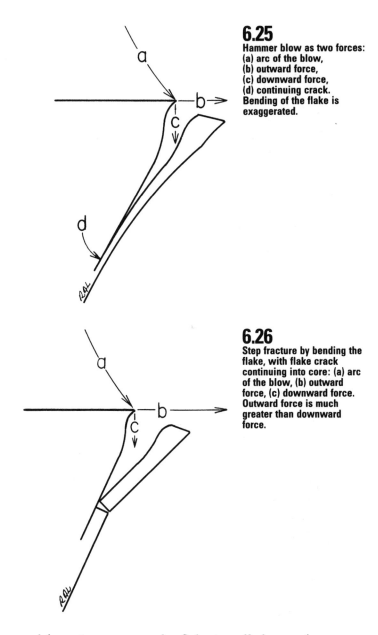

6.25
Hammer blow as two forces:
(a) arc of the blow,
(b) outward force,
(c) downward force,
(d) continuing crack.
Bending of the flake is
exaggerated.

6.26
Step fracture by bending the
flake, with flake crack
continuing into core: (a) arc
of the blow, (b) outward
force, (c) downward force.
Outward force is much
greater than downward
force.

1968). If the outward force is too great, the flake is pulled away from
the core too rapidly, and snaps when it is bent beyond its endurance
(see Sollberger 1986). Sometimes you can even see the fracture plane
extending into the core as a crack that ran part way under a step fracture, before the flake broke off and the downward force was terminated
(Figure 6.26). Accordingly, if you are getting lots of step and hinge frac-

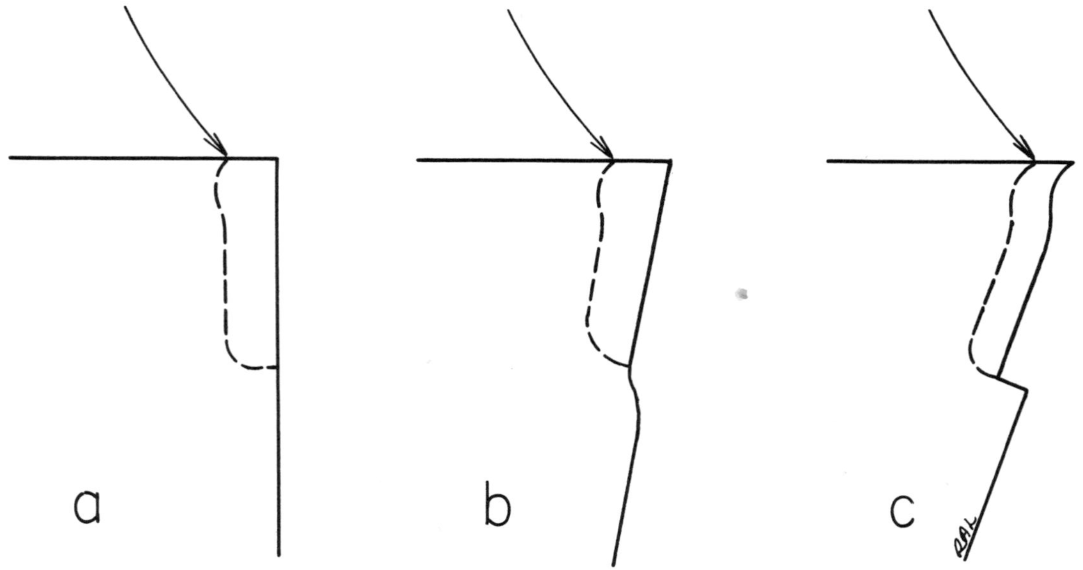

6.27
Causes of hinge terminations: (a) platform angle close to 90 degrees, struck with insufficient force; (b) flake runs into preexisting lump; (c) flake runs into existing step or hinge scar.

a

b

c

tures on cores where the angles and surfaces should be good, it is probably because you are pulling the hammerstone toward you at the instant of impact. This is a common fault of beginners, and I catch myself doing it sometimes when I am particularly anxious about the accuracy of a blow on a small platform. I find myself tightening up and forgetting to keep a loose swing and natural follow-through. Logically, low angles of blow also increase the chance of a step or hinge, but I have rarely seen this problem in beginners.

Step and hinge fractures also seem to occur when the force of a blow is simply not sufficient to remove a long flake—the crack follows a shorter path to the core surface by hinging. I suspect that bending is usually involved too. Step and hinge terminations become more likely as the exterior platform angle gets closer to 90 degrees (Dibble and Whittaker 1981), partly because the force needed to detach a flake also increases (along with flake size) and also because the fracture plane of a flake from a 90-degree platform is running nearly parallel to the surface of the core instead of at an angle that encourages an easy exit (Figure 6.27a).

Steps and hinges also interfere with subsequent flakes. When a flake stops short, subsequent flakes on the same surface may run into the step or hinge left on the core. When a flake runs into a large mass of material, much more than was being separated by the fracture plane that started at the point of percussion, it often stops, and the flake breaks off at the edge of the increased mass, making an even larger step (Figure 6.27c). Similarly, you cannot flake into a depressed area or concavity on a core's face or into a large bulge or lump (Figure 6.27b). Repeated step terminations may produce a *stack* or *plateau* on the face of a core, and the failure to remove such a problem is often the reason for discarding a core or biface (Figure 6.28; see also Figure 8.34).

A large, thick flake may run deeply enough to pass under steps and other obstacles, and with proper platform preparation, even a relatively small flake can be oriented so as to remove a large mass. This problem will be discussed at some length in the section on biface thinning. On simple percussion cores, here are the best options:

1. Avoid flaking into either depressions or bumps—follow ridges and regular, slightly convex surfaces.
2. If you get one step, don't make it worse by flaking into it.
3. One way of removing such problems is to strike a large flake. This will often remove a major part of your core, however, and so may not be a good solution.
4. Alternatively, remove the obstacle from a different platform (Figure 6.29).

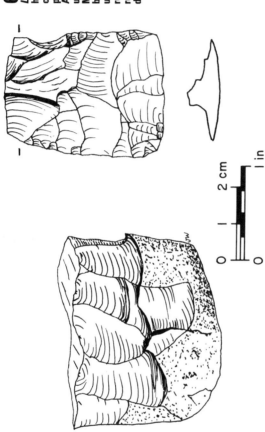

6.28
Left, flaws and repeated hinge and step fractures caused discard of this prehistoric chert core from Arizona. *Right,* this unfinished chert point from Mississippi was probably broken during repeated and unsuccessful attempts to remove the plateau left by repeated step terminations during soft-hammer thinning.

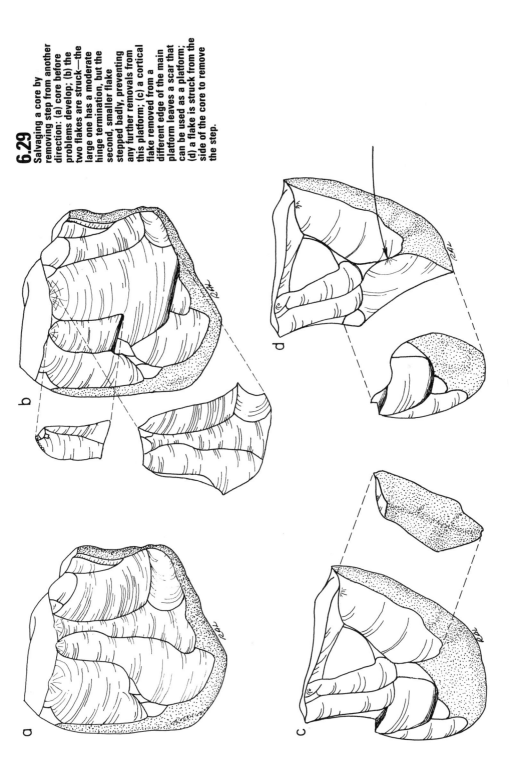

6.29
Salvaging a core by removing step from another direction: (a) core before problems develop; (b) the two flakes are struck—the large one has a moderate hinge termination, but the second, smaller flake stepped badly, preventing any further removals from this platform; (c) a cortical flake removed from a different edge of the main platform leaves a scar that can be used as a platform; (d) a flake is struck from the side of the core to remove the step.

a

b

c

d

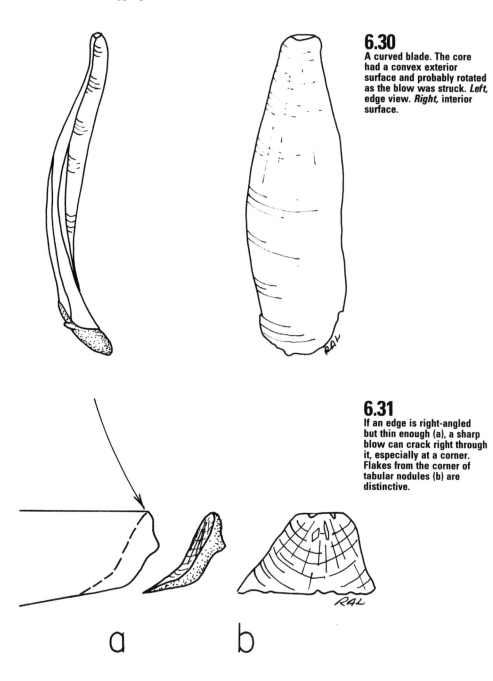

6.30
A curved blade. The core had a convex exterior surface and probably rotated as the blow was struck. *Left,* edge view. *Right,* interior surface.

6.31
If an edge is right-angled but thin enough (a), a sharp blow can crack right through it, especially at a corner. Flakes from the corner of tabular nodules (b) are distinctive.

a   b

CURVATURE

The fracture plane that separates a flake from a core follows approximately a straight line, but will curve under certain conditions. The shape of the core affects flake curvature (Andrefsky 1986). If the core is flat, the fracture will be fairly flat. If the outer face of a core is smoothly convex, the fracture will continue to pass under a certain mass and will partly follow the curvature of the core (Figure 6.30). If the core moves when struck, rolling under the force of the blow, this can also produce a notably curved flake.

STARTING A CORE

Some kinds of material come in angular lumps, and it is easy to find some edge that forms an angle of less than 90 degrees. However, on many potential cores, suitable platforms are few. Rounded and right-angle edges are common problems. For instance, most natural nodules of chert and flint are rounded, and right-angle platforms occur on the edges of tabular flint, broken flakes, snapped bifaces, and plate glass.

If a right-angle or rounded edge is thin enough, a sharp blow can sometimes crack right through it (Figure 6.31). Most cores will have some place on them where this can be done, and once the first flake is struck, the scar it leaves can serve as a platform for further work.

If you have an edge on a core that makes an angle of less than 90 degrees, it is logical that you can strike flakes off it from either side, and we have seen how this may be used to improve an unsatisfactory platform surface. If you flake from only one side, your core is unifacial—that is, flakes come off only one face of the core. It can equally well be bifacial if you strike flakes in both directions, covering both faces. This may be a useful way of getting the most flakes out of a piece of material, by avoiding problems on one face, for example. In addition, many tools, even very early and simple ones, were bifaces. Producing a bifacial edge on a piece of material is useful in platform preparation for simple flake cores, as a flaking strategy for flake cores, and as a basic starting point in manufacturing some kinds of tools, which will be discussed as "turning the edge" in the next chapter.

Many cores end up as *multidirectional* or *amorphous* cores, with flakes removed opportunistically in many directions from many platforms. It is more efficient, when possible, to flake consistently in one direction from a single platform (see "Blades," Chapter 9), but as cores become smaller and flaws or errors interfere with one face or another, it is often possible to remove flakes from other directions.

Occasionally you may run into a nodule that is essentially a sphere. There are two ways to deal with this. One is bipolar percussion. In *bipolar flaking* (Sollberger and Patterson 1976a; Hardaker 1979; Koba-

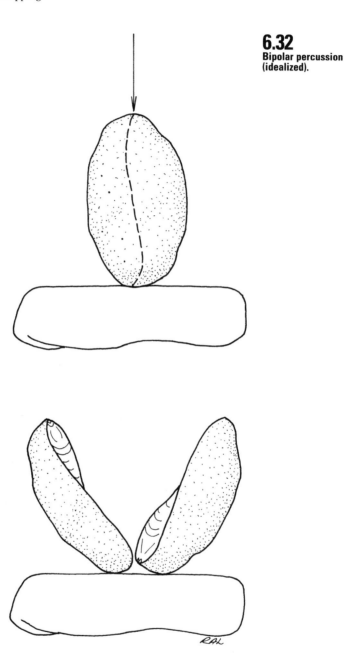

6.32
Bipolar percussion
(idealized).

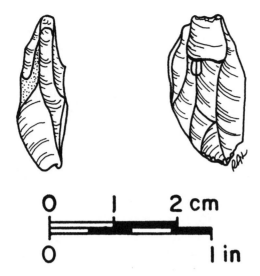

6.33
Bipolar obsidian core from Lizard Man Village, Arizona. The core is 2.3 centimeters (⅞ in.) high.

yashi 1975) the core is rested on a hard surface that serves as an anvil, and a blow straight down on top of the core drives it down on the anvil (Figure 6.32). This may produce cones simultaneously at the point of percussion and the point of contact with the anvil, and tends to split or shatter the core (Figure 6.33). A roundish core may split up into sections like an orange. The fracturing force is almost purely compression (Cotterell and Kamminga 1987), which is ideally very stable and predictable but in real knapping situations with irregular cores is extremely hard to control (Sollberger and Patterson 1976a). Nevertheless, this technique was common in some prehistoric stone industries (Flenniken 1981; White 1968), usually where rounded cobbles were the prevalent raw material. As bipolar flaking is hard to control, it is not ordinarily recommended.

A related technique for dealing with rounded nodules is the so-called *split cone* technique (Crabtree 1972a). Instead of resting the core on an anvil and getting a bipolar fracture, the core can be rested on a yielding surface, such as sand or a padded leg, and struck a very hard blow at right angles to the surface. The material at the point of the blow is compressed and acts rather like a wedge to split the piece. The fracture surface has a rather odd, flattened compression bulb, which is often crushed or sheared. Rounded nodules can be split this way, leaving flat surfaces for platforms. This technique is also useful for breaking a very large nodule into more manageable sections (Titmus 1980). However, it is harder than it sounds, and not likely to succeed the first few times you try. The penalty for trying and failing is of course incipient cones in your piece of material.

SUMMARY: NINE ESSENTIALS

The main variables to keep in mind in hard-hammer percussion flaking are these:

1. The platform must have an angle of less than 90 degrees.
2. The striking angle must be less than 90 degrees.
3. Use an easy, natural swing and follow through on the blow.
4. A great deal of force is usually not necessary.
5. Aim at a spot about 3–6 millimeters (⅛–¼ in.) from the core edge, or about as far in as you would like the flake to be thick.
6. Try to strike above a ridge on the core face and not above a step, depression, or lump that will stop your flake.
7. Trim your platforms for best results.
8. The platform angle, the platform depth, and the shape of the surface of the core are the most important factors in determining the size of your flake.
9. Above all, think about what you do. Observe your setup and talk to yourself about why you are doing it that way and what you think the result will be. Look at the result and see if you were right, and if not, why not. You can even use a crayon to draw the outline of the flake you expect on the core before striking it. When you are beginning, this is good practice, and when you are fairly consistent, it makes a good demonstration of the predictability of a good knapper's flaking.

EXAMPLES

Example 1: Simple Flake Core

A rounded lump of obsidian is selected to demonstrate beginning a core on a difficult piece (Figure 6.34a). The first step is to break the nodule open with a heavy blow, using a large hammerstone (Figure 6.34b). This requires some force and may leave the split cone mentioned above or, in this case, a very large bulb of percussion. The scar left by this first large flake provides a platform, and flaking begins anywhere there is a suitable less-than-90-degree angle, formed by the scar surface as platform and the cortical exterior of the core. The second flake (Figure 6.34c) was intended to follow a rounded ridge on the face of the nodule, but the blow fell too far in, and the flake expanded. The third flake followed the corner of the core and was much straighter but still irregular (Figure 6.34d).

Example 2: Retouching a Scraper

A thickish flake can be easily retouched into a scraper by unifacial percussion flaking (Figure 6.35). Most of the edge has an angle of less than 90 degrees, and even where the edge is not a good platform, it is

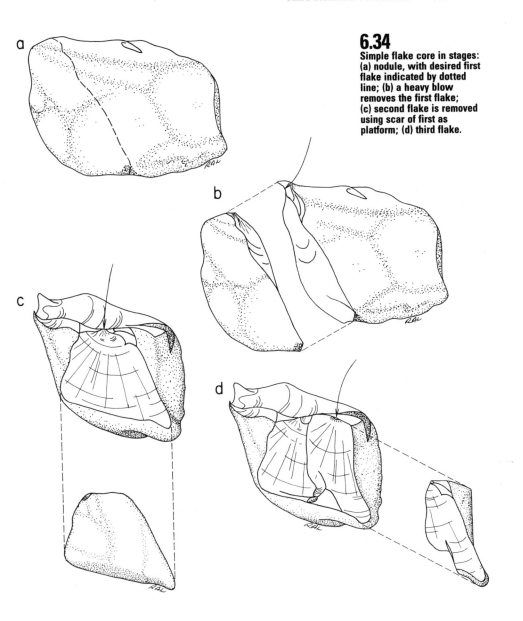

6.34
Simple flake core in stages: (a) nodule, with desired first flake indicated by dotted line; (b) a heavy blow removes the first flake; (c) second flake is removed using scar of first as platform; (d) third flake.

thin enough to be flaked right through. A light hammer is used, and the blows fall only about 1–2 millimeters (1/16 in.) from the edge. They are evenly spaced about 5–10 millimeters (1/4–1/2 in.) apart.

It may sound silly, but for a beginner, retouching scrapers is a good exercise. Practice working around the edge, striking rhythmically but not rapidly, and trying to remove a consistently spaced, similar-sized flake with each blow. End with a smoothly curved edge that forms a

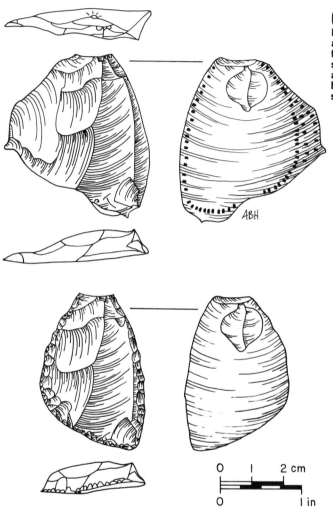

6.35
Retouching a flake to make a scraper. *Top,* unretouched flake. Dots on interior surface to the right show approximate location of blows. *Bottom,* finished scraper.

consistent, steep edge angle. This will improve your hand-eye coordination and the habit of using a loose, easy swing through the target.

Example 3: Making a Burin
Burins are typical tools of Upper Paleolithic Europe (Figure 3.7) and are also found in many other lithic assemblages. Most are by no means spectacular (many people do not even recognize them), but making burins provides practice in platforming, accurate striking, and predicting the path of a flake along a ridge. A burin flake, or *burin spall,* runs along an edge rather than on a surface. The scar left by the removal of the edge often intersects the flake surface at a right angle, leaving a

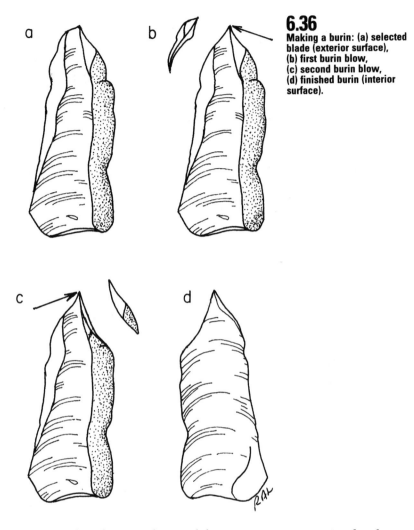

6.36
Making a burin: (a) selected blade (exterior surface), (b) first burin blow, (c) second burin blow, (d) finished burin (interior surface).

strong but sharp edge that can be used for scraping or grooving hard materials (e.g., Movius 1968; Semenov 1973; Crabtree 1973b). Burination can also be used to remove a sharp edge, leaving a flat surface that makes a safe finger rest (Vaughan 1985).

In the example here (Figure 6.36), a previously made blade is selected. A flake would do as well. One corner of the distal end serves as the platform for the first burin blow. The first burin spall removed leaves a sharp, straight, right-angled edge along one edge of the blade. A more complex burin, called a *dihedral burin*, can be made with a second blow. Using the first scar as a platform, the second blow removes the distal end of the blade, and leaves a sort of chisel tip, suit-

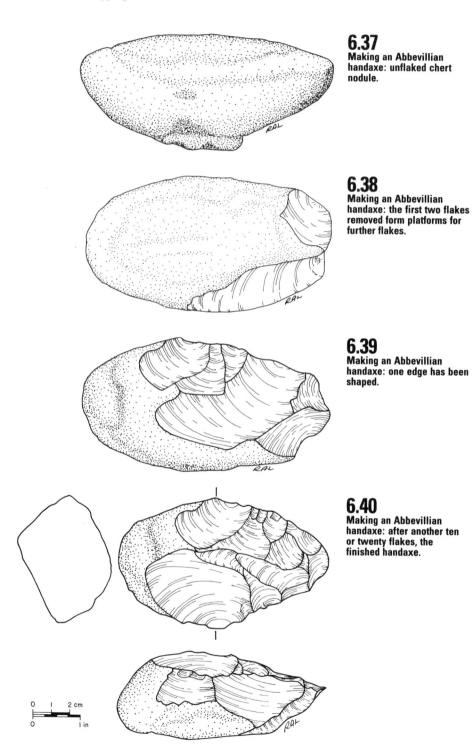

6.37
Making an Abbevillian
handaxe: unflaked chert
nodule.

6.38
Making an Abbevillian
handaxe: the first two flakes
removed form platforms for
further flakes.

6.39
Making an Abbevillian
handaxe: one edge has been
shaped.

6.40
Making an Abbevillian
handaxe: after another ten
or twenty flakes, the
finished handaxe.

0   2 cm
0   1 in

able for grooving or engraving bone or wood. If needed, a notch can be made partway down the blade to stop the burin spall and prevent it from overshooting—turning inward and cutting the blade in half.

Example 4: Abbevillian Handaxe

A very simple biface starts with a medium-sized, flattish nodule of chert (Figure 6.37), weighing about 625 grams (4.56 oz.). A rounded, but thin spot on the edge is selected for the first blow. Two flakes are struck using the thin edge as a platform (Figure 6.38). When the nodule is turned over, the long scar serves as a platform for several more flakes that shape one edge (Figure 6.39). Another dozen flake removals work the edge bifacially, except for an area left unworked at the base for easy holding if the handaxe is used (Figure 6.40). The edge is wavy and jagged, and the tool is thick except at the tip. This is typical of hard-hammer percussion bifaces, although I intentionally did not thin this one as much as is possible. When you can make a crude handaxe like this, congratulations are in order—you have reached the early *Homo erectus* stage in your knapping abilities.

Example 5: Levallois Flake

The Levallois technique was often used by the Neanderthal makers of some Mousterian industries (Figure 6.41; see also Figure 3.5). A large surface is prepared for the removal of a single flake by flaking around the edges of a core and preparing a platform at one end. The shape of the final large flake is partly determined by the way the core is prepared, and a good Levallois flake is large and flat, with a sharp edge all around—a better tool than the average flake struck off an irregular core. The finished Levallois flake usually has scars from the preparation flakes running in toward the center of the exterior surface, and a large platform often prepared by facetting, with a large bulb resulting from the use of a hard hammer. Some Levallois flakes were also made long and bladelike, or triangular. Van Peer (1992) provides a detailed discussion of Levallois strategies and variability.

I selected a good-sized nodule of chert, weighing 820 grams (29 oz.; Figure 6.42). Although a bit knobby, it had a convenient shape: a wide upper surface, slightly convex, with a reasonably good angle for platforms around much of the edge.

The edge is worked bifacially, with two major goals in mind. The upper surface should be covered by flat flakes, maintaining a gently convex surface without steps, hinges, or other irregularities. The edge around the core should be even and below the level of the final platform, which is prepared at one end. The opposite end especially should be below where the flake is expected to terminate, or it will overshoot and remove the end of the core. In other words, you are making a thick,

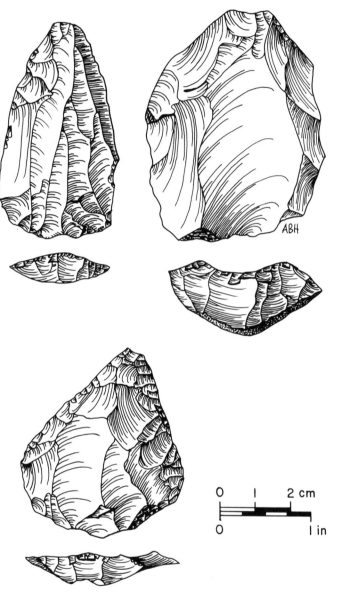

6.41
Levallois core (right) and two Levallois flakes. Note facetting of platforms. The bottom flake has been retouched and could be classified as a Mousterian point. These specimens have a history. They were collected around the turn of the century in Somaliland (Africa) by H. W. Seton-Carr, an English big-game hunter and archaeologist who sent them to a friend in the classics department at Grinnell College. Seton-Carr later went down with the Titanic.

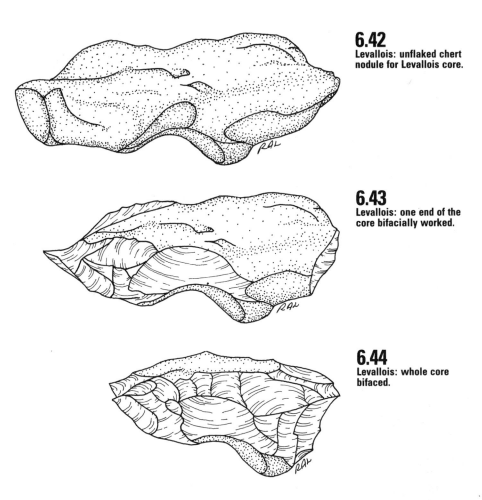

6.42
Levallois: unflaked chert
nodule for Levallois core.

6.43
Levallois: one end of the
core bifacially worked.

6.44
Levallois: whole core
bifaced.

steep-edged biface. Bifacial techniques will be discussed in detail in the following chapters. In Figure 6.43 one end of the core has been worked bifacially. In Figure 6.44 the whole perimeter is steeply bifacial, and much of the upper surface has been prepared by large, flat flakes. Figure 6.45 shows the last of these. I did not quite succeed in removing all the cortex from this surface.

The platform for the Levallois flake is prepared at one end. It is prepared mostly by facetting to produce an angle close to 90 degrees. As you will remember, this helps to give the flake maximum length. The facetting is also used to isolate the platform. To remove a large flake from a platform close to 90 degrees, a hard blow is necessary. If a Levallois core is large enough, the surface and platforms can be reworked after the first flake and another Levallois flake removed. Figure 6.46

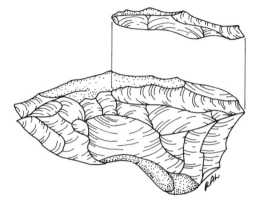

6.45 Levallois: the last preparation flake removed from the core surface.

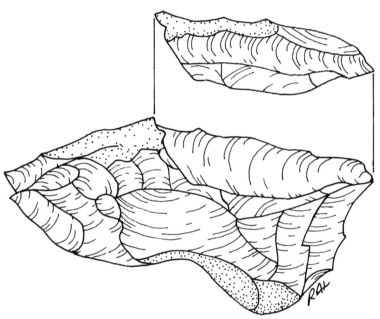

6.46 Levallois: the Levallois flake is struck.

shows the final Levallois flake and core, and Figure 6.47 gives the conventional surface and platform views. Note the steep facetted platform, and compare this flake to the prehistoric specimens in Figure 6.41.

If you have mastered all of the examples above, you have qualified for your BNA (Bachelor of Neanderthal Arts). In other words, you can replicate the complete stone tool kit of many of our early ancestors, which means you can make all the basic stone tools you might need for survival. Most of this stuff is not very showy, but if you are good at hard-hammer percussion, you can adapt it to make some things like projectile points and thinner bifaces that are usually easier to do in

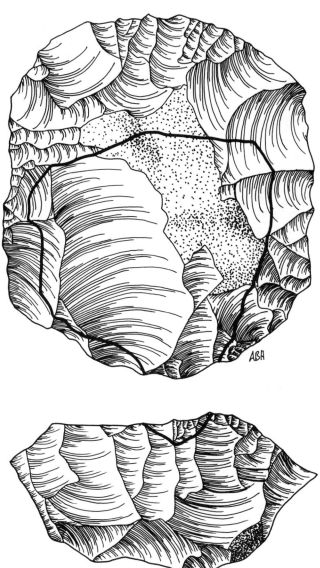

6.47
Surface and platform of
Levallois core. Flake is
shown by heavy line.

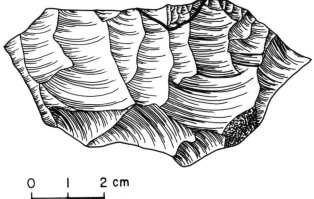

0   I   2 cm

0   I in

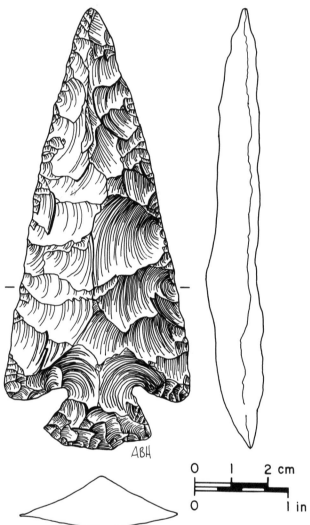

6.48
Obsidian biface point by
Amado Ortega Vidal,
Mexico, 1990.

ABH

0   1   2 cm

0   1 in

other ways. For example, the large obsidian point in Figure 6.48 was made by a modern Mexican knapper. The deep bulbs of percussion, large short flake scars, frequent edge crushing, and thick triangular cross-section are typical of bifaces made by hard-hammer percussion. The large notching flakes were probably removed by indirect percussion. Compare this piece to bifaces of similar size made by soft-hammer percussion, which have large, flat flake scars with small negative bulbs, and a thin cross-section (e.g., Figures 1.4a, 2.6, 3.8, 8.22). A knapper who is really good at hard-hammer percussion can, however, duplicate the effects of soft hammers.

7
PRESSURE FLAKING

His arrow head he quickly maketh with a
little bone, which he ever weareth at his bra-
cert, of any splint of a stone, or glasse in the
forme of a heart, and these they glew to the
end of their arrowes.
—Captain John Smith (1624:31)

The pressure-flaked "arrowhead" is the most characteristic American stone artifact. Even people who know nothing else about prehistory recognize "arrowheads." Small bifacially flaked projectile points (to be more technically precise) are one of the artifacts that give archaeological remains from this continent their distinctive flavor.

Even the early explorers like John Smith were impressed, sometimes against their will. The Norse sagas of the discovery of Vinland relate how Thorvald, son of Eirik the Red, discovered stone tools on an exploring trip somewhere along the northeastern coast of North America. After he and his crew killed a group of natives they found resting under canoes, they were attacked by a large band with bows and arrows. They escaped, but Thorvald was mortally wounded by an arrow. He is said to have pulled it from the wound, remarking as he did so, "This is a rich land we have found, there is fat around my entrails" (Magnusson and Palsson 1965:60, 102). He then died, leaving his last words as an unwitting testimony to the efficiency of stone tools and a foreshadowing of the rest of Native American history.

When the early archaeologists began to study stone tools in nineteenth-century America, learning how to make arrowheads was of course one of their interests, and pressure-flaked projectile points were the most complex stone tools still being made by the time they got around to recording native knappers. As we have seen, stone flaking was considered a "lost art" for years, although actually a number of anthropologists and others learned some knapping. Part of the problem was simply the need to build up a body of knowledge and the vocabulary to describe it. For instance, the British prehistorians learned what knapping they knew from gunflint knappers and forgers like "Flint Jack," who worked exclusively by percussion and were admittedly unable to reproduce the fine arrow points of the Neolithic period and

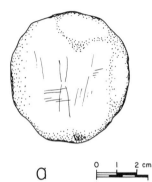

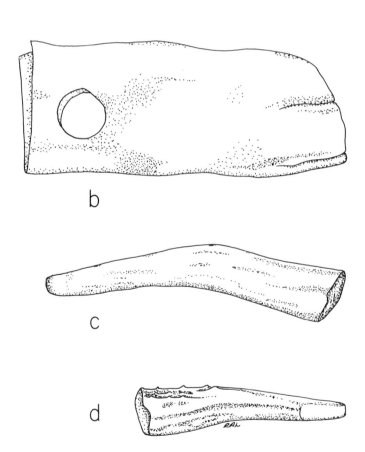

7.1
My basic pressure-flaking
tool kit: (a) small,
flat sandstone hammer/
abrader, (b) leather hand pad
(doubled for extra
protection), (c) antler tine
pressure flaker, (d) antler
tine flaker with chisel tip for
fine work and notching.

a

b

c

d

Early Bronze Age. It was only when surviving stone age technologies outside Europe began to be reported that this gap in knapping knowledge was filled, and even then there were some difficulties.

In 1895 Frank H. Cushing, an eccentric genius who taught himself knapping, tried to describe pressure flaking. As he put it, removing flakes involves "twistingly wrenching them off by a most dextrous motion, which I can exhibit, but cannot adequately describe or illustrate (Cushing 1895:318). I believe we can now be a good deal more helpful.

In the history of lithic technology, hard- and soft-hammer percussion preceded pressure flaking. In making complex flaked stone tools like spear points or bifacial knives, the manufacturing sequence usually proceeds through the same sequence of hard-hammer, soft-hammer, and pressure work. Nevertheless, it is easier to learn pressure flaking before soft-hammer percussion, preferably at the same time as you learn basic hard-hammer percussion.

The principles of pressure flaking are very similar to those of soft-hammer percussion, which will be discussed later. The difference is that force is applied by pressing the flaker against the stone rather than striking it. This means that you can't apply as much force, but accuracy is greater. When one is learning to knap, it is better to start with pressure flaking because it is easier. You can see what is happening and apply the principles at a lower level of hand and eye skill. Suitable tools and raw materials are easier to find, and even the beginner can make a simple arrowhead to be proud of (for a little while, anyway).

TOOLS
Pressure-flaking tools are easy to get or make. You need a flaker, protection for your hands, and a small stone abrader. My basic kit is shown in Figure 7.1.

A lot of knappers use the tine of a deer antler as a pressure flaker. Antler can be found in the woods (on a deer if you hunt or shed if you don't), bought at swap meets or flea markets, and begged from friends who hunt if they're willing to give up trophies. If you are alert, you can sometimes find road-killed deer with antlers, but be aware that in some states it is against the law to collect road kills without a permit, so check local ordinances and look both ways before you cross the highway.

The only really necessary modification to a tine flaker is cutting it off the rack and occasionally resharpening it as it dulls with use. This is the most common kind of flaker found in archaeological sites (e.g., Olsen 1979, 1980; Ritchie 1969; Benson 1980) and is well known ethnographically (see Ellis 1939; Holmes 1919).

If you can't get antler, there are alternatives. My first flaker was a splinter of beef bone hafted in a wooden handle (Figure 7.2a). Com-

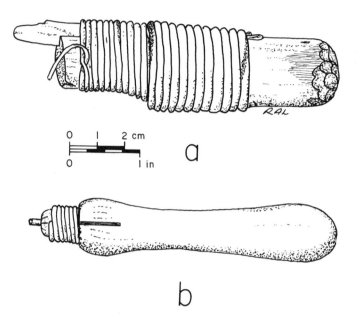

7.2
Alternate pressure flaker forms: (a) my first pressure flaker—a splinter of beef bone in a wooden handle, (b) copper wire in a file handle.

pound flakers like this are also common in recent and prehistoric times (e.g., Goddard 1903–1904; Guernsey and Kidder 1921:97; Hester 1974; Muto, Mehringer, and Warren 1976). Ishi favored a compound flaker tipped with a soft iron nail, and many modern knappers use copper wire. A short length of heavy-gauge copper wire can be set in a file handle or other hafting for a cheap, durable, and effective tool obtainable at any hardware store (Figure 7.2b).

Many knappers prefer copper over antler, partly because it is a bit harder and requires less frequent resharpening. If you are working tough material, or setting up tough platforms to remove large flakes, copper is easier to use. The sharper, harder tips of copper pressure tools allow more precise flaking and make it easier to detach flakes. A prehistoric American tool that is probably a flaker, made of native copper, from the Early Woodland period (1000–500 B.C.) has been found in New York State (Ritchie 1969:185), and others are reported for Minnesota (Romano and Altiere 1992). Copper may have been used in some of the fine pressure flaking of Egypt and Scandinavia as metal began to be available there in their Early Bronze Ages. The use of copper for flaking may be authentic for some cultures, although you would not expect a scarce and expensive material to be used much when other things would do as well. Copper also leaves metallic marks on some stone, which I find annoying.

It is also possible to use hard wood, but this requires more skill, some slightly different techniques, and a lot of resharpening. Some of the fine Australian flaking was probably done with wooden flakers

(Crabtree 1970). Shell also works, as does stone (Patterson 1981b; Semenov 1973), but both are really too hard. Because they don't indent enough, it is hard to remove long flakes and avoid crushing platforms.

Of all the above, my personal preference is for antler, partly because I am used to it and like it and partly because antler (or bone, which is very similar) was most likely to have been used by most prehistoric knappers, and is therefore the best material to use in serious replication, unless there is real evidence for the use of copper, shell, or other materials.

I mostly use a short-handled flaker, but it is also possible to attach a longer handle to give more leverage or add the pressure of body weight (see "Working Position" below).

I have already expressed my feelings about safety. If you pressure flake into your bare palm, you will cut yourself to shreds, and while a few gory nicks may enhance your macho image, having your arm in a sling or stitches in your hand is inconvenient, to put it mildly. Many of the ethnographic accounts of pressure flaking mention pads, and there are prehistoric examples (e.g., Benson 1980), so the ancients were no tougher than we are. Gloves limit your ability to feel a piece and hold it, so the most common rig is a small pad with a hole for the thumb (Figures 7.1, 7.5). This stays firmly on the hand, across the palm, but with the fingers free. Most knappers don't worry about eye injury in pressure flaking, but I recommend that the glasses stay on. It is surprisingly easy to flick flakes into the air and at yourself, either by a mistake in pressing against the tool, or in preparing platforms, or by tiddly-winking them off the pad on your hand. A tiny flake that is merely an annoyance anywhere else is a danger in your eye. If you get one in your eye, don't rub it; go wash it out immediately. Ishi, who apparently worried a good deal about knapping safety, would "pull down the lower lid of the eye with his left forefinger, while with his right hand he slapped himself vigorously on the top of the head . . . to dislodge the glass fragment" (Kroeber 1961:184). The only results I have ever got from trying this are tears of pain that may or may not wash out the flake. Note also that Ishi and other American Indians liked to flake glass, and Ishi's knapping kit included a protective pad like that described above.

The other tool you should have is a small hammerstone or abrader. It should be rough, like fine-grained sandstone, hard limestone, fine basalt, or even carborundum. This will be used to rub and abrade the edges of the piece you are flaking to prepare platforms.

RAW MATERIAL

Pressure flaking usually begins with a flake or a partially worked biface. For learning, start with a fairly thin and even percussion flake. A

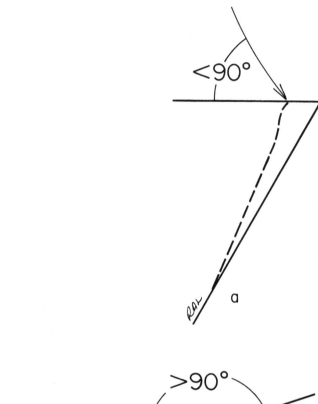

7.3
The differences between
(a) hard-hammer percussion
flaking and (b) pressure
flaking; c = centerplane.

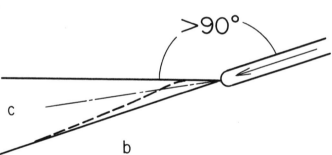

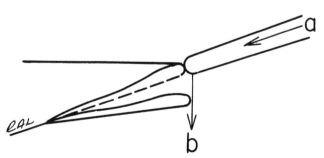

7.4
Pressure-flaking forces:
(a) main force component
detaching flake,
(b) downward force that
begins crack and flake
detachment.

fragment of a glass bottle or a sherd of windowpane works too. In fact, a number of knappers, myself included, did much of their first learning on glass simply because it was all that was readily available. Glass has other advantages: it is very homogeneous, so you won't run into annoying flaws, and the flake scars are very clear, so you can see what is happening. It is a little brittle, which isn't so good because it is easier to break things, but the brittleness also means that less force is required to flake it, which gives you more control. Edges on glass crush easily, so it is important to prepare platforms properly. For the beginner, anything that forces you to slow down and think about platforms is good.

FIRST PRINCIPLES

Pressure flaking differs from hard-hammer percussion in a number of ways. First, you are applying force by pressing rather than by striking. Second, the platform is not a flat surface, but an edge. Third, the direction of the force is very different.

In hard-hammer flaking, the blow is struck behind the edge on the flat platform surface. In pressure flaking, pressure is applied with the flaker against the edge itself (Figure 7.3). The platform angle—in this case, the angle formed by the edge itself, is still less than 90 degrees and actually is usually much less.

In hard-hammer flaking, the angle of the blow is less than 90 degrees to the platform surface, which makes it approximately perpendicular to the centerplane of the piece. The main force in pressure flaking is applied almost parallel to the centerplane or slightly away from it, but following the surface of the piece (Figure 7.3). Actually, there are two components to the pressure-flaking force. Most of it should be directed as above, inward, parallel to the centerplane of the piece, along the surface in the direction you want the flake to go. But there is also a downward force that helps to start the flake (Figure 7.4).

To make this work, set the tip of the pressure flaker against the edge of the piece as if you intend to split your flaker. The edge should be properly prepared: (1) less than a 90-degree angle, (2) sharp enough to cut into the flaker just a bit so that downward force can be applied without the flaker slipping, but (3) dull enough not to crush under the first pressure (see "Platform Preparation" below). Press firmly into the piece in the direction the flake is to go, building up force, then add a slight downward motion, and the flake will detach with a sharp crack. Too much downward force will produce only short flakes, and too much inward force may crush the edge without removing a flake. Beginners almost always make short flakes, usually because they use too much downward force.

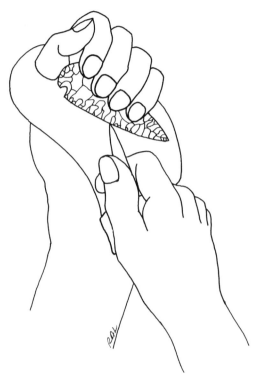

7.5
A normal hand position in pressure flaking. Left hand is protected by leather pad and should be rested on leg.

WORKING POSITION

There are a lot of possible variations, which I will discuss later. For now I will describe a simple, basic position that everyone uses at least some, and which many rely on almost completely.

Put a leather pad over your palm. Lay the piece to be worked on the pad over the heel of your hand, and hold it down firmly with your fingers (Figure 7.5). It should be supported on the fleshy heel of your hand, especially the part of the edge you are flaking. If you bridge the piece over the crease in your palm (the "lifeline") and press on it, it is very likely to break (see Figure 7.39). I like to work seated, bent over with my wrists supported on my legs (Figure 7.6). This gives strength and stability. One of the problems I have seen in beginning knappers is the tendency to rest their elbows on their knees, or even to flake without supporting their arms at all. As soon as they apply pressure, everything starts to wobble, or the piece is pressed down into the palm, the palm turns, the angle of force changes, and only a small short flake is removed. Not only is everything very stable with the wrists and backs of hands supported on the legs, but the full force of the arms and some of the weight of the upper body can be applied to remove large flakes. I also sometimes press my legs together to add force.

7.6
A basic sitting position in pressure flaking.

BEGINNING

The first step is to inspect the flake you are going to work, and think about it a minute. What do you want to do with it? Visualize the finished piece. Is it possible? What problems (thick spots, flaws, right-angle edges) are you going to have to avoid or overcome? Thinking ahead is essential and will become more and more a habit. Each step should not only accomplish its immediate task, but should also prepare the piece for the next, or lead logically to it.

When you know what you want to do, start preparing the edge. If you have a thin, sharp edge from a feather termination on a flake, remove this by rubbing it with your small hammerstone abrader or with the edge of your flaker (Figure 7.7, see also Figures 7.15, 7.16). If you try to flake a very thin, sharp edge, it will just crush anyway, and leaving it on the flake is begging for a cut finger. Crush the feather edge off by rubbing or shearing toward the interior surface of the flake, leaving an edge that is beveled toward the interior surface and slightly dulled.

Now use this edge as the platform and remove a series of flakes from the exterior face of the flake. These first flakes need not be long. Try to make them even and avoid steps and other errors. When you have flaked along as much of the edge as possible, trim and abrade the edge

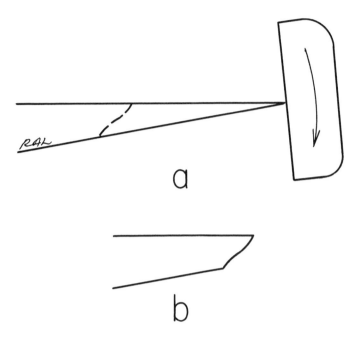

7.7
Removal of thin feather
edges by (a) abrading,
leaving a tougher edge,
which is beveled and
dulled (b).

in the same direction, then turn it over and flake the other face. When you have done this, you will have a bifacial edge along the thin parts of the edge of your piece.

The next step is dealing with any edge that is particularly thick, or right-angled, as on a piece of glass. This is called *turning the edge*, or *bifacing*, and as before, the goal is to end up with a sharp, bifacial edge on which you can set up platforms for further flaking to cover the faces of the piece.

If the right-angled edge is thin enough, you can sometimes flake right through it from one side or the other (Figure 7.8), especially at a corner. This gives an edge which is beveled to one face, and can now be flaked in that direction.

It is also possible to press flakes off a right-angled platform. This may thin a right-angled edge enough to give you a better starting point (Figure 7.9). The disadvantage is that, unless you are very careful, flakes from a 90-degree platform are likely to end in a step or hinge, especially when flaking on a smooth face like the surface of a piece of glass. Steps or hinges will cause problems later when you try to run flakes across the faces of the piece.

Most edges have some place to start that is not a right angle and provides a suitable platform. Begin here, and work into the right-angled edge. Starting wherever there is a suitable platform, work along the edge; each flake from a suitable, less-than-90-degree platform will re-

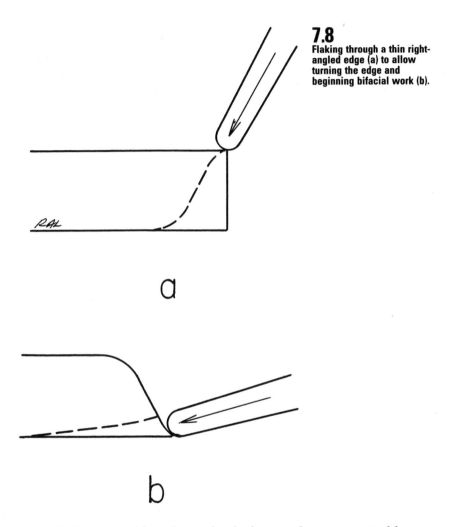

7.8
Flaking through a thin right-angled edge (a) to allow turning the edge and beginning bifacial work (b).

move part of the unsuitable right-angle platform and set up a suitable platform for a flake from the opposite side of the piece. This is best understood by looking at Figure 7.10. After each flake (or a couple of flakes) the piece is turned over, and the scar from the last flake serves as the platform for the next, until the entire right-angled edge has been removed, leaving a sharp bifacial edge with suitable platform angles. Crabtree (1972a) refers to the process above as "alternate flaking" and uses "turning the edge" for what I describe as "beveling." Some readers may object to using "bifacing" as a verb, but both turning the edge and bifacing in the sense used above are in common use among knappers, so I will continue to use them without further apology. Daniel Webster need never know.

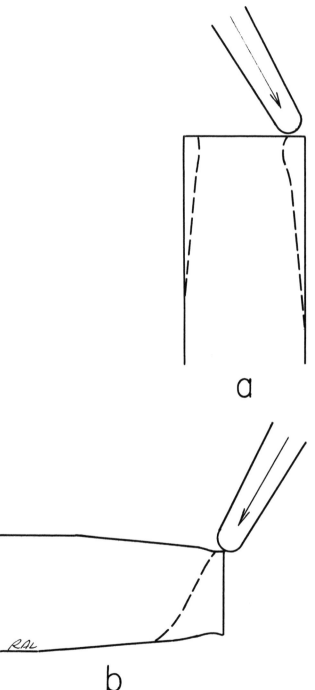

7.9
Thinning a right-angled edge
(a) before flaking through
it (b).

a

b

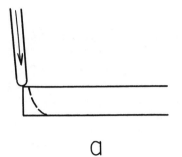

a

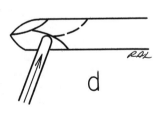

b

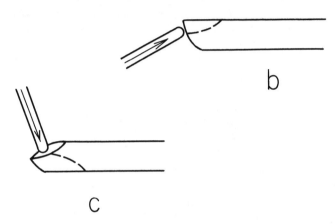

c

7.10
Turning the edge: (a) flaking
through initial right-angled
edge; (b) beginning on other
face; (c) returning to first
face for first thinning flake;
(d, e) using each flake scar
on edge as platform for next
flake off opposite face.

d

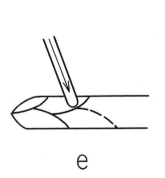

e

Turning the edge is the way to overcome most edges with unsuitable platforms—angles of 90 degrees or more, strong rounded edges, lumps, bumps and humps, and areas where you crushed the platform or put steps in it. You do have to be careful to avoid crushing the platform or grinding it round. If you crush the rather small platform left by the removal of the previous flake along a right-angle edge, you may have to back up and work into it again, turning the edge again a bit deeper into the faces of the piece until you can set up new platforms.

Turning the edge works a piece on both faces, and is usually the first step in producing a biface, either a pressure-flaked arrowhead or a percussion-flaked handaxe. Most of the flakes removed in turning an edge will be short and unevenly shaped, and will not run very far onto the faces of the piece. Once the process is completed, it provides platforms all along the edge, which can then be prepared for removing flakes that run farther across the faces of the piece.

PLATFORM PREPARATION

Having turned the edge and removed thin, sharp edges, you are now ready to begin flaking the piece to thin it and shape it. For this, you need to run flakes across the faces and well in from the edges. At first you will echo the lament of Nels C. Nelson (1916:401): "Not having experimented very much, I am unable to say why Ishi proceeds as he does, but he gets results which I cannot imitate, try as I will. Ishi removes thin and fairly slender chips that extend two-thirds or more across the face of the flake, while my chips are thick and short. Consequently, his arrowpoints when finished are thin and shapely, while mine, much to his disgust, are thick and clumsy affairs."

I will give you a head start and tell you two things Nelson had not figured out. I have already mentioned the importance of inward pressure in the direction of the flake. This is necessary to drive a flake a long distance across the face of your piece. Even more important is a good platform that allows you to apply the right pressure, and I will emphasize again the importance of preparing proper platforms.

Remember that in pressure flaking the platform is the edge itself. Ordinarily the edge is beveled so that it is closer to one face than to the other. Usually you will want to remove flakes from this face (Figure 7.11). This doesn't mean that you are a slave to chance and can flake only where the platform edge is just right. Platforms can be controlled and adjusted to give you what you want, and as we have seen in hard-hammer percussion, the platform is the single most important variable that you control.

The ideal pressure-flaking platform in most situations is slightly above the face from which you intend to remove a flake and consider-

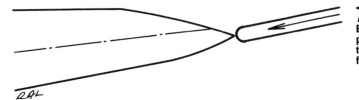

7.11
Beveling of the edge. Proper
platform position is below
the centerplane, close to the
face to be flaked.

ably below the other face of the piece you are working (Figure 7.11).
You can think in terms of an imaginary *centerplane* (Callahan 1985)
through the tool (Figure 7.12). The platform should be at or below the
centerplane. If the platform is too far below the centerplane, flakes will
be too small; if the platform is above the centerplane, flakes will be
short and the likelihood of bending and breaking the piece increases.

A bifacial edge is preferable to a unifacial edge where the face of the
tool forms one side of the platform (Figure 7.13). Extreme bevels should
also be avoided. If your platform is too close to the face, the flakes you
remove will tend to be either thin and short, or they will be likely to
end in a step or a hinge. This is similar to what happens with platforms
that are close to 90 degrees. If you flake a unifacial bevel the other way,
toward the face farthest from the edge, it is difficult to make the flake
run up onto the flat face. Usually it just follows the previous flake scars
on the bevel, which gives a thin, short flake and increases the angle of
the edge but does not change the position of the platform. A proper
bifacial edge, on the other hand, allows a thicker, longer flake that
extends onto the flat face of the piece and thins it.

When you remove a flake from one face, the platform area on the
edge moves back toward the other face of the piece. It is thus easy to
adjust the position of the platform. If you do not want to flake on a
surface and need to move the platform away from it, you can remove
short flakes from the edge, toward the face you want to move away
from (Figure 7.14). This can be done by flaking, shearing with the pressure flaker (Figure 7.15), or buffeting with your abrader (Figure 7.16). In
flaking, you remove short flakes, pressing almost entirely down on the
flaker. *Shearing* involves crunching flakes off the edge with the side of
your flaker. *Buffeting* involves using the abrader in one direction, away
from the face you want to flake, which pulls off flakes (if you press
hard enough), and also dulls the edge, which will be discussed soon.

Once you have removed a flake, you have a fragile overhang on the
platform above the negative bulb of percussion, just as we have seen in
hard-hammer flaking. This overhang makes an edge that is too weak
to allow another flake off either face unless the overhang is removed
and the platform prepared. In pressure flaking and most bifacial work,
you will want to remove flakes from the other face next, so you remove

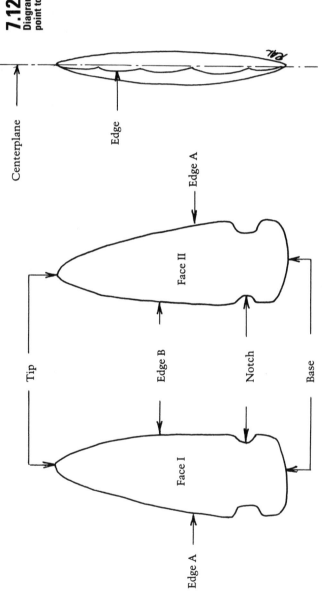

7.12
Diagram of pressure-flaked point to show terminology.

Centerplane

Edge

Edge A

Tip

Edge B

Notch

Base

Face II

Face I

Edge A

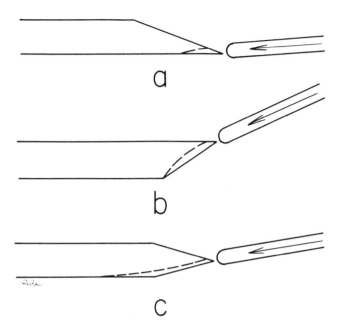

7.13
A bifacial edge is better than a unifacial edge. A unifacial edge (a) produces only a short flake because the platform is too close to the face of the piece. The same unifacial edge turned over and flaked to the opposite face (b) increases the angle of the edge but does not change the position of the platform, so it is difficult to get flakes to run up onto the flat face of the piece. A proper bifacial edge (c) allows a flake that extends onto the flat face, thinning the piece.

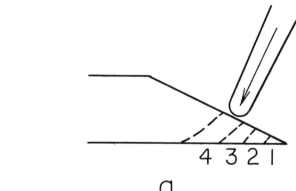

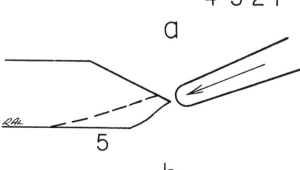

7.14
Changing the position of the platform: (a) as each short flake is removed (1–4), the platform on the edge is shifted farther from the bottom face of the tool and upward; (b) finally the platform is close enough to the centerplane that more force can be directed inward and a longer flake can be removed.

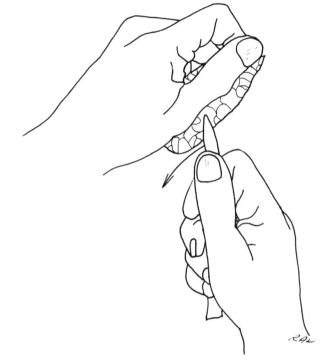

7.15
Changing the position of the platform by shearing with edge of pressure tool.

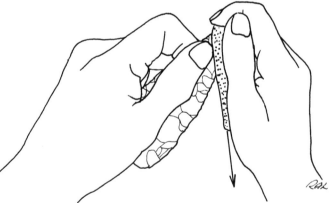

7.16
Changing platform position by buffeting with abrading stone.

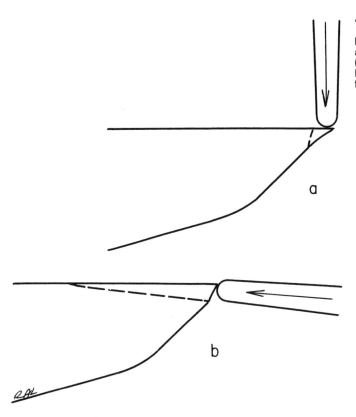

7.17
Removing the overhang above a negative bulb (a) toughens the edge and bevels it for a subsequent flake (b).

the overhang by flaking, shearing, or abrading in the same direction as the flake you just removed—in other words, to the face opposite the one you will work next (Figure 7.17). Not only are you removing the overhang, but you can also adjust the platform toward the face you want to work, as described above.

Pressure flaking platforms need to be both sharp and strong. The platform is the edge, and it should be sharp enough to dig into the pressure tool a bit; otherwise, the flaker will just slip off before you can apply enough pressure to detach a flake. On the other hand, a very sharp platform is too fragile to support much pressure and pass it on to the flake. Abrading the edge a bit dulls the platform and strengthens it. You can abrade away from the face you want to work, as mentioned above, if you want to adjust the platform position. Even if the platform is right with respect to the faces, some knappers try to have a very small bevel right on the edge of the edge, so to speak, in the same direction as the main bevel (Figure 7.18). The effect of this is to increase the platform angle and make it easier to direct the force across the face of the piece. I generally don't worry about this, but it may help

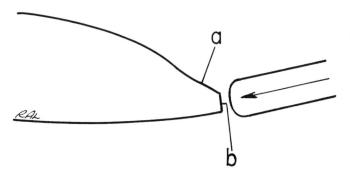

7.18
Bevels on the edge: (a) main bevel, (b) small bevel.

you, in which case you should use the abrader gently so that it does not pull off flakes, but only grinds or sands the sharp edge off the platform. If you don't want to adjust platform position, but just want to dull it, the platform can also be ground by rubbing the abrader back and forth along the edge, as if you are cutting the abrader. Rubbing toward the next face to be flaked is usually to be avoided unless you need to bring the edge back toward the centerplane to get a larger flake or if you have just removed flakes from that face and want to do another series off the same face. In this case, you should remove the overhanging fragile edge left by the previous series.

It is possible to strengthen a platform too much, dulling it to the point where the flaker slips off, or until you simply can't apply enough force to start a long flake. It is usually possible to remove a short flake by pressing down on this platform, as described above in turning the edge, and this may be what you have to do to start again at that spot. But perhaps it is the ideal place to remove a crucial flake, and you have a perfect platform except that it is too strong for you to remove a flake with any control. In that case, you can weaken the platform a bit by isolating it. The amount of force needed to detach a flake depends heavily on the amount of material the initial crack must break through. The amount of force you are applying to a particular platform also depends on how big that platform is—in other words, how much of the edge of the piece is in contact with the tip of your flaker. This is one reason why it is good to keep your flaker tip sharpened. A sharp tip gives you more precision and also concentrates the pressure on a smaller area, which reduces the force needed to start a crack. Isolating a platform has something of the same effect. By flaking a small notch on each side of the platform, you reduce the area of the edge in contact with your flaker and the distance the initial crack must break through the edge of the piece (Figure 7.19). Be careful not to isolate too much.

Beginners usually make platforms too weak or forget to prepare them at all. As a result, their flakes are short and irregular. As your confidence and strength grow, you will find that strong platforms and

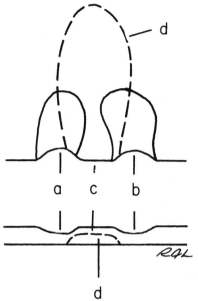

7.19
Isolating a pressure platform. Two small flakes (a, b) have been removed from the upper face to isolate the desired platform (c). The desired flake (d) will be removed from the opposite face. *Above,* view of the top side of the piece, with the desired flake (on the invisible underside) indicated by the dashed lines. *Below,* view of the piece edge-on.

larger flakes are much more efficient. You should usually set up the strongest platform you can handle, and refuse to be timid. This is especially important if you want to get beyond the elementary stages of pressure flaking and to work toward making large pieces, thinning, and patterned pressure flaking.

THINNING

As you should remember from the discussion of hard-hammer flaking, the last important variable you need to control is the form of the surface from which you intend to remove the flake. Flakes tend to follow ridges and high points, and this is why a skillful knapper can set up a consistent series of even flakes to cover the surface of a projectile point with a rippled pattern of flake scars. On the other hand, flakes will step or hinge when they run into an excessive hollow or up against a sudden lump. Such problems need to be removed carefully and the whole piece thinned evenly.

It is hard to thin by pressure flaking. Pressure flakes tend to be short and fragile, so they don't remove much mass. They aren't strong enough to carry much force, and will hinge or step or crush if you expect too much of them. This is especially true as you are beginning. Once you have some experience and can produce long, even flakes, you will be able to thin small pieces fairly well. This is one of the few parts of flintknapping that really does require some strength. Don Crabtree specialized in pressure flaking, and people who knew him spoke with

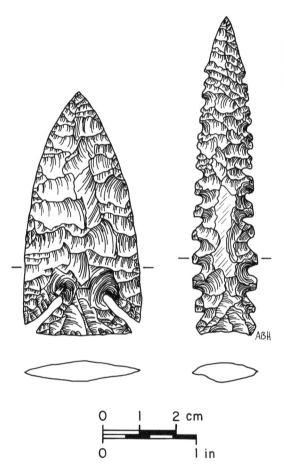

7.20
Left, deeply notched point, heat-treated chert, Carl Doney, 1990. *Right,* serrated point, heat-treated Burlington Chert, John Whittaker, 1990.

```
0      1      2 cm
0             1 in
```

awe of his forearms. The strength is mostly needed to hold a piece steady while applying pressure, and the key to successful thinning is to apply as much inward pressure as possible in the direction the flake is to go, while using as little downward pressure as will serve to start the flake. Proper platform preparation helps make this possible, but it will be better to discuss that in the context of soft-hammer percussion in the next chapter. Once you have mastered simple pressure flaking, go on to try some soft-hammer percussion, or at least read about it and apply the platforming principles to pressure flaking.

NOTCHING

Many of the familiar American projectile points and some other stone tools have notches and other elaborations that are usually made by a special application of pressure-flaking techniques (Figure 7.20).

Notches are begun by flaking as usual, then repeatedly removing

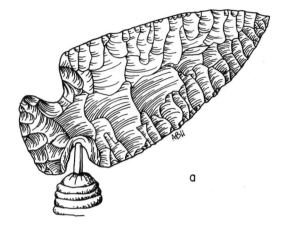

7.21
Notching: (a) pressure tool
is on the face of the point in
the notch, not just against
the edge; (b) pressure is
applied mostly downward;
(c) notching flake has a
characteristic shape.

a

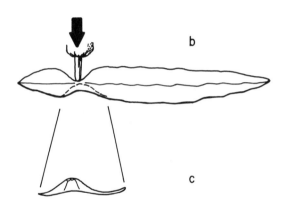

b

c

flakes from both faces of the point at the place on the edge where the
notch is to be. A very sharp pressure tool is needed here if you want a
narrow or deep notch. You can use either a very sharp tip on your
flaker, which is rather weak in bone and antler, or a flaker with a wide,
flat tip like a screwdriver. The notch should be made with two small
flakes rather than one. This gives you a second chance should you
crush a platform, which is easy to do as the notch gets deeper. Once
you get into the notch you will be removing short, broad flakes rather
than long ones, using a good deal of downward pressure. It will be difficult to bevel the edge inside the notch, and your platforms will often
be at the centerplane. The edge itself will often be either quite fragile,
overhanging the last removal, or duller and more crushed than desirable. You will often find it best to place the flaker slightly above and
behind the edge in the notch (Figure 7.21). This means that most of the
flaking pressure will be downward and that it will require a lot of force.

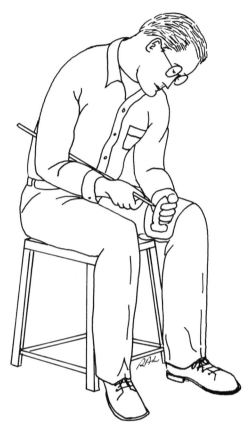

7.22
Pressure flaking with long compound flaker and arm or chest pressure.

Good judgment is called for to avoid trying to flake from too far in, which will usually result in bending and snapping a delicate area at the most frustrating time—after you have worked hard on the piece and almost finished it. Careful support of the whole piece, especially around the notch, will help prevent bending fractures. Some knappers prefer to notch with the point lying flat on a leather pad on a table. Notching flakes are quite distinctive (Figure 7.21c), and the process and results are discussed at greater length by Titmus (1985) and Austin (1986).

OTHER PRESSURE-FLAKING TECHNIQUES

I have described a simple and basic pressure-flaking position, which is the one I use almost all the time. There are alternatives and variations, and it may eventually be worth your while to experiment with some.

If the flaker is hafted in a long handle, it is possible to bring a lot more force to bear by pressing with the upper arm, shoulder, or chest (Figure 7.22). Modern knappers call these long compound flakers "Ishi

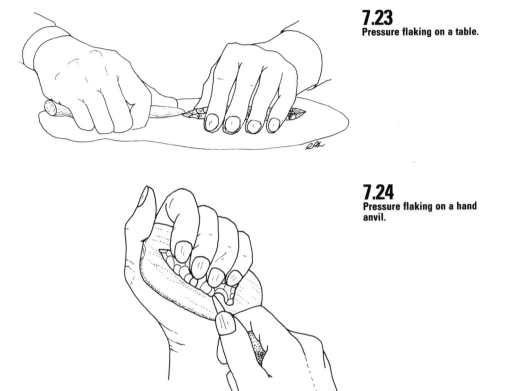

7.23
Pressure flaking on a table.

7.24
Pressure flaking on a hand anvil.

sticks"; they were used by a number of the California tribes as well as other people (Schumacher 1877; Goddard 1903–1904). However, the more pressure you use, the more difficult it is to steady the piece you are working on. If you do not steady it enough, the pressure will tend to turn it, and the force, instead of running a long flake across the face, will remove only a short flake. In attempting to hold a piece firmly, you may squeeze and bend it too much. This will snap it, especially if you are putting a lot of pressure on it with the flaking tool as well.

Supporting the piece you are flaking helps solve these problems. Some knappers like to flake on a table or other surface, laying the piece flat on a piece of leather or other material that gives a soft, gripping surface, but does not leave a hollow under the piece that might allow a bending fracture (Figure 7.23). An alternative is a small, flat piece of wood held in the hand, which I call a hand anvil (Figure 7.24; see Soll-berger 1979), or a thick, stiff pad of leather or rubber. Hand anvils and pads are particularly useful for small, fragile pieces that are difficult to hold and easy to break.

SUMMARY: SIX ESSENTIALS

Let us summarize the basic principles of pressure flaking as described so far:

1. Pressure is applied to the *edge* of the piece.
2. The edge, which is the platform, should form an angle of less than 90 degrees.
3. Place the pressure flaker on the edge, apply force into the edge in the direction the flake is to go, and then detach the flake by adding a bit of downward force. The longer the flake desired, the more inward force is needed.
4. The edge must be dull enough not to crush but sharp enough to keep the flaker from slipping off.
5. Biface all right-angle and thick edges. Prepare the platform on bifacial edges by flaking, shearing, and abrading.
6. The platform on the edge should be below the centerplane of the piece.

APPLICATION: SMALL TRIANGULAR POINTS FROM THE SOUTHWEST

Small, light, triangular arrow points are common all over the continent from late prehistoric times up until their replacement by metal points. There is a great deal of variation in shape and presence or absence of notching, serration, and other details. Some of the variation reflects change through time and the contrasting styles of different peoples, but even within small areas there is a lot of variation in points, reflecting the differences between small groups of people and individual knappers, short-term "fads" and stylistic changes, and the effects of differences in material, knappers' skills, and so forth (all these issues will be discussed at more length in Chapter 11).

The particular points I will illustrate as examples come from Grasshopper Pueblo, a village of about 500 rooms and perhaps 1,000 people in Arizona, dating from about A.D. 1300 to 1400. I will discuss this site and the points from it at length later to illustrate some problems of archaeological interpretation. Here I will demonstrate the manufacture of a modern replication and show some archaeological specimens that illustrate the same things.

I subdivide the manufacture of points into a number of stages. Archaeologists argue about whether sequential stages really exist in the manufacture of stone tools or the mind of the knapper, or are merely imposed on the process by archaeological classifications (e.g., Bradley 1975; Callahan 1979b; Collins 1975; Flenniken, Patterson, and Hayden

1979; Magne and Pokotylo 1981; Patten, Sollberger, and Patterson 1978; Patterson 1977). Stages are usually defined by major changes in a knapper's goals and procedures as manufacture of a tool progresses. Most knappers find some kind of staging concept useful for thinking about stone tools and for teaching knapping (e.g., Callahan 1979a, 1985; Waldorf 1984). Especially when you are beginning, sticking to a methodical set of procedures and stages will help you. Most knappers, however, do not follow stages in any very rigid way, and when we apply our definitions to archaeological specimens, we are making our own interpretation of what the prehistoric knapper was doing or trying to do at the point when the piece we are analyzing was abandoned. This means that there is some subjective judgment and ambiguity involved, and we usually find it necessary to make some arbitrary definitions in order to classify and describe.

I use five stages, numbered from 0 to 4: blank, edged blank, preform, unfinished point, finished point. As I illustrate the sequence of making a small side-notched point, I will define the stage and its goals in ideal terms first, then describe the actual point and how it fits or differs from the ideal, and discuss knapping strategy and procedure. My replication sequence was drawn as I flaked, and I have tried not to pretty it up too much. Doing a detailed step-by-step drawing like this, by the way, makes a very good exercise in seeing and understanding what you do when you knap.

Stage 0: The Blank

The first step in making a projectile point is selecting a piece of material to work with. I have already discussed this in general terms. Here you are looking for a small flake. It should be flat rather than curved, or you will have to remove a lot of material at both ends to get a straight point (Figure 7.25). It should not be much thicker than the point you want to end with, but it should be about twice as wide and 25 percent longer. This gives you enough space to thin out the bulb at the proximal end of the flake, thin other thick spots, and shape the point. Too large a flake means that much more extra material to remove.

I refer to this as Stage 0 because it is usually not possible to recognize an unworked blank in archaeological sites. In rare instances where a prehistoric tool kit is found with finished and unfinished points, and flakes of the right size to become points, we can call those flakes blanks with some assurance. In most situations, lots of material is mixed together, and it is not possible to read the minds of dead knappers and decide which flakes they would have made into points had not fate intervened.

The flake I selected for this replication (Figure 7.26) is 43 millimeters

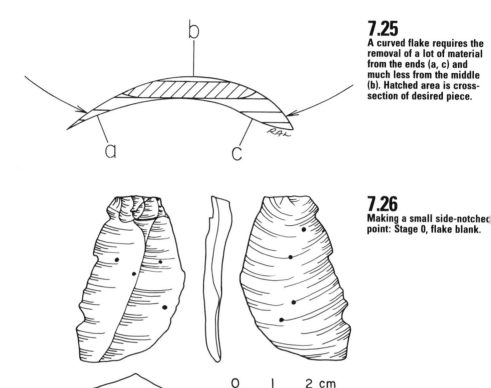

7.25
A curved flake requires the removal of a lot of material from the ends (a, c) and much less from the middle (b). Hatched area is cross-section of desired piece.

7.26
Making a small side-notched point: Stage 0, flake blank.

long, 25 millimeters wide, and 7 millimeters thick (1.7 × 1 × .28 in.) at its thickest point. It weighs 6.7 grams (.24 oz.). It was struck with a hard hammer from a nodule of Redwall Chert, the material used at Grasshopper. This piece is a little grainy and has some small fossils, indicated as dots on the drawings to help you stay oriented. It is a good size, but a little too thick, with a ridge on the exterior that will be a bit of trouble. The base of the point will be at the bottom of the flake, because removing more material from the platform end will let me eliminate the twist and thin the thick bulb and platform.

Stage 1: Edged Blank
The first thing to do with the flake is to prepare the edges, as discussed earlier. The sharp feather edge is removed by crushing and rubbing with my abrading stone. The thick edge at the platform is turned by pressure flaking. The whole edge is then flaked to make it bifacial all around.

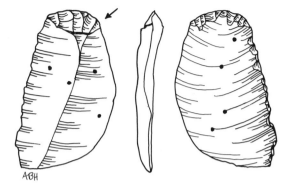

7.27
Stage 1, edging the blank. Edges have been ground, edge A and what will be the tip have been flaked on the interior (Face II), and the original flake platform has been removed. Arrow indicates desirable platform and ridge to remove part of the step near the tip on Face I.

To begin the edging process (Figure 7.27), I have ground the feather edges rather severely, working unifacially toward the interior of the flake. This is because I want to remove the first flakes from the interior surface, but the feather edge is well below the centerplane and I need to move the edge away from that surface and closer to the centerplane to make my platforms. The first series of flakes should come off the interior face because flakes on the exterior face would not be able to run across the slightly concave surface up to the ridge, and would crush and step. Flakes off this surface will have to be intentionally short until enough of the width is removed to get closer to the ridge. This gives you some idea of how far ahead you have to think. I have also begun removing the thick platform end by turning the edge there, to produce a bifacial edge from which I can remove longer flakes for thinning.

The final edged blank (Figure 7.28) has had all edges flaked, mostly bifacially, and the thick edges at both ends bifaced. An opportune combination of a platform with a good ridge allowed me to remove a long flake from the exterior face (arrow in Figure 7.27, scar in Figure 7.28) that took off part of a troublesome step, even if that was not part of the ideal stage sequence. If you look at the piece end on (Figure 7.28 top and bottom at left) you will see how strategy is affected by the position of the edge. At the platform end, flakes from the left edge can be removed only from the interior, but on the right edge the distance to the ridge is shorter and the surface is less concave, so a strong platform will allow a flake to follow the previous flake scar up onto the ridge. At the distal end of the piece, flakes can be removed only from the interior face.

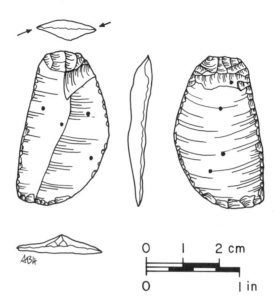

7.28
Stage 1, edged blank finished, with mostly bifacial edges. Arrows (end-on view) show directions of next flakes.

Stage 2: Preform

During this stage, the goals are to thin and regularize the piece, and begin to shape it. I proceed as systematically as possible by shearing and abrading all around the edge, producing an edge that is beveled below the centerplane and provides platforms all around for a series of flakes off one face. When I have flaked the first face, I shear and abrade in the other direction and flake the second face similarly. I do this several times, beginning to remove more material at the tip end as I begin to shape the preform, but concentrating on thinning out the thicker areas to leave a regular cross-section.

After the first series of flakes (Figure 7.29), the shape begins to take form. I have decided how to orient the point and have made a straight edge at the distal end of the flake that will be close to the final base of the point. This means more material will have to come off the left edge (looking at the exterior face) than off the right. Now that the very thin edges of the blank have been removed, it is possible to detach larger flakes and begin to thin across the whole of the interior face and up onto the ridge on parts of the exterior face, as the enlarged view shows. Initial results are visible in the final preform (Figure 7.30) after a second series of large flakes. Note that there is still thinning to do on this preform, so it does not entirely fit my ideal description. Because the edge is uneven and thinning is still needed, flakes will have to be selected to solve these problems, preventing perfect regularity. The strategy at this point is to remove more from the interior face to get the edge closer to the ridge and at the centerplane. Then it will be

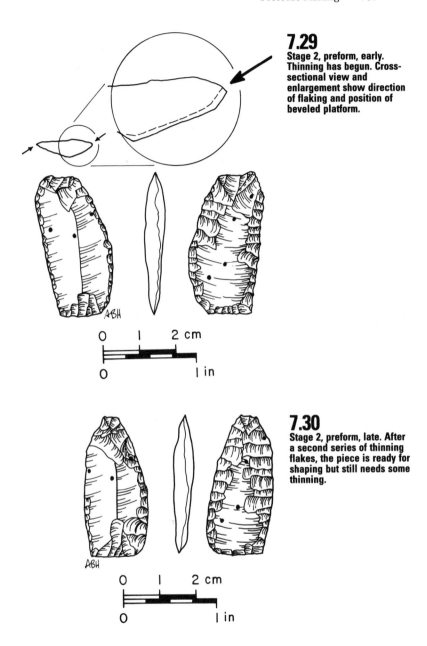

7.29
Stage 2, preform, early.
Thinning has begun. Cross-
sectional view and
enlargement show direction
of flaking and position of
beveled platform.

0   1   2 cm

0   1 in

7.30
Stage 2, preform, late. After
a second series of thinning
flakes, the piece is ready for
shaping but still needs some
thinning.

0   1   2 cm

0   1 in

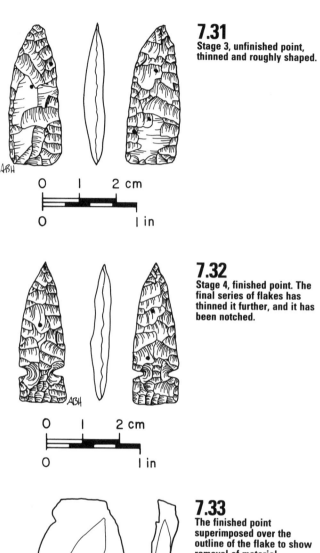

7.31
Stage 3, unfinished point, thinned and roughly shaped.

7.32
Stage 4, finished point. The final series of flakes has thinned it further, and it has been notched.

7.33
The finished point superimposed over the outline of the flake to show removal of material.

possible to flake across the exterior surface and remove the rest of the ridge.

Stage 3: Unfinished Point
Beginning with the preform, which is fully bifacial and regular, the emphasis shifts to shaping, while continuing to thin as necessary.

The unfinished point (Figure 7.31) has nearly its final outline shape and is ready for a final series of flakes and then notching. Thinning was pretty successful except for one step on the right edge of the exterior face that will leave a slightly thick spot in the center of the point. At this point I switched to a pressure flaker with a smaller point, ground my platforms so that they were quite strong, and was careful about flake spacing to get as even a pattern of scars as possible.

Stage 4: Finished Point
On the best points at Grasshopper, a final very regular series of flakes was removed from each face to leave a regular pattern of scars. Then the base was thinned, and the edges carefully touched up to remove any jaggedness and platform remnants. Some of the Grasshopper points were notched, others were not (see Figures 7.37, 7.43, 7.44). Mine has side notches, made as described earlier.

My finished point (Figure 7.32) is well within the range of points at Grasshopper, but a bit thicker than most because I started with a slightly thick flake to show how thinning progresses. It weighs 2.4 grams (.08 oz.) and measures 36 millimeters long, 13 millimeters wide, and 5 millimeters thick (1.4 × .5 × .2 in.) About two-thirds of the flake mass was reduced to dust and small flakes (Figure 7.33). Not counting time spent drawing and taking notes, it took me about five minutes to edge the blank, another fifteen minutes to preform it, ten more to reach the unfinished point, and a final eight minutes to finish and notch the point. I work faster when I am not being so careful and thinking so much, and slower when I am trying to produce a really fine piece.

Although the Grasshopper points are small and light, they were effective weapons. The term "bird points" applied by some collectors has never made sense. A stone point is fragile, and only lasts a few shots at best (Titmus and Woods 1986). Even when the game is struck, the point may break. A sharp wooden tip is adequate for birds and small game and much more durable, especially when one is likely to miss frequently. Despite the small size of many prehistoric arrow points, they were frequently used in areas where the main game was deer (as at Grasshopper) or even bison, and are occasionally even found embedded in the bones of large game and human victims. Modern experi-

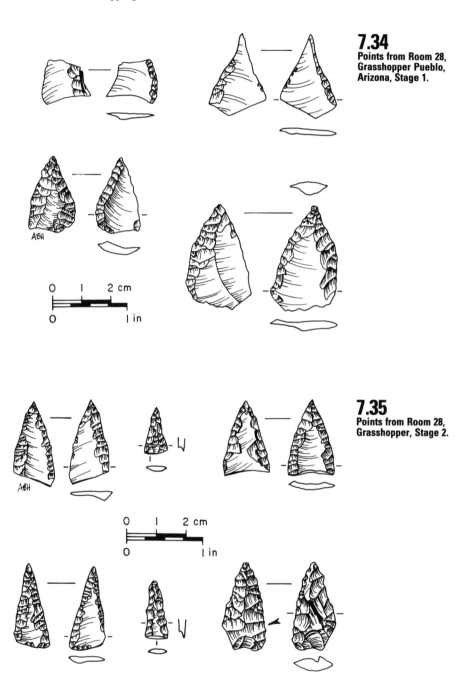

7.34
Points from Room 28,
Grasshopper Pueblo,
Arizona, Stage 1.

7.35
Points from Room 28,
Grasshopper, Stage 2.

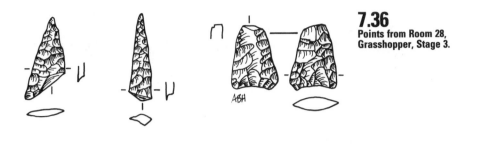

7.36
Points from Room 28,
Grasshopper, Stage 3.

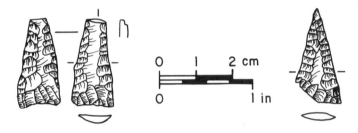

ments support their effectiveness. They may be a bit smaller than we would use today, but prehistoric bows were usually smaller and lighter than modern hunting tackle, and people relied on getting very close and expected to track wounded animals.

PRESSURE-FLAKING PROBLEMS

A few archaeological specimens from Grasshopper Pueblo will further illustrate the sequence of manufacture and some of the problems you are likely to encounter (Whittaker 1984, 1987b). A series of points and fragments from Room 28, where one knapper made a large number of points and little else, illustrate the stages described above (Figures 7.34, 7.35, 7.36, 7.37). You can see the progression of a point in manufacture. The preference at Grasshopper seems to have been to finish the tip before the base. I find it better to finish the base before making the tip any more fragile than necessary.

Figure 7.38 shows idealized views of the kinds of breaks common on small points at Grasshopper. Most breaks on specimens from the site are snap breaks caused by bending (Figure 7.39). Bending fractures are usually not hard to identify (Sollberger 1986; Cotterell and Kamminga 1979, 1987; Tsirk 1979). You will soon recognize them from your own painful experience. They are either approximately right-angled at both faces, or right-angled at one face, while the other shows a lip or the scar of a lip, much like a hinge fracture. This is because when a stone tool is fractured by bending, the lower surface is stretched and pulled

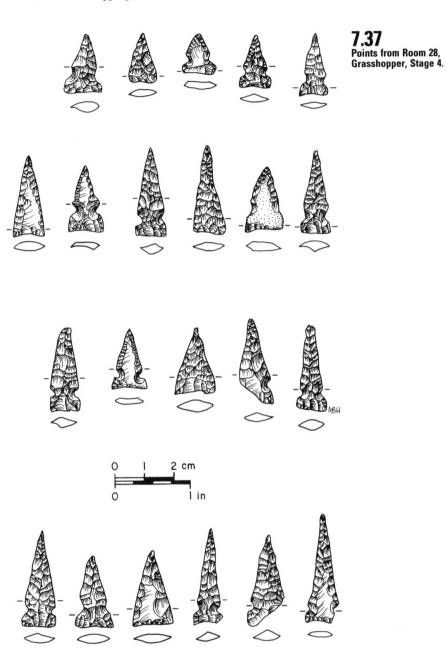

7.37
Points from Room 28,
Grasshopper, Stage 4.

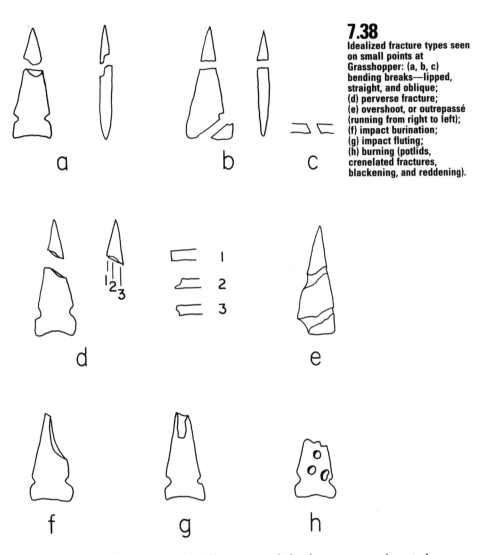

7.38
Idealized fracture types seen on small points at Grasshopper: (a, b, c) bending breaks—lipped, straight, and oblique; (d) perverse fracture; (e) overshoot, or outrepassé (running from right to left); (f) impact burination; (g) impact fluting; (h) burning (potlids, crenelated fractures, blackening, and reddening).

apart to make the right-angled fracture, while the upper surface is being compressed (Figure 7.40). This is the most common kind of manufacturing failure in making small points, and the smaller and thinner the point, the more difficult it is to flake it well without snapping it. Notice one point in Figure 7.36 and two in Figure 7.37 whose corners broke with bending fractures during either the first or the second notching.

Another kind of break is the overshoot, or outrepassé. In an example in Figure 7.35 a rather thick and flawed preform was finally discarded after a flake (indicated by arrow) ran too far and took off the far corner.

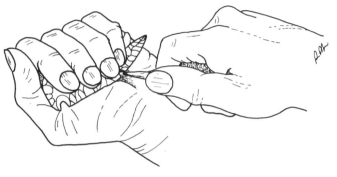

7.39
Bending fracture in pressure flaking. The point was pressed and flexed by fingers and the pressure tool in the center of the palm, where it was not well supported. The leather pad on the left hand has been left out to show this—don't knap unprotected.

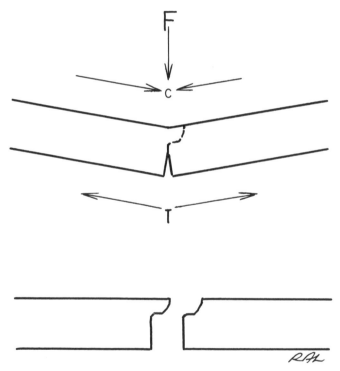

7.40
Bending fractures. F = downward force, c = compression on the top surface, T = tension on the bottom surface, producing the lipped fracture below.

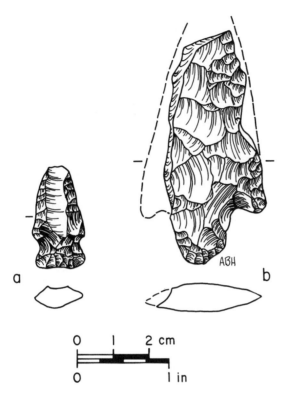

7.41
Impact fractures: (a) impact flute on a Late Woodland point from Iowa; (b) severe burination of an Early Woodland Waubesa point from Iowa (Whittaker and Kamp 1985).

This may happen to you if you make a platform too strong or too close to the centerplane on a small point. Sometimes a flake "plunges" like an overshoot, but nearer to the middle of a piece, in which case it is called a *plunging* or *perverse fracture*. These are probably influenced also by bending stresses, and they often look similar, but with a more complex fracture surface and sometimes a flake scar leading into the fracture.

Bending fractures can occur on projectile points during manufacture and through accidents and use after they are finished. However, there are distinctive breaks that tend to occur only during use, when a stone point strikes a hard object like a bone if the hunter aimed well, or a tree if he did not. A couple of examples from Iowa (Figure 7.41) illustrate *impact fluting* and *impact burination*. In the first, the impact has detached a flake that runs from the tip down toward the base on one face; in the second, the flake runs along an edge. Usually there is crushing at the tip as well, and sometimes tip crushing is the only damage. These patterns have been confirmed experimentally (Bergman and Newcomer 1983; Bradley 1974; Frison 1978; Titmus and Woods 1986; Woods 1987).

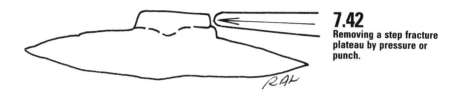

7.42
Removing a step fracture plateau by pressure or punch.

Another common problem that you will experience, especially at first, is the failure to thin a point. Beginners often suffer from starting with a flake that is too thick, or too narrow in relation to its thickness. Repeated step and hinge terminations in trying to thin a point can leave a large, thick plateau with no platforms from which to remove it (see Figures 6.28, 8.34). These can occasionally be removed by using the edge of the plateau as a platform (Figure 7.42). This is risky: sometimes it breaks the piece, occasionally it produces a deep hinge or ripple, and frequently it just crushes the edge of the plateau.

Do not despair when you ruin a point. The knapper in Room 28 whose work we have been discussing left ninety-three points behind him. Eighteen of them were finished and unbroken; almost all the rest had been broken by bending or perverse fractures. Of course, we cannot know how many points he finished and took away, but when I and four other knappers replicated Grasshopper points, we finished twenty-nine points out of fifty-six attempts, a success rate of 52 percent. Individually, our success rates ranged from 36 percent to 80 percent and were influenced by our different levels of skill as well as individual preferences in such things as the thickness of the points and the depth of notching. A knapper with years of experience at making these points should probably expect better than 80 percent success, and the simple versions of Grasshopper points, like most of those from Room 28, take only fifteen to thirty minutes to make. Some of the very fine points probably occupied the knapper for over an hour, and are of course much more likely to be broken in manufacture as well.

I will discuss the archaeological interpretation of points from Grasshopper Pueblo further in Chapter 11. For the moment, let me point out that in this one site there is a great range in the form and quality of the ubiquitous small triangular projectile point. A few examples (Figures 7.43, 7.44) will suffice to show you that then, as now, there were good knappers and mediocre, experts and beginners, and a variety of acceptable point styles.

PATTERNED PRESSURE FLAKING

As you increase in skill, your flaking will become more systematic and regular. The height of pressure-flaking skill can be seen in the patterned pressure flaking common in a number of prehistoric cultures

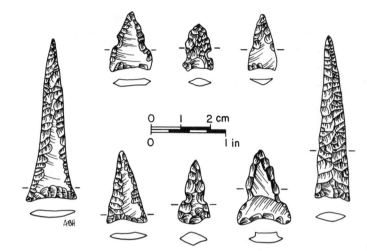

7.43
Selected points from Grasshopper Pueblo, Arizona. Note the range of forms and quality of flaking in a single site with a span of one hundred years or less; all local chert except top row center (obsidian) and bottom right (slate).

(see Figures 3.16, 7.46, 7.51). Patterned pressure flaking leaves a pleasing, rippled surface covered with regular flake scars, and the patterns can be varied, as the illustrations show. The Danish flint dagger shown in Figure 7.45 is an example of intentionally decorative use of skillful flaking. The Danish daggers were made in a variety of styles during the Late Neolithic (ca. 1800–1500 B.C.), and the finer specimens are some of the most impressive flint work ever done. Some appear to have been utilitarian knives and show evidence of use and resharpening, while others probably circulated as items of status and were included in burials and offerings. Some appear to have been imitating or inspired by the early bronze daggers of northern Europe. The one shown in Figure 7.45 is a small but well-flaked example of a "Type V" dagger (Callahan 1981; Lomberg 1973; Müller 1902; Waldorf 1988).

A number of other works discuss fine pressure flaking in general and in particular prehistoric industries (e.g., Callahan 1981; Green 1975; Kelterborn 1984; Patten 1978; Sollberger 1976). Here I will outline the principles, and you can begin to experiment for yourself.

For even pressure flaking, you need a very regular preform. Unless you maintain a perfect contour and faces without steps and other flaws, you cannot do consistent, patterned pressure flaking. Cross-sections for patterned pressure flaking are usually convex, or even diamond-shaped (Figure 7.46), so that the pressure flakes will tend to run to the center of the face or a bit beyond and feather out smoothly. You do not want a thin, flat cross-section because flakes will spread out and terminate in steps on a flat surface. Excessive thinning too soon makes patterned pressure flaking difficult. One way to get a perfect cross-section and, more important, a perfect surface for even flaking is to

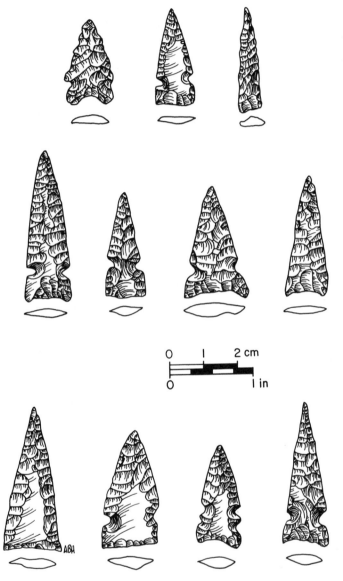

7.44
Further variation in points from Grasshopper; all of local chert except top left (obsidian).

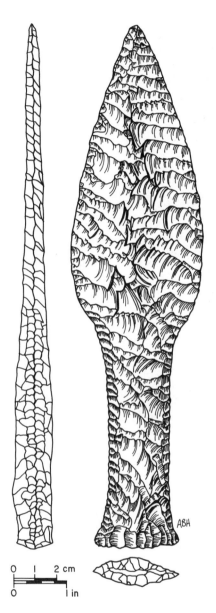

7.45
Flint dagger, Late Neolithic, Denmark. Drawn from Lithic Casting Lab Cast N-3.

ABH

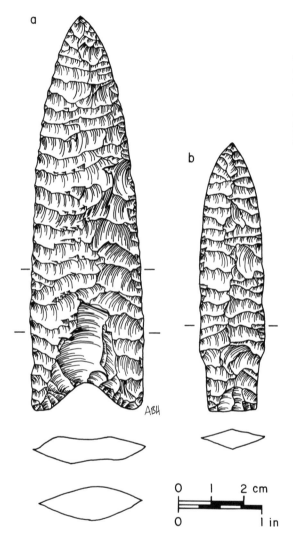

7.46
Patterned pressure flaking
on two points with typically
thick cross-sections:
(a) Dalton-Meserve point
(Late Paleo-Indian–Early
Archaic) from Missouri.
Drawn from Lithic Casting
Lab Cast A-3. (b) replica
of Eden point (Late
Paleo-Indian), John
Whittaker, 1990.

grind the faces of the piece. This is the technique used by Scott Silsby
in the precisely pressure-flaked point in Figure 7.47 and by Jim Hopper
(Figure 1.6b). The Predynastic Egyptian knife in Figure 7.51 was also
carefully ground, and typically has only one face pressure-flaked, the
other being left smooth.

Platforms should be set up as a continuous edge, along which the
flakes are spaced so that they overlap each other 30 to 50 percent (Figure 7.48). The first series of flakes on the first face leaves a serrated
edge, and unlike most pressure flaking, this should not be removed and
ground, although it may be necessary to bevel and grind the serrations

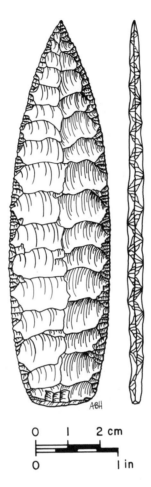

7.47
Patterned pressure-flaked point by Scott Silsby. The original was flaked on a ground obsidian blank, using a copper pressure tool. According to Silsby, it took "about three hours of *concentrated* work." Drawn from Lithic Casting Lab Cast MM-1.

themselves. When the piece is turned over to work the other face, the tips of the serrations serve as the platforms for the series of flakes here (Figure 7.49). If this is done correctly, the fracture begins with a small lip on the pressure flake (similar to many soft-hammer percussion flakes; see Chapter 8), and the serrations are broken off, leaving a slightly sinuous and very sharp edge, as in the example by Errett Callahan (Figure 7.50). I refer to this as the Paleo-Indian style of patterned pressure flaking, as some of the early points from North America are flaked this way. Note that there are almost no negative bulbs at the edges where the flakes begin. This lack of bulbs led to one of the most ludicrous misinterpretations of a stone tool ever published. E. E. Blackman (1932) decided that parallel-flaked Paleo-Indian points could not have been made by pressure flaking, but were finished by painting glue

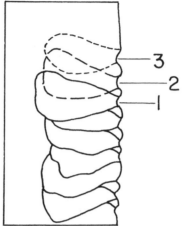

7.48
Overlap of scars in patterned pressure flaking. Three numbered flakes are shown in sequence, each removing the forward edge of the previous one.

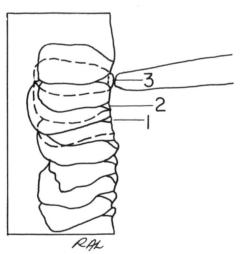

7.49
Patterned pressure flaking, Paleo-Indian style. Serrations left by flaking the first face were used as platforms for flakes off the other face. Initiation of the flake by a bending fracture removes the serration and much of any negative bulb and produces little or no new bulb, so the edge is left sharp and straight. Numbers indicate three flakes in sequence (shown with broken lines) that are being removed from the (invisible) face opposite that shown. The edge below the numbers has not had the second face flaked.

7.50
Patterned pressure-flaked
obsidian point by Errett
Callahan, 1988. This point
took one hour and forty-one
minutes to make, going
through the stages discussed
in this chapter. Note that
there are no negative bulbs
and no need to trim the
edges.

ABH

0   1   2 cm

0   1 in

on the surfaces. As the glue dried, it pulled off flakes in even rows. Try it if you like, but do not be surprised if all you get is a sticky biface.

Another style of fine pressure flaking, which I find somewhat easier, can be called "Gerzean," after the Gerzean ripple-flaked knives (Figure 7.51). In these knives and in Silsby's point (Figure 7.47) a thicker platform was prepared along the edge, and the pressure tool rested on the platform as much as on the edge itself. Because of this, the flakes began with a small bulb (Figure 7.52). The flakes were also larger and spaced farther apart than is usual in the Paleo-Indian style.

In most patterned pressure flaking the flakes will be smaller and closer together. After each flake, part of the platform between it and the next flake can be trimmed away. This helps to guide the next flake and prevent it from spreading out too soon. It also has the effect of straightening the edge and thinning out the "deltas" between flake scars. If both faces are to be flaked, the edge can be beveled in the opposite direction after the whole edge is flaked on the first face.

In the Gerzean example shown, the flakes are so far apart that their bulbs do not overlap, and some of the negative bulbs can still be seen

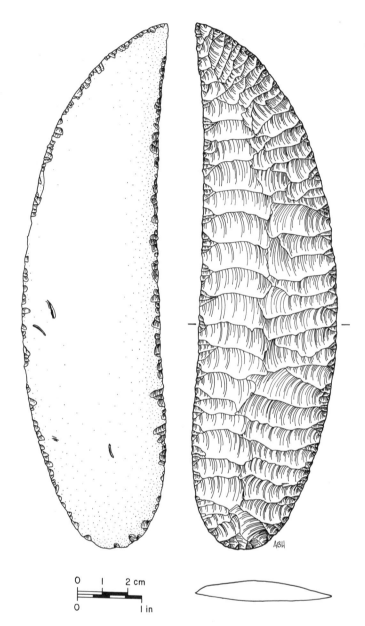

7.51
Gerzean ripple-flaked knife.
Drawn from Lithic Casting
Lab Cast EG-2.

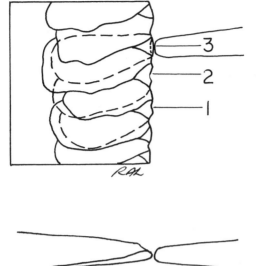

7.52
Patterned pressure flaking, Gerzean style. A dull or ground platform and Hertzian cone initiation were used to remove a second series of flakes (broken lines) from the opposite (invisible) face. Flakes are spaced farther apart and leave negative bulbs and platform remnants. The platform remnants on the upper face are shown untrimmed.

along the edge. Some of the tiny scars thinning the deltas overlap the major pressure-flake scars, so on this piece the platform trimming was done last, thinning and sharpening the edge and giving a serrated effect that was carefully emphasized by delicate retouch on the opposite face. No attempt was made to prepare the edge for a series of flakes on the second face.

The Gerzean ripple-flaked knives (Bradley 1972; Hoffman 1987; Kelterborn 1984) are some of the finest flint tools ever made (Figure 7.51). The Gerzean period between about 3300 and 3100 b.c. was the end of the Predynastic period in Egypt, when wealth and power were becoming concentrated in the hands of local leaders, beginning developments that led to the rise of the pharaohs and the unified Egyptian kingdom (Hoffman 1979). Many of the Gerzean knives known today were looted and sold in the early days of Egyptian archaeology, so we often do not know where they were found.

The knife illustrated is fairly typical. It was begun by percussion-flaking a thin blank of fine tabular flint. This was then ground to shape over both faces, one of which was left unflaked. There are a few remnants of the percussion flake scars left on the ground face—a few ripples that went too deep to be obliterated. The pressure flaking was done with great care, and the flakes removed are so large that it is likely that some sort of long flaker was used to add the pressure of chest or arms. As copper was becoming increasingly common in the Gerzean period, a copper-tipped pressure tool may well have been used.

If you look closely, you can see from the overlap of flakes that the left edge of the rippled face was flaked first, from tip to base, then the right edge, from base to tip. A perfectly straight edge was not desired on the Gerzean knife, so after the deltas were retouched with small flakes, the resulting serrations were deepened by small flakes removed from the ground face.

The Gerzean knappers were obviously very skillful and were surely specialized craftsmen, leaving extensive evidence of mines and production sites (Weisgerber 1987). They produced finely flaked forms that were clearly for use as well as the ripple-flaked form shown. Knives like this would have been excellent for butchering, but rather fragile. The perfection of the work and the fact that the specimens found by legitimate excavation are usually grave goods argue that at least some of these marvels were not ordinary tools, but prestige goods that may have also had religious significance (Needler 1984; Midant-Reynes 1984). A few famous examples were embellished by handles of carved ivory or gold-sheathed wood (de Morgan 1926:144; Aldred 1965:35), which has led art historians to illustrate them instead of dismissing them as mere stone tools.

8

SOFT-HAMMER PERCUSSION AND BIFACES

At this came the executioner, the Nacam,
*with a knife of stone, and struck him with
great skill and cruelty a blow between the
ribs of his left side under the nipple, and he
at once plunged his hand in there and seized
the heart like a raging tiger and snatched it
out alive.*

—Bishop Diego de Landa
(1582, in Tozzer 1941:119)

The knife that cut the heart out of Aztec and Maya sacrifices was personified as a god, or actually several related gods (Brundage 1979). Among the Aztec, the flint knife, *tecpatl* (Figure 8.1), was an aspect of Tezcatlipoca, the central god of Aztec mythology, and in some stories the gods all sprang from a flint knife. *Itztli*, the obsidian knife, was one form of the terrible goddess Itzpapalotl, Obsidian Knife Butterfly, and several of the Aztec goddesses wore knives as skirts or carried them on their backs like babies. Sacrificial knives are often shown with faces, or even as animated gods chasing and devouring human victims. Actual tools used in sacrifice are hard to identify (Hester and Shafer 1987; Robicsek and Hales 1984). Those used in human-heart sacrifice seem to have been finely worked flint or obsidian bifaces, often decorated with carved wooden or mosaic handles. Finely worked stone knife blades were common offerings in temple foundations and other ceremonial deposits in the Great Temple in the Aztec capital of Tenochtitlan (Moctezuma 1988:98), where they were sometimes placed in the mouth and nose of skulls. The Maya also flung sacrificial knives (Figure 8.2) into cenotes, or natural wells, and buried knives and amazing *eccentrics* (Figure 3.20) in ceremonial contexts at Maya centers such as Copan (Stuart 1989) and Altar de Sacrificios (Willey 1972). Iannone (1992) suggests that eccentric lithics were symbolic representations of gods and noble ancestors, and were used to display and reinforce the status of the ruling elite.

8.1
Aztec date glyph "1 Flint Knife" from the Temple Stone, Mexico City. The flint knife with a face is flanked on the right by a stream of fire and water representing war, and on the left by a smoking obsidian mirror motif emblematic of rulers and the god Tezcatlipoca. The date 1 Flintknife begins the third thirteen-year period in each fifty-two-year cycle of the Aztec calendar, symbolizes the patron god Huitzilopochtli, and represents the traditional date (A.D. 1168) for the Aztec migrations to the Valley of Mexico (Brundage 1979; Pasztory 1983). A small piece of stone can carry a large load of meanings.

Among North American groups such as the Yurok Indians of California, large obsidian or chert bifaces were objects of prestige and wealth, displayed at ceremonials, inherited by one's descendants, and jealously guarded (Kroeber 1905, 1925; Rust 1905). All over the world, large bifaces were recognized as the epitome of the knapper's skill, and today, when modern knappers fall to boasting, chances are they will proclaim the thinness of their bifaces, and the even flaking achieved on them, with almost poetic eloquence.

DEFINITIONS

As we have seen, a biface is, strictly speaking, any tool worked on both sides. Modern American usage applies this term most often in Paleolithic archaeology to handaxes and in American archaeology to relatively large bifacial tools that are also called knives or blades as well as to the early stages of manufacturing such tools. Most projectile points are bifacially worked, but are rarely referred to as bifaces. The term "blade" should be used only for the special type of flake and not for what I will call bifaces. As most American archaeologists use the term biface, it also usually implies a tool that is worked at least partly by percussion. Knappers use "to biface" as a verb, meaning either to turn an edge (as discussed in Chapters 6 and 7), which makes a piece bifacial, or more generally to mean working a bifacial tool by percussion, usually to thin it.

The most common and effective technique for making bifaces is soft-hammer percussion using a bone, antler, or wooden hammer, also called a *billet* or *baton* or *percussor*. Bifaces, including some of considerable refinement. can also be made by hard-hammer percussion. Some

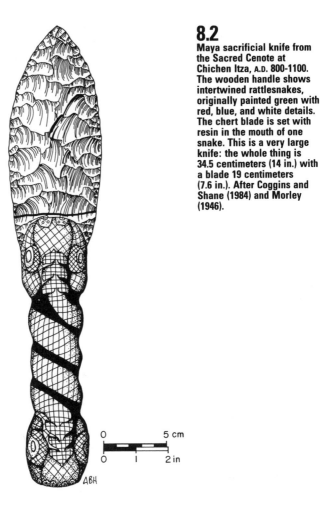

8.2
Maya sacrificial knife from the Sacred Cenote at Chichen Itza, A.D. 800-1100. The wooden handle shows intertwined rattlesnakes, originally painted green with red, blue, and white details. The chert blade is set with resin in the mouth of one snake. This is a very large knife: the whole thing is 34.5 centimeters (14 in.) with a blade 19 centimeters (7.6 in.). After Coggins and Shane (1984) and Morley (1946).

knappers also use indirect percussion, sometimes with copper tools (Frank 1992). My experience is with soft-hammer direct percussion, and this is what most knappers use.

Billets of organic material do not preserve well in most archaeological sites, and few of the stone-using peoples who survived into historic times did much soft-hammer percussion. As a result, it took a long time for soft-hammer percussion to work its way into the mainstream of flintknapping and the archaeological literature. Coutier (1929; Cabrol and Coutier 1931) seems to have been the first to publish experiments with batons of wood and bone, but it is plain, from most early mentions of the technique and the failure of early experimenters to duplicate some kinds of tools, that it was not well understood (e.g., Pond 1930; Ellis 1939). François Bordes is probably the one most re-

sponsible for the revival and present flowering of soft-hammer techniques in modern knapping, although others were also involved.

Now we recognize soft-hammer percussion by distinctive features of
the flakes and tools produced as well as by occasionally finding the
batons themselves. Soft-hammer percussion is an ancient technique,
as some Acheulean handaxes show. It was eventually used over most
of the world, although it rose and fell in popularity through time, and
was used extensively by some people while their neighbors ignored
it. Modern knappers probably overemphasize soft-hammer percussion
and tend to forget, both in replication and in analysis of archaeological
sites, that there are other ways of producing similar effects.

TOOLS

Soft, as in "soft hammer," just means softer than hard—that is, antler
or wood as opposed to stone—and relatively elastic as opposed to relatively inelastic. It does not mean that you will not mind if you hit your
finger instead of the core. There is a wide range of hammer hardness—from quartzite and chert at the hard end of the scale to basalt,
sandstone, limestone, copper, antler and bone, and, finally, wood.
Speaking of soft-hammer (or baton or billet) technique usually implies
the use of wood or antler. It also implies certain techniques and results,
but first let us discuss the tools themselves.

Like most modern and prehistoric knappers, I use antler. Deer antler
is easiest to get and is good for small to medium hammers. Elk and
moose antler is larger, and moose is especially heavy and dense, so
these are prized for larger batons. The beginner will do fine with deer.

Shed antler is perfectly all right if it is not too old and weathered.
Fresh antler may be a bit heavier and less likely to chip and wear out.
If you do not find many antlers in your neck of the woods, try friends
who hunt, taxidermists, swap meets and flea markets, and those un-
appreciative folk who hang antlers on their summer cabins to dry in
the sun and rot in the rain. I never see a fine rack on some would-be
woodsman's gable without thinking about returning at night with a
rope or ladder, but so far conscience has restrained me.

Antlers can also be improved by modern tricks. Old dry antlers can
be soaked in glue to harden them. An antler hammer can be weighted
by drilling out a hole and filling it with lead. A smaller section can be
mounted on a long handle like a modern hammer head, which improves leverage and accuracy for some people. I have always preferred
a simple antler base with a minimal amount of shaping and smoothing.

If you can't find antler, hard wood will do. It wears faster and is a
little harder to use than antler, but for flaking the very toughest and
the very most fragile materials, wooden batons are actually better than
antler. In any case, for the beginner's needs, wood is easy to find. A

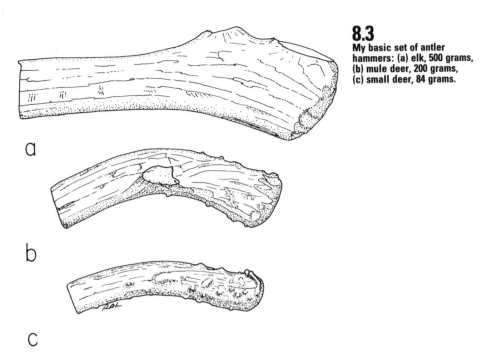

8.3
My basic set of antler hammers: (a) elk, 500 grams, (b) mule deer, 200 grams, (c) small deer, 84 grams.

a

b

c

well-seasoned limb of oak, hickory, or any other hard wood, cut into pieces about 20 centimeters (8 in.) long and 2.5–5 centimeters (1–2 in.) in diameter makes fairly good soft hammers. Hammer, axe, and pick-axe handles from the local hardware store work too.

You will eventually want some different sizes. My basic set that I use a lot consists of three antlers (Figure 8.3). The large one is elk and weighs about 500 grams (1 lb.). This is suitable for big bifaces like large handaxes. The middle-sized one is the one I use constantly, for large to medium-sized bifaces typical of American prehistory, large projectile points and knives. It is mule deer and weighs about 200 grams (7 oz.). The smallest deer antler weighs about 84 grams (3 oz.) and is useful for thinning small bifaces, as in the later stages of making a large point. The two smaller sizes are what you will need to begin.

The hammers shown are made from the crown of the antler, where it attaches to the skull and the bone is most dense. You can also use sections of the beam, but they wear out faster. The tines are good for small hammers, but mostly as pressure flakers (Figure 8.4). I grind off most of the burrs around the crown, and grind a smooth, rounded surface to start with, but you will notice that all my hammers which have been in use awhile have flattened facets. These develop with wear, and many knappers prefer to keep grinding a rounded end for a more precise strike. I find that I do just as well using the facets and the edges of the facets. Antler hammers are well known archaeologically in some parts

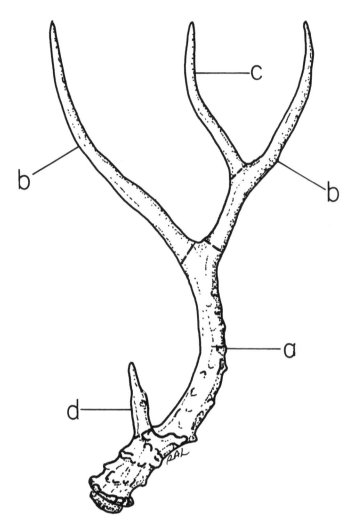

8.4
Typical antler, showing
how to cut it up: (a) medium
to heavy hammer, (b) tine
flakers and light hammers,
(c) small-tine pressure
flaker, (d) discard. If not
shed, cut it off right at the
skull. Grind off sharp edges
where you hold tools.

of the world (e.g., Frison 1982; Holland 1988; Olsen 1979; Shafer 1985)
and can be identified by the distinctive faceting wear, the tiny flakes
embedded in the facets, and the polish that develops where the hand
grips them.

Some modern knappers use copper billets and get very good results.
Large pieces of copper can sometimes be found in junkyards, and a
wide variety of copper tools can be bought at some knap-ins. Some
other metals will work too; I have seen aluminum and even nickel
billets. Lead is too soft.

Some knappers make a lot of bifaces with soft, tough hammerstones.
Hard limestone pebbles are especially good, and these are found ar-

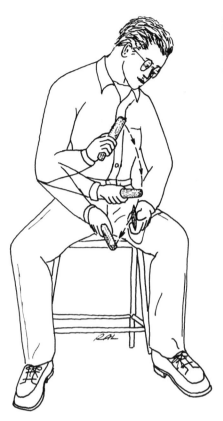

8.5
Soft-hammer percussion, sitting, with biface held in the left hand and left wrist steadied on the leg.

chaeologically as well (Shafer 1991). The distinction between hard and soft hammers is difficult to maintain both in the tools themselves and, as we shall see, in the resulting flakes. The beginner will find, as many advanced knappers do, that antler is easier to use than soft hammerstones. Antler is also what I am most familiar with, so I will emphasize it in my descriptions.

You should already have the other equipment you will need. Glasses and a glove on your holding hand are of course recommended. A leather pad for your leg will be appreciated, and you will need a small abrasive stone for preparing platforms.

BEGINNING

Most knapping is easiest to do sitting down. As in hard-hammer percussion, I like to have my legs about level and feet planted firmly. Most knappers work bifaces either "freehand" or supported on their thigh. For small pieces, it is easy to hold them in your hand, with your hand or wrist steadied on your leg (Figure 8.5). Your fingers support the biface, and your thumb holds it down. The flake comes off parallel to

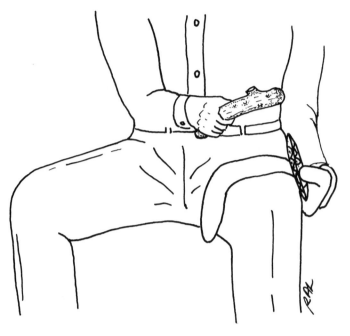

8.6
Soft-hammer percussion
with a large biface pressed
against the outside of the
thigh.

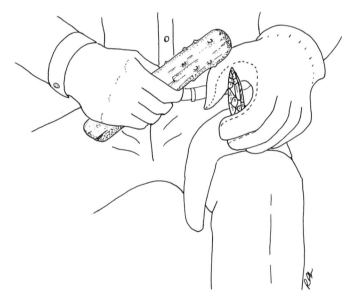

8.7
Soft-hammer percussion
with a biface standing on
edge on the thigh.

your fingers, so wear gloves and be careful. The alternative, as in hard-hammer percussion, is to support the biface on the outside of your thigh, or even lying on top of your thigh. A pad protects your leg both from miscalculated flakes and from the follow-through part of the blow (Figure 8.6). This is especially useful for large bifaces. Another variation is to stand the piece up on your thigh and let your thumb catch the flake (Figure 8.7). In any case, it is very important to support the biface for two reasons. First, your accuracy is improved if the piece is steady and if it does not shift too much when struck. Second, a blow flexes and vibrates a biface, so it is easy to break a thin biface that is not properly supported. The larger your biface, the more important this support becomes.

If you are just beginning, take a piece of material (a large flake is good) and strike some flakes off it, using the baton in the same way you use an ordinary hard hammer. Now try turning the edge, as discussed in Chapters 6 and 7. You will notice that the soft hammer requires a good deal more force in the blow than a hard hammer. When you have acquired a preliminary feel for swinging your soft hammer and a little accuracy, stop. Now you are going to start doing everything differently, and that requires a bit of explanation.

SOFT-HAMMER PRINCIPLES AND RESULTS

A soft hammer is particularly useful in thinning, flattening, and shaping bifaces because it is the easiest way of removing large, relatively flat and thin flakes with small bulbs of percussion. This is because when a soft hammer strikes a core, it compresses slightly, and the force is spread out and transmitted more slowly and evenly. The kind of flakes produced by a soft hammer are necessary if one is trying to produce a large, thin tool with extensive working and with a straight edge. The hard-hammer Oldowan and Abbevillian handaxes shown earlier (Figures 3.2, 6.40) have wavy edges, a result of the large bulbs of percussion usually produced by a hard hammer. If you want to progress to a more sophisticated Acheulean handaxe with flat, flaked surfaces and a straight edge, soft-hammer percussion is the best technique to use.

BIFACE THINNING FLAKES

A *biface thinning flake* or *soft-hammer flake* tends to differ from flakes struck off ordinary cores or flakes struck using a hard hammer (Figure 8.8). Ideally, a biface thinning flake should be relatively thin and flat, with a tendency to expand in width from the platform. The bulb of percussion is relatively flat, or "diffuse." The platform is often very small and should have a small lip on the interior, which, as we will see, is a remnant of the edge of a biface. Platforms may be exten-

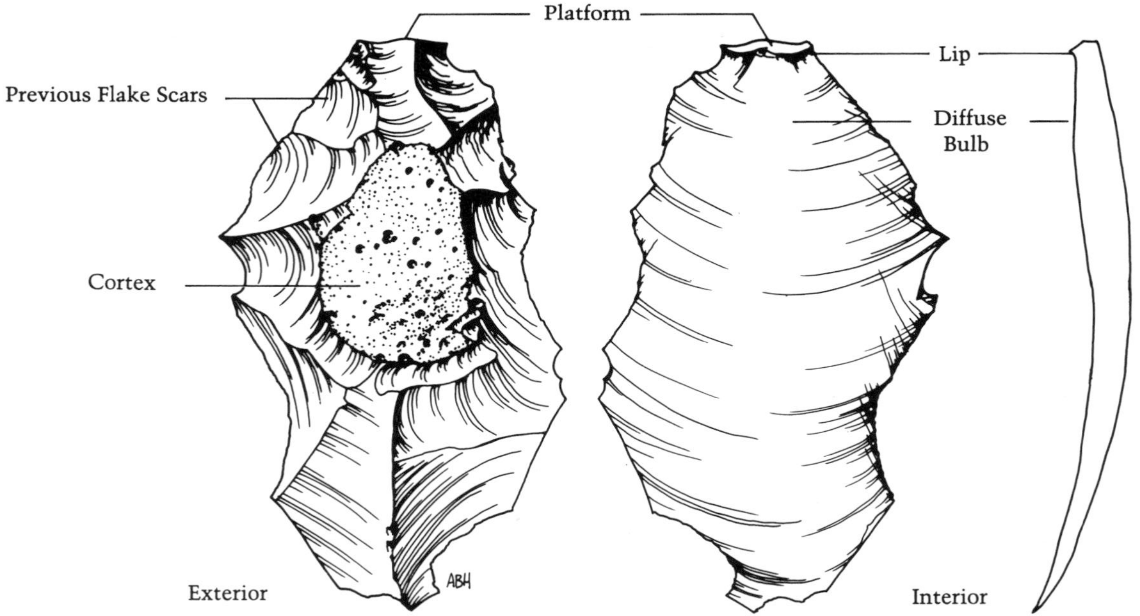

8.8
Features of a biface thinning flake.

Lip

Diffuse
Bulb

Interior

Platform

Previous Flake Scars

Cortex

Exterior

ABH

sively prepared, often rounded and reduced by abrasion. There are often several flat scars on the exterior of the flake from previous thinning flakes. Frequently the platform is crushed by the blow, and thin flakes are often broken. Biface thinning flakes are often somewhat curved.

Not all of these traits are present on every flake. The trait most characteristic of soft-hammer percussion seems to be the frequent lipping of the interior of the platform (Crabtree 1972a; Newcomer 1971; Ohnuma and Bergman 1982). As a group, the traits above are considered characteristic of soft-hammer percussion because they are common in an assemblage of flakes produced by soft hammer, but relatively rare in an assemblage of hard-hammer flakes. However, all these traits, singly or in combination, can be produced by hard-hammer percussion. Soft-hammer assemblages tend to look different from hard-hammer assemblages partly because different hammers were used, but equally because it is easier to make bifaces with soft hammers and cores for ordinary flakes with hard hammers. Bifaces and cores tend to have different kinds of platforms and produce different kinds of flakes, regardless of the hammer used (Bradley 1978). A skillful knapper can use hard and soft hammers almost interchangeably. In fact, some knappers prefer a hammerstone for most of their biface work, often a relatively soft hard hammer such as limestone. The copper billets favored by some knappers now are a bit harder than antler but softer than most stone. I recommend a soft hammer of antler or wood through personal preference and because it is easier to learn to use a soft hammer and get consistent results.

A soft hammer can also be used as if it were a hard hammer. However, because it requires much more forceful blows, it is difficult to do some things, such as removing large flakes from tough materials. The principles of hard-hammer flaking discussed in Chapter 6 should be mastered and kept in mind, but ordinarily a soft hammer is best used on a different kind of tool (bifaces) and in a somewhat different manner, which uses principles closer to those discussed for pressure flaking. This is why I recommend learning to do pressure flaking before beginning soft-hammer percussion.

In hard-hammer percussion, I stressed that the blow should fall at an acute angle to the platform (Figure 8.9). Also, with a hard hammer, it is often enough to allow the weight of the hammerstone to provide the force of the blow, with very little muscular exertion in addition.

A soft hammer is different and often requires a blow of considerable force to detach a flake. This means that a bit more practice is required for control. Also, in making bifaces, the blow contacts the platform at a different angle, at times even appearing to be much greater than 90 degrees.

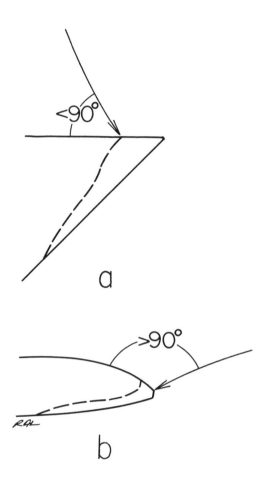

8.9
The angles of blow for
(a) hard-hammer percussion,
(b) soft-hammer biface
flaking.

FRACTURE THEORIES

What follows is my theory of soft-hammer percussion. There is some evidence to support it, but I would stress that no controlled experiment has been done and subjective observations are difficult to confirm, so these ideas are open to argument.

When a hard hammer is used, fracture in a flake begins, or *initiates*, at a relatively small point at or very close to where the hammer contacts the core. This can be seen in the incipient cones where a core has been struck but no flake detached, and in the points of percussion, the small, crushed areas on the platform of flakes that show where the hammer actually struck.

A hammer of antler or wood is much more elastic and compresses slightly on contact with the platform, so the soft hammer actually contacts a larger area on the platform. All else equal, a fracture (especially a cone-like fracture) is more likely to initiate at the smaller point of

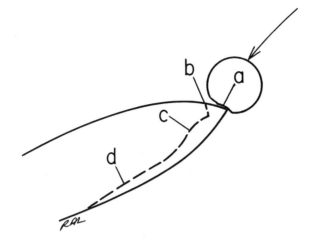

8.10
A schematic view of how a soft hammer removes a flake: (a) soft hammer compresses, contacts large area; (b) fracture initiates as a vertical crack (bending fracture) beyond the actual contact; (c) percussion force produces a bulb; (d) crack continues until flake is detached.

contact. If the contact area is large enough, the fracture will not initiate there at all; rather, the force applied will often exceed the tensile strength of the material at some other point. In other words, the force bends the material until it breaks, and a recognizable bending fracture ensues. These have already been discussed in Chapter 7.

The phenomenon of bending fracture helps us interpret the lipping that is a common feature on the platforms of soft-hammer flakes (Figure 8.10). The soft hammer compresses to contact a relatively large platform area, and the fracture initiates slightly behind the contact area as a small bending fracture. After the fracture initiates, it acts as an ordinary conchoidal fracture, producing a bulb on the flake, and the downward and outward force of the blow continues the crack on into the biface until a flake is detached.

The relationships between bulbs and cones and other flake features and their relationships to features apparently originating as bending fractures are not well understood. Cotterell and Kamminga (1987) argue that the diffuse bulb on soft-hammer flakes is not really a bulb at all, but a feature of bending fractures as they change from the right-angled break at initiation to the flatter fracture surface produced as the rest of the flake is detached. Soft-hammer percussion, however, involves percussion forces as well as bending forces, as is shown by the other features of the flake, and I suspect that the bulb is at least partly a true bulb of percussion.

A series of illustrations drawn from real flakes (shown in cross-section) demonstrates the relationship of lipping to bending fractures. Figure 8.8 shows an ordinary large biface thinning flake, thin and flat, with a small lip and a well-defined bulb of percussion. Figure 8.11 compares a normal biface thinning flake to what I call an *edge-bite flake*.

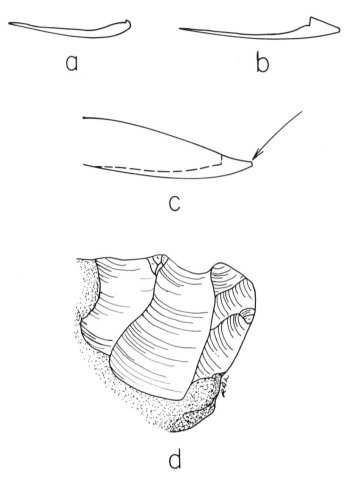

8.11
Edge-bite flake compared with ordinary biface thinning flake: (a) ordinary biface thinning flake, (b) edge-bite flake, (c) biface and edge-bite flake in cross-section, (d) face of biface with edge-bite flake removed.

The edge-bite flake is thin and flat, an ordinary biface thinning flake but with an exaggerated lip. The initiating fracture was not near the point where the hammer struck the platform (the edge of the biface), but even farther in than usual. This is a common mistake in working bifaces, where either the platform on the edge is made too strong to allow a fracture to start there, or the blow falls too far in from the edge. In either case, the fracture initiates well in from the intended platform and removes an ugly bite from the edge of the biface. An archaeological example can be seen on the Solutrean laurel leaf in Figure 3.8. The third step along this continuum is a full bending fracture (Figure 8.12). In this case, the blow intended to remove a thinning flake went wide and struck well in from the platform. The biface bent under this stress until it broke, even farther in from the platform. Note that the right half of the biface is a sort of flake, with a lip larger than the rest of the flake.

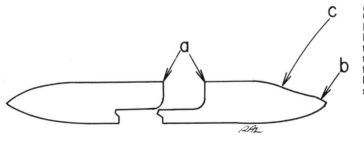

8.12
Bending fracture (a) of a biface, showing relationship to lipping of ordinary biface thinning flake and edge-bite flake. Fracture was caused by a blow aimed at b striking c.

THE BLOW

By now you have noticed that the platforms in biface flaking are different from those worked in ordinary cores. Instead of the blow falling on a platform *surface*, it now falls on the *edge*. As in pressure flaking, biface platforms are usually edges, rather than surfaces, and this is a crucial difference that strongly affects the nature of the resulting flake. It also makes it very hard to relate biface platforms to the discussion of platform angles and striking angles in Chapter 6.

Let us begin with the angle of the blow. Exactly what happens is unclear, as it is difficult to observe a moving hammer with any precision or to measure the angle at which the blow is struck. This is compounded by the fact that the hammer swings in an arc rather than a straight line.

Most knappers would say that the angle of the blow to the platform surface is considerably greater than 90 degrees (Figure 8.9). It is difficult to be precise about this, but I would say the striking angle is about 100 to 110 degrees to the upper surface of the biface, or 130 to 150 degrees to the centerplane of the biface mass. Another way to think of this angle is to consider the direction of the blow to be roughly parallel to the fracture—that is, to the flake that will come off. Other knappers see this differently (e.g., Callahan 1979a; Young and Bonnichsen 1984). If we treat the upper face of the biface as the platform surface, we notice that while the angle of the blow is definitely obtuse, the platform angle is still acute—in fact, much less than 90 degrees on an ordinary biface. However, even this is difficult to measure precisely on the rounded surfaces of the biface edge.

The soft hammer seems to act to change the formation and direction of the crack so that the effect is like a blow struck at almost 90 degrees on an imaginary platform of almost 90 degrees. This produces a long flake, driving the force into the material so that the flake runs along the face. If we treat the biface edge as an ordinary hard-hammer platform and use any kind of hammer to strike a blow at an acute angle to the real platform surface (the surface instead of the edge of the biface),

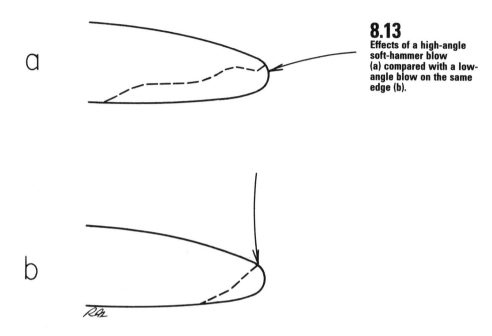

8.13
Effects of a high-angle soft-hammer blow (a) compared with a low-angle blow on the same edge (b).

we will detach a flake that begins at the same point, but it will be much shorter (Figure 8.13).

Whatever is actually happening in soft-hammer percussion on bifaces, the model above is a good one for learning how to do it. Here are the most important things to remember: (1) you will be striking the edge rather than the surface, and (2) you will be striking at an extremely obtuse angle to the platform surface, roughly parallel to the desired flake fracture. This is of course something that you should have trained yourself *not* to do in ordinary percussion flaking, where a blow into an edge will usually just crush it. In soft-hammer percussion the edge will still take the brunt of the blow, and the crack that begins the flake is expected to start a little way in from the edge. This means that the edge has to be strong enough to endure the force of the blow without crushing and pass the force on into the material to detach a flake. This is why many soft-hammer flakes have abraded platforms. Abrading the edge of a biface removes a thin, sharp edge and leaves a rounded, thicker, stronger edge for better platforms. We will return to platform preparation in a moment.

A few more points about the blow. It has to be a lot harder than a blow with a hammerstone on an ordinary platform. In fact, you have to put some muscle force into it, and a bit of a snap of the wrist. The surface area of the flake—that is, the area the fracture has to separate—is relatively large, and the flake is long for its small platform.

The soft hammer compresses and spreads its force out, and the crack begins as a small arc rather than a point, as in hard-hammer percussion. This means that the initial crack requires more force too. Also, you have to make the platform strong so that it will not crush under the blow. You *want* the fracture to initiate in from the actual point of contact—but not too far in (if the platform is too tough, you will get an edge-bite flake, or a fractured biface, or, if you are lucky, nothing at all).

Although you need to hit harder, you still need an easy, natural swing with a follow-through. Adding force makes the blow harder to control, and the proper combination of force and accuracy is physically the hardest part of flintknapping to master.

If you hit a strong platform properly but with too little force, the flake will often terminate in a hinge, or it will not be completely detached. If you hit too hard, your flakes will probably shatter, and you may get a lot of crushed platforms and step-fracture terminations. You are likely to put dangerous stresses upon your biface as well.

You can think of the blow as coming almost straight down on the platform, or parallel to the fracture, but in fact there is an arc to the blow. As in pressure flaking, you can think of the force as two components: a major downward force that drives the crack into the material and a slight pulling force that seems to help detach the flake.

If there is too much downward force or if the angle of blow is too high, too closely paralleling the fracture, the risk of an overshoot flake or a bending fracture of the biface is increased. If there is too much arc to the blow, or if you actually jerk the baton back as it strikes the edge (which some beginners do), the flake is likely to be pulled away from the biface, bending until it snaps and leaving a step on the biface. If you do manage to drop the blow so that it actually falls straight into the piece without any arc at all, you will crush the edge of the platform, usually without getting a good flake. Nor should you drag the end of the hammer across the remnants of the platform as the flake is detached, since this will crush the edge and make future platforms more difficult to prepare.

Smaller hammers are better for smaller pieces than are large hammers. If the head is too large and clumsy, even if you get the flake you want, you may crush areas of platform to either side of the one you need. If the hammer contacts some other area of platform before it hits your target, it will throw off your aim. A light hammer is also better on a small biface because a slow, heavy blow with a large hammer will move the biface too much before the fracture initiates, whereas a lighter blow at a higher velocity will initiate a fracture without jarring the biface out of position.

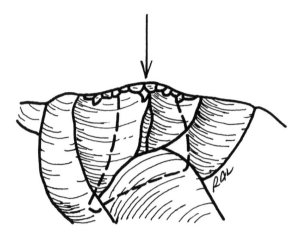

8.14
Flakes tend to follow existing ridges between flake scars. Note platform isolation.

PLATFORMS

As I have already said, biface platforms should be abraded or otherwise prepared to be strong enough to carry the force of the blow and initiate a flake without crushing. The thin, sharp edge that is desirable on the finished biface is not a good platform.

As in all flaking, prepare platforms where the surface morphology of the biface will allow a proper flake. Do not put them over an extreme concavity or a large hump that the flake cannot pass. Try to prepare platforms where there is a ridge for the flake to follow (Figure 8.14).

It is often good to isolate a platform (Pelegrin 1981; see Chapter 6). This makes it easier to see and aim for, and prevents your hammer from striking edges around the target platform, which could deflect your blow. Isolating the platform also makes it a little weaker. The crack initiates at or near the point of contact and has less material to pass through, and since the contact area is smaller, the force is not diffused. This means that you can strike with less force and more accuracy. Isolating the platform a bit helps you prepare a platform that is tough enough to carry the blow and not crush, but one that will crack where you want it to and not edge-bite or fracture the biface. Although you can get away with little or no platform preparation in much casual biface work, proper platform preparation and isolation is especially important in thinning and in doing fine, even percussion work, as on the Solutrean laurel leaf bifaces (Figure 8.15).

The shape of the platform and its position with respect to the two faces of the biface are also important. For thinning bifaces, I think in terms of three types of biface platforms, which I call "normal," "flat," and "steep." (On a smaller scale, these can be applied to pressure flaking as well.) These three types of platforms are also related to different types of blows and are useful in different situations, although it should

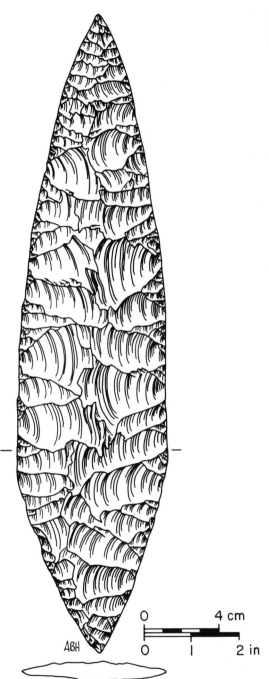

8.15
A fine Solutrean biface, Volgu, France. Note the even size and spacing of large percussion scars. Redrawn with permission from original by Errett Callahan.

0   4 cm

0   1   2 in

ABH

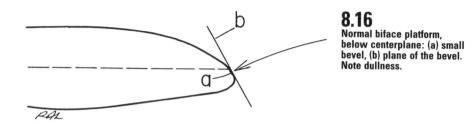

8.16
Normal biface platform, below centerplane: (a) small bevel, (b) plane of the bevel. Note dullness.

be remembered that they all grade into one another. (For a rather different conception of platforms, see Callahan 1979a.)

A *normal* biface platform should be positioned on the edge of a biface, suitably dulled, and struck at a high angle (Figure 8.16). The dulling can be done by rubbing with a hammerstone, either down (trimming), up (facetting), or parallel to the edge, or any combination. Trimming and facetting can also be done with the soft hammer, brushing it lightly across the edge or pressing it against the edge and dragging it up or down. In all of these, the effect is to remove thin, sharp edges, leaving a stronger edge to receive and transmit the force of the blow. If it is abraded with the hammerstone, the edge may even be dulled and rounded. I also find it best to put a slight bevel on the last 2–5 millimeters (1/16 in.) of the edge itself.

The position of the platform is also important (Figure 8.17). The centerplane is where most of the finished edge will be. However, the edge can be below, at, or above the centerplane. With a normal biface platform, I find it easier to remove a good thinning flake if the platform is closer to the face off which the flake will come—that is, below the centerplane (Figure 8.17a). Flakes from a low platform like this will tend to be thin and run close to the surface of the material, usually terminating near any central ridge. This is a good type of platform for refining the edges and faces of a biface.

A more centered platform (Figure 8.17b) can produce a longer, thicker flake that removes more material and is thus a better platform for thinning and flattening a biface. With a more centered platform it is easier to get a flake to run past the center of the face and cut under any central ridge, which produces a flatter cross-section. However, this sort of platform puts more stress on a biface and is more likely to end in a hinge or step, or overshoot and remove part of the opposite edge.

Having said that, it is only fair to note that some other knappers recommend the exact opposite—centered platforms for short flakes and low platforms for long, deep thinning flakes (e.g., Callahan 1979a). I think this is because the flake is affected not just by the platform position, but by the small details of angle of blow, the relative force of downward and inward components of the blow, beveling of the edge, and so forth. All of these interact in complex ways, are very hard to

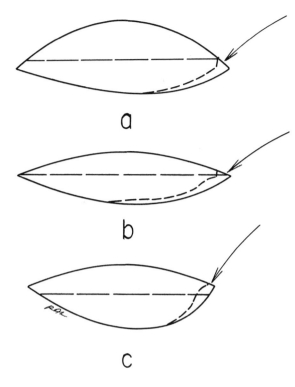

8.17
Normal biface platform positions: (a) below centerplane—easier but shorter flake; (b) close to centerplane—longer flake but greater stress; (c) above centerplane—short flakes, frequent steps, hinges, crushing, bending fractures.

observe accurately, and are both performed and perceived differently by different knappers. You will have to develop your own preferences in the end.

Normal biface platforms that are too high (Figure 8.17c)—that is, above the centerplane of the biface—are usually not satisfactory. The proper high-angle soft-hammer blow, on a high platform, will often crush the edge or produce a short, hinged flake. A less direct, more acute angled blow will remove a flake, but it will be shorter than a flake from a centered or low platform that is struck a direct blow. High platforms also mean greater stress on the biface and are a common cause of fracture.

There are some situations where placing the platform above the centerplane and striking at a more acute angle is useful. This is what I refer to as a *flat* biface platform. Flat platforms are especially useful in the early stages of work on a biface, when the edge has been turned but there are still large lumps or thick areas close to the edge (Figure 8.18).

Notice several things about Figure 8.18, which was drawn from an actual specimen. The platform is well above the centerplane of the biface and the surface from which the flake is being removed, but the flake cuts through a large mass of material. A flat platform like this

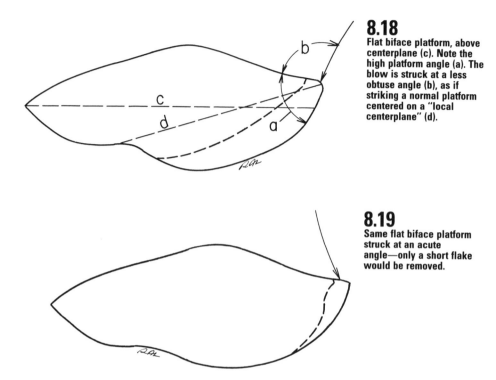

8.18
Flat biface platform, above centerplane (c). Note the high platform angle (a). The blow is struck at a less obtuse angle (b), as if striking a normal platform centered on a "local centerplane" (d).

8.19
Same flat biface platform struck at an acute angle—only a short flake would be removed.

should have a fairly high angle, in this case, close to 90 degrees. It was prepared by both facetting and trimming, and the edge itself was heavily abraded to strengthen it. All this required a terrific wallop with a heavy billet. The blow is not at such a high angle to the edge and centerplane, but is still 90 degrees or a bit more and roughly parallel to the desired fracture. It may be easier to visualize this situation by considering a "local centerplane" for only the right half of the biface. Seen this way, it looks like a normal biface platform on the centerplane, struck at a more obtuse angle, as before. As in a typical biface situation, the soft hammer contacts the strong abraded edge of the platform rather than the platform surface.

The angle of the blow here is crucial. An obtuse angled blow will behave much as described, but a flake can also be detached by an acute angled blow on the same platform (Figure 8.19). It will, however, be much shorter and will fail to remove the desired mass. The flat biface platform is a difficult platform to judge and set up, and it requires a relatively heavy blow, but it is very useful in working thick edges, a common situation.

A third useful platform type is the *steep* biface platform (Figure 8.20). A steep platform is rather like a giant bevel on a normal platform. Usually below the centerplane, the edge is worked to a fairly

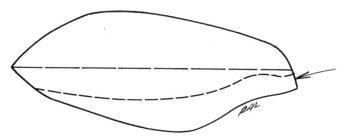

8.20
Steep biface platform. An angle close to 90 degrees is formed at the edge by large bevel. The edge and platform are below centerplane.

steep angle, and the bevel surface also forms an angle of close to 90 degrees with the centerplane. Steep platforms are especially good if a thick flake is needed—for instance, to remove lumps and large masses of material that are not close to the edge. This is most often necessary in the early stages of biface manufacture. While steep platforms are useful in biface work, they do not really conform to the soft-hammer pattern I have described.

In its extreme form, as drawn above, the steep platform behaves as an ordinary hard-hammer platform with a high exterior platform angle. In fact, it can be struck with a hard hammer just as well as a soft hammer. If you use copper, limestone, or other relatively hard soft hammers, you will use steeper platforms and stronger platforms in general. Limestone hammers and steeply beveled platforms were the strategy used by the Maya knappers who made large agricultural and woodworking bifaces in the Late Preclassic at Colha (Shafer 1991:40). Steep platforms also resemble the platforms on Levallois flakes, most of which appear to have been struck with hard hammers. The high exterior platform angle, close to 90 degrees, allows the flake to achieve maximum length, and a large platform gives a thick flake that will cut through considerable mass.

Notice that on steep platforms the blow is no longer falling primarily on the rounded platform edge, but rather contacts the platform surface at an angle of 90 degrees or less, just as in hard-hammer flaking. This kind of platform is prepared primarily by facetting (also a common trait of Levallois flakes) to produce a large, strong platform with a high exterior platform angle. Because the blow falls on the platform surface rather than on the edge, abrading the edge is not really necessary. Having seen this kind of platform, you should have a better idea of how a biface can be thinned by hard hammer alone as well as why it is difficult to distinguish completely between hard hammer and soft and between biface and core flaking.

BIFACE STAGES

Since at least 1890, when Holmes recognized some crude bifaces as early stages in the manufacture of more refined tools, manufacturing

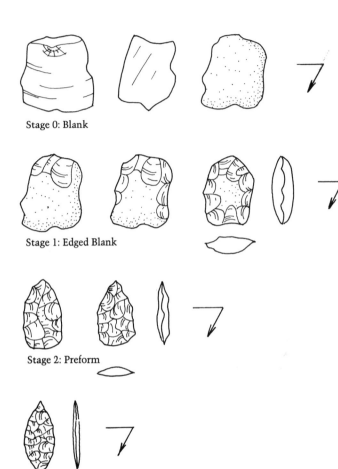

8.21
Idealized biface stages.

Stage 0: Blank

Stage 1: Edged Blank

Stage 2: Preform

Stage 3: Refined Biface

Stage 4: Finished Biface

sequences have been described in terms of stages (e.g., Collins 1975; Callahan 1979a; Whittaker 1984). There has been a good deal of argument about whether stages really exist in the knapper's mind in working a biface or are just figments of archaeological classification (Magne and Pokotylo 1981; Patten, Sollberger, and Patterson 1978; Flenniken, Patterson, and Hayden 1979). The manufacturing process is continuous, with changes produced by the accumulating effects of small removals. There are also points in the continuum at which the tool used, the force applied, the size of the flakes removed, or the goal of the removal changes. Modern knappers do think in terms of stages, and prehistoric knappers may have; we will never really know. Nevertheless, stages in both modern and prehistoric material can be recognized and defined by major changes in technique or apparent goals, and the stage concept is useful both in analyzing archaeological remains and in teaching the art of flintknapping.

The stages I am going to suggest for biface knapping (Figure 8.21) are very close to those used by some other knappers (e.g., Callahan 1979a) and conform to those used for pressure flaking in Chapter 7. I define stages in terms of the finished product that results from the goals and techniques used in each stage. This is an archaeological approach; others prefer to define stages from the knapper's point of view, emphasizing the goals and techniques rather than the results. I will discuss ideal stages first, then provide some examples.

Stage 0: Raw Material and Blank
The first step is to choose a suitable piece of material. Try to make it easy on yourself if possible: if you want a large, flat biface, don't start with a small, round nodule. Bifaces are (and were) often made from flattish nodules or tabular pieces of material. A large flake is also good, and usually has sharp edges that provide an easy beginning point. Remember that in thinning a biface, you will also lose a lot of width, especially at first, so the thicker your starting piece is or the thinner you want it, the larger it should be to begin with.

Stage 1: Edged Blank
The goal of this stage is to produce a blank with bifacial edges to allow further working. Archaeologically this is the earliest stage that can be reliably defined, and even after some working it is still difficult for an archaeologist to know what the knapper intended to make, unless a complete sequence of worked and unfinished pieces is found with examples of the finished product (Whittaker 1984).

In the first stage of bifacing, begin at a spot where a suitable platform exists and turn the edge as described earlier, working both sides alternately to remove unsuitable platforms and leave a sharp, wavy, bifacial edge with suitable platforms all around the blank. A flake with sharp, feathered edges offers lots of easy places to begin bifacing, but you should start by dulling the edge with your hammerstone, since the thin feather edge is not a good platform and gives you an excellent opportunity to cut your holding hand.

Initial bifacing can be done with either a hard or soft hammer. Unless I am trying to replicate a particular technology, I often use both. The hard hammer is good for thick platforms on tough material, and the soft hammer is versatile, good for blows on platform surfaces in turning thick edges and for blows on thinner edges that turn the edge and begin thinning at the same time.

When you are done, the blank will still be fairly thick, with width-thickness ratios around 2.00—that is, twice as wide as thick. The edge should be bifacially worked all around and suitable for further reduction. Because of the thickness, the edges should form relatively steep angles, 50 to 80 degrees or so. An edged blank is similar to some early handaxes.

Stage 2: Preform

In making the preform, the emphasis shifts to primary thinning. This is most easily done with a relatively large billet. Instead of removing short flakes at the edges, you are now attempting to make the flakes run across the faces of the biface, at least to the middle, and to remove the major irregularities of the faces. Get rid of as many problems as you can, concentrating on removing bad hinges and steps, major humps and knots, and cortex or other exterior surfaces.

When you are done, you should have a biface with a smoothly biconvex or lenticular cross-section and fairly straight and centered edges with angles between about 40 and 60 degrees. It will still be relatively thick, with a width-thickness ratio of about 3.00 to 4.00—that is, three to four times as wide as it is thick. Most important, it should have regular faces without major flaws, or further thinning and refinement will be difficult.

Good Acheulean handaxes look like this. In later cultures first- and second-stage bifaces are sometimes called quarry blanks and are in fact often found in quarry contexts (e.g., Holmes 1890, 1919; Singer and Ericson 1977), used as an economical form for the transport or trade of material. By this point in reduction, flawed pieces have been discarded and much of the least useful mass of the original material has been removed. What is left is a compact and versatile form that is a useful tool just as it stands, and can easily be refined to produce both useful flakes and a large, finished biface of many different forms.

Stage 3: Refined Biface

Once the piece is fairly regular and looks as if it may be worth refining, concentrate on removing large, flat flakes that run past the middle of the face, and thin the biface faster than it loses width. It is also important that you avoid major errors and keep the faces regular. You are still removing large flakes, which means stressing the biface, which is getting thinner and more fragile. All this means that you must pay careful attention to platforms and surface contours. As the biface gets smaller, you may want to shift to smaller hammers too, and be careful to give the biface adequate support. At the same time as you are concentrating on thinning, do not forget to work toward the outline shape you want.

At the end of this stage you should have a biface with a flattened cross-section, a width-thickness ratio of 4.00 or above, and thin edges with angles around 25 to 45 degrees.

Stage 4: Finished Biface

Finishing a refined biface can be simple or complicated. You may refine the form only a little by trimming off jagged edges and old platform remnants. Or you may want to modify the base for hafting with notches, or serrate the edge. Folsom and Clovis points at this stage underwent several more episodes of preparation and fluting, which could also be considered separate stages (Patten 1980; Callahan 1979a; Flenniken 1978; see Chapter 9).

A variety of techniques can be used in finishing. Either careful percussion with the soft hammer or pressure flaking are common. Figure 8.22 shows four soft-hammer bifaces with different styles of flaking and different finishes. The first (Figure 8.22a) is a triangular biface from Grasshopper Pueblo, worked entirely by percussion. The major goal of the knapper seems to have been a thin piece of regular shape. In Figure 8.22b we see a more or less contemporary biface from a nearby site in Arizona (Whittaker, Ferg, and Speth 1988). It is made of a banded Wyoming chert. The percussion scars are very regular, and by running them past the midpoint of each face, the knapper achieved a thin, flat cross-section. The edge was carefully finished by pressure flaking. Figure 8.22c shows a replica of an Early Archaic point by modern knapper George Eklund. The percussion work thinned the piece, which was then shaped and finished by extensive pressure flaking. The large scars on the left are from the percussion work; the smaller scars on the right edge are from beveling the edge by pressure. Sometimes pressure retouch removes the evidence of percussion thinning, as in Figure 8.22d, a piece made by Bob Hunt. Such a large biface is unlikely to have been made by pressure alone, and in this case a few remnants of large, flat

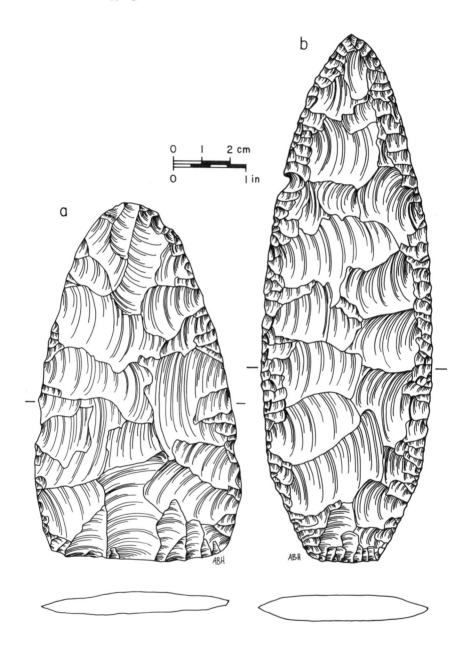

0   1   2 cm

0   1 in

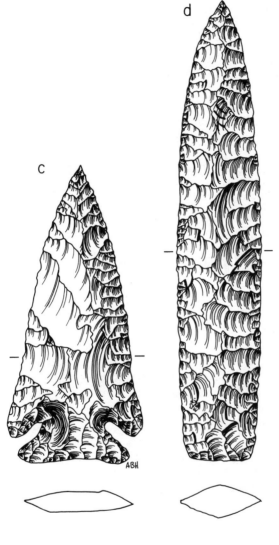

8.22
Four different soft-hammer bifaces: (a) Grasshopper Pueblo, Arizona, 1300s, Redwall Chert; (b) Q-Ranch Site, Arizona, 1300s, Wyoming Tiger Chert; (c) George Eklund, 1990, chert; (d) Bob Hunt, 1990, Burlington Chert.

percussion scars remain, although careful and unusually large pressure retouch on a narrow piece has removed most of them. Both of the modern pieces were flaked with copper tools.

KNAPPING STRATEGY AND OTHER CONSIDERATIONS

By outlining the sequence of stages above, I am not implying that you should necessarily work in discrete, inflexible stages. One important rule is not to throw away opportunities. For instance, if while turning the edge you find yourself in position to remove a long thinning flake, you may want to do so.

Thinking in stages may help you work more efficiently, but this is a matter of personal preference. One of the most instructive demonstrations I ever watched was a Hopi carver making a wooden kachina doll. Every cut he made required the minimum effort and efficiently prepared the way for the next cut. This is how you should think of your knapping. Each flake, or each goal, such as removal of a lump, needs to be prepared for. Sometimes this is simple platform preparation, sometimes it requires thinking several or even many flakes ahead. Each flake that is removed has consequences for later flakes, making them easy or causing problems that have to be overcome. At each stroke you must be thinking of the whole biface. This kind of awareness is very difficult to come by, and I am frequently dissatisfied with my own. I also remember that in my earliest flaking I had trouble even remembering which face I wanted to work next and why, and would get confused because everything looked the same. Your ability to plan ahead will develop with experience.

To thin a biface, you must sacrifice some width, because each blow removes part of the edge. To remove a flaw will also cost you width as you prepare platforms. The thinner a biface becomes, the more fragile it gets, and some platforms or attempts to remove particular flakes may put dangerous stresses on a biface. You are always faced with decisions: accept an imperfect biface or take a risk to improve it. Especially at first, taking risks is the only way to learn what works and what does not, the only way to understand and improve your capabilities.

In my knapping strategy (see the example to follow), I usually like to work on one face of a biface at a time. I adjust a whole edge by trimming and facetting, until it is fairly straight and at the right level in relation to the centerplane. Then I take a series of flakes off the one face before setting up the edge for a new series, usually on the other face. If I am being careful, I also adjust the platform for each flake individually and try to work in sequence from one end of the biface to the other. Ideally, the edge of each flake scar in a series provides a ridge for the next flake to follow. Platforms can also be isolated and improved by removing a little of the edge to each side with a pressure flaker, especially when the edge has the thin overhang left at the bulb of the previous flake scar. A similar procedure has been discussed and illustrated in the section on patterned pressure flaking in Chapter 7. If you prepare platforms properly and flake carefully, you can produce a very regular biface with evenly spaced flakes like the Solutrean biface in Figure 8.15. It isn't always possible to work so systematically. It depends on the problems you encounter and the problems you make for yourself.

EXAMPLE: A BASIC BIFACE

I chose to work with a flat slab of chert from the Glen Canyon area (Figure 8.23). Natural fracture planes produced a tabular piece of stone that was a good size and shape, and I heat-treated the whole slab successfully. The disadvantages of natural slabs like this are the right-angle edges and the tendency to have fracture planes and flaws concealed in them. As it happened, this one broke almost immediately when I started working it, as shown by heavy dotted lines in the figure. Crystal pockets are also visible, but caused less trouble.

I began by turning the edge with a small hammerstone, and two large pieces broke off at flaw lines. This considerably reduced the size of the biface I could make, but I comforted myself with the thought that this was not my fault. Figure 8.24 shows Face I of the Stage 1 blank after about ten minutes of work with both the hammerstone and the medium antler hammer shown in Figure 8.3. It is not completely bifaced yet, and the edge is very uneven. Figure 8.25 shows the biface after another series of flakes was removed around the whole edge on Face I. This represents another ten minutes of work using the antler hammer, which will be the only hammer used from now on. The edge is completely bifaced and some thinning begun; this specimen is at the end of Stage 1. As most of the flakes were struck off the face shown, the edge is below the centerplane and I have beveled it (note small flakes along the edge) to set up the next series of thinning flakes. Most of these will be detached from Face II.

Face II is shown in Figure 8.26 after another twenty minutes of work, removing two series of flakes from this face and leaving the edge beveled and ready to remove the next series from Face I. I would call this a preform, and the goal of most flakes is thinning, removing as much thickness and as many problems as possible with each blow.

Figure 8.27 follows another ten minutes of knapping and shows Face I again, after a single series of large thinning flakes has removed the last traces of the old natural fracture surface. These flakes also made the cross-section more even and left Face I quite flat, although Face II is still somewhat convex. Note the position of the edges. They are still close to the face, above the centerplane.

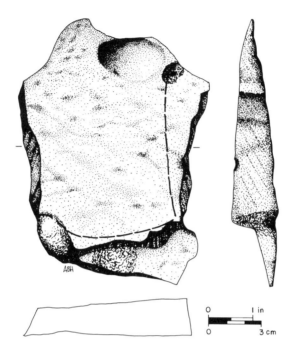

8.23
Stage 0, blank, Face I. Heat-treated natural slab of chert from Glen Canyon, Arizona. Dashed lines indicate subsequent fractures.

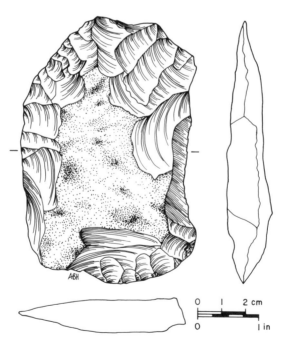

8.24
Stage 1, edged blank. Face I after ten or fifteen minutes of work. Some material was lost by breakage before the piece was partially bifaced, using both hammerstone and antler hammer.

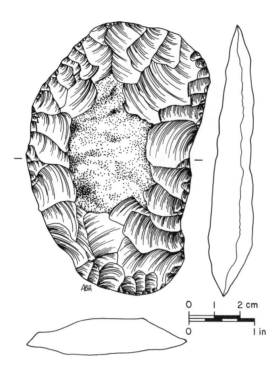

8.25
Stage 1, edged blank, final. Face I after another ten or fifteen minutes of work, using only an antler hammer. The piece is completely bifaced, and thinning has begun.

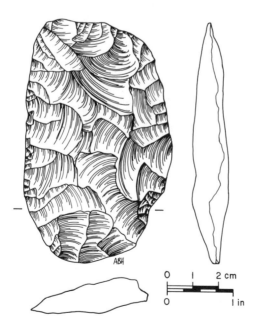

8.26
Stage 2, preform. Primary thinning is in progress on Face II. Two series of flakes have been removed in about twenty more minutes of work.

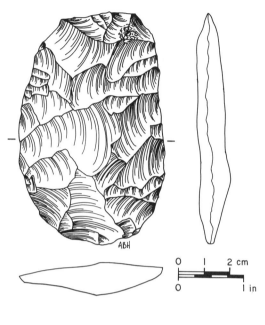

8.27
Stages 2 and 3, preform/
refined biface. Face I has
been further thinned by a
single series of large flakes,
after another ten minutes of
work.

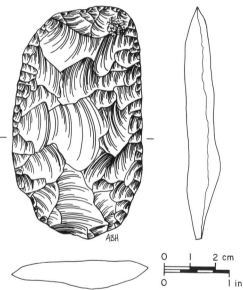

8.28
Stages 2 and 3. Face I is
unchanged from Figure 8.27
except by preparation of the
edge for removal of flakes
from the opposite face.

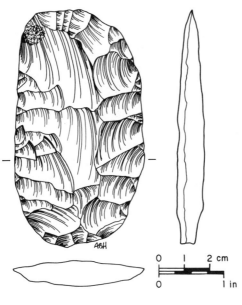

8.29
Stage 3, refined biface. Face II after removal of a series of large, careful flakes—another ten to fifteen minutes of work.

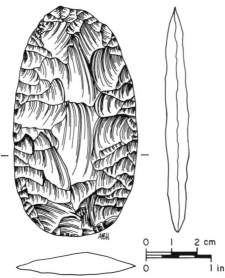

8.30
Stage 4, finished biface. Face II after another ten or fifteen minutes. One to two series of smaller flakes were removed from both faces to regularize the shape and to straighten and center the edge.

In Figure 8.28 the edge has been prepared on Face I for the next series of flakes off the other face. The only change from the previous figure is the removal of many small, short flakes, which lower the edge below the centerplane, closer to Face II, from which the next thinning flakes will be struck.

After ten more minutes a single series of regular flakes has been carefully removed (Figure 8.29), leaving a Stage 3 refined biface that is thinned and regular and can now be finished into a variety of forms.

I chose to finish the biface very simply by removing a couple of additional series of small flakes from all edges and both faces. This made the shape symmetrical, straightened and centered the edges, and removed all platform remnants (Figure 8.30). I now have a finished biface, suitable for use or for further finishing, perhaps by pressure flaking to make a large point.

BIFACE PROBLEMS: PREHISTORIC MISTAKES

Knappers are proud of fine bifaces because they are difficult to make. A small flaw in the material or a moment of carelessness and the biface is marred or shattered. A look at a few archaeological examples will illustrate some of the common errors. They should also encourage you—the ancient experts made mistakes too. We can only speculate about what they said when a biface broke after an hour's work, but we can often be pretty sure what went wrong if we examine the fragments.

Again I will use examples from Grasshopper Pueblo to illustrate both the stages of manufacture discussed above and the kind of problems you are likely to run into in making large bifaces. Other good archaeological discussions can be found (e.g., Shafer 1985), and Callahan (1979a) has published excellent illustrations and descriptions of similar material from his own replicative experiments.

Room 246 at Grasshopper was a large room in the heart of the pueblo, surrounded by other rooms. On the ground floor was a heap of knapping debris and other rubbish. Room 246 was probably a communal room used by one clan for ceremonial storage and male craft activities, including knapping. There were arrow points that appeared to have been made by a number of different knappers and more than seventy fragments of large bifaces with debitage from their manufacture, plus a variety of other stone tools and related artifacts. Large bifaces are relatively rare in the Southwest, and while a few others were found at Grasshopper, only Room 246 out of more than one hundred rooms excavated contained extensive evidence of biface manufacture. The bifaces are made of the local high-quality Redwall Chert, and their concentration and similarities suggest a single knapper, although there is no way to be sure of this.

The two most common reasons for biface discard, both prehistorically and among modern knappers, are fracture, most often a bending fracture, and failure to thin, often related to step or hinge terminations of some flakes. Figure 8.31 shows a Stage 1 biface. This specimen illustrates how hard it is to apply stage concepts. Although I class it as an edged blank, not all the edge has been bifaced yet, and thinning has already started. There is a large hinge on one face, but at this point it would not be hard to remove. The angled break across one end might be the reason for discard, as it leaves the piece rather small for what the knapper was probably trying to achieve. Other pieces show that the goal was a large, thin lanceolate or crescentic knife form, 15–30 centimeters (6–12 in.) long.

The second example (Figure 8.32) is half of a good Stage 2 biface. Thinning was well advanced when it suffered a bending fracture. There are remnants of abraded platforms at several points along the edge. The large flutelike flake was struck from the fracture surface, perhaps as the first blow of an attempt to thin the piece for a smaller biface.

As mentioned earlier, bending fractures result from flexing the biface by pressure or a blow. Although a biface like the one in the figure is thick and relatively strong, the longer it is, the more likely it is to flex and break if not properly supported. Also, at this stage, the knapper is attempting to thin the biface by removing large flakes, and is thus setting up strong platforms and striking heavy blows. Blows at the ends of a long biface are especially likely to flex or vibrate the biface and snap it.

The three fragments in Figure 8.33 probably all resulted from a single blow on this Stage 3 biface. The knapper in Room 246 liked to set up very strong platforms. They are often isolated and heavily ground. This helped produce large flakes but is also one reason why there are many bending fractures and edge bites. In this case the platform was strong and the blow was probably a bit too high. The curved fracture across the bottom of the biface is a perverse fracture beginning at a small but distinct cone and running down through the biface. In effect, the poorly aimed blow burinated the biface, and the stresses of a hard blow on a tough platform also flexed the biface, producing a second fracture at the upper end as well as probably aiding the perverse fracture.

In the last example (Figure 8.34) the knapper was plainly being frustrated by a stack or plateau of step fractures near the center of the piece on the face shown. Note that the thick spot rises well above the desired centerplane of the biface, but the original platforms were probably at or near the centerplane when they needed to be closer to the level of the lump to be removed. As a result, the first flakes ran into the mass

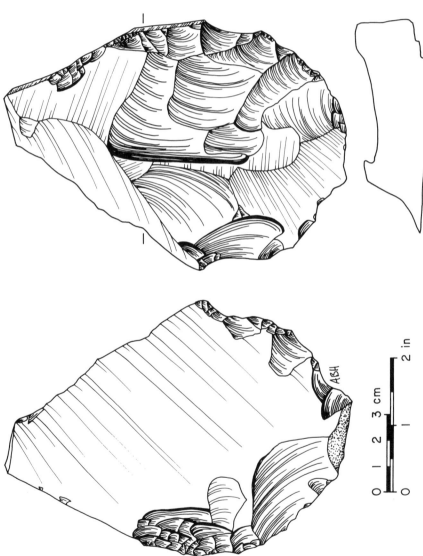

8.31 Stage 1 biface from Grasshopper Pueblo, Room 246. Arizona State Museum specimen.

ABH

0   1   2   3 cm

0   1   2 in

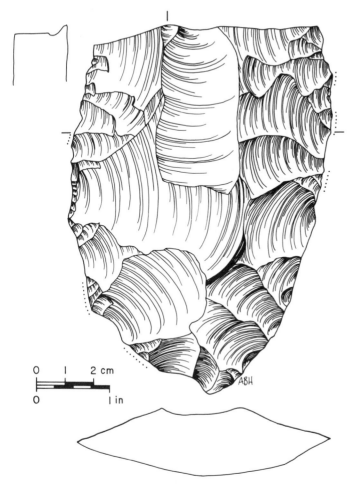

8.32
Stage 2 biface from Room
246, with bending fracture.
Dots indicate ground
platforms on the edge.
Arizona State Museum
specimen.

0   l   2 cm

0   l in

of the lump and could not remove it, so they broke off, leaving a step plateau. Having failed to thin the biface from one edge, the knapper did the right thing by attacking the lump from the other edge. A deep-enough flake could have passed under the plateau and removed it, coming out at the base of the steps on the other side. However, to get at the plateau he should have removed flakes from the other face, reducing the width of the biface and bringing the edge past the centerplane and closer to the level of the plateau. He probably did not want to lose so much width and took a risk instead, setting up extra-strong ground platforms in the hope that they would let him remove a large-enough flake. In vain—after a couple more step terminations, he missed or struck a platform that was too strong, and the biface flexed and broke. Note that the center was pulled down and the ends bent upward—the lips on both bending fractures are on the opposite face of the central

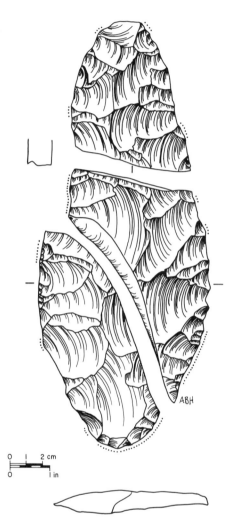

8.33
Stage 3 biface from Room 246, broken in three pieces by bending and perverse fractures. Dots indicate ground platforms on the edge. Arizona State Museum specimen.

piece, the face that would have been up, where the material was compressed by bending. This could have happened if the biface was not properly supported, resting loosely on the soft flesh of a leg, or held in the hand with the ends jutting out.

That was a long story to tell from a single stone tool, but although some of it is guesswork, it is all very likely. With these examples and what has been said earlier, you should be able to recognize some of the errors you will make and figure out how to avoid them.

SUMMARY

The most important principles of soft-hammer knapping can be summarized as follows:

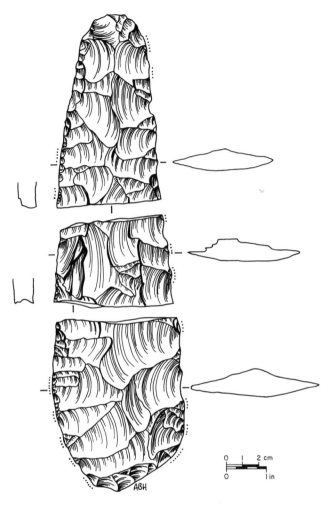

8.34
Stage 4 biface from Room 246, broken by bending fractures during attempts to remove a step plateau. Dots indicate ground platforms on the edge. Arizona State Museum specimen.

1. Platforms are generally on the edge of the piece.
2. The edge that is the platform should make an angle of less than 90 degrees.
3. The blow is an arc, with most of the force directed into the edge to detach a long flake, but with a little of the force working downward to begin the flake detachment.
4. Platform preparation is extremely important. Good platforms should usually be below the centerplane, ground strong enough to transmit force, and isolated.
5. The biface should be supported or it will break.

9

BLADES AND FLUTING

My experiments in flintknapping have led
me to conclude that the making of this point
[Folsom] probably took more time, patience,
and skill than any other projectile point
of comparable size.

—Don Crabtree (1966:3)

Even Don Crabtree considered fluted points a challenge, and when I finally completed my first acceptable fluted point after many unsuccessful tries, I felt I had achieved a diploma of sorts. Crabtree was not the only American knapper who felt that fluted points represent the pinnacle of knapping skill. If you can produce a good Clovis or especially a Folsom point (see Figures 3.14, 3.15), you have not only mastered the making of fine bifaces by percussion and pressure, but also developed the ability to flute them, which involves careful preparation and detachment of large, specialized flakes.

As we have seen, blades are long, straight flakes with roughly parallel edges, useful for a variety of tools and common in many Old World industries. They were also important in Mesoamerican prehistory (e.g., Clark 1987; Gaxiola and Clark 1989; Hester 1978), and although blade industries were less common in North America, there were a number of distinctive traditions (e.g., Arnold 1985, 1987; Green 1963; Hofman 1987; Morrow 1987). American knappers are usually not much interested in blades, probably because they do not excite the imagination the way a projectile point does. They are deceptively simple in form, and, besides, many knappers have a somewhat parochial affection for the lithic tools of their own region. However, blades make excellent tools for woodworking and cutting up game, and can be retouched to make a variety of other tools, including projectile points (Figure 9.1; see also Figures 3.6, 3.7, 3.9, 3.13, 3.22). Because blades and fluting involve the same principles, they will be considered together here.

BLADES

Blades and fluting flakes are both long, straight flakes. We have already seen that flakes tend to follow ridges on the surface of cores; the es-

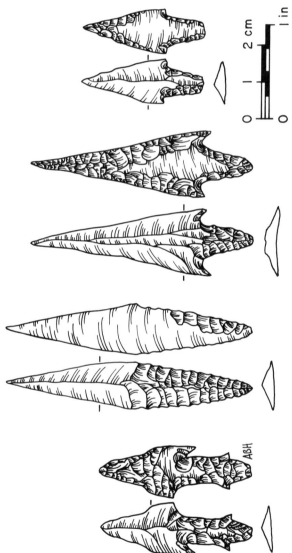

9.1
Arrow points made on blades, Pre-Pottery Neolithic of the Middle East (after Perrot 1968). Steep retouch on the exterior face forms the base; flat retouch on the interior face shapes the tip and reduces the curvature of the blade.

2 cm

1 in

sence of blade making is the development of a ridge system for the blades to follow. Once the first blade is successfully detached, the edges of its flake scar form ridges that other blades can follow, and if the core and the knapper are good, it is possible to work around and around a core, removing blades like paring an apple (see Figure 3.19). This is a very efficient use of material—more edge per pound can be made by blades than by any other means (Sheets and Muto 1972).

Setting up the first ridge can be the main problem in making blades. There are several solutions. Some kinds of material lend themselves to making blades. The edges and corners of tabular material often provide good ridges for starting a blade core (Figure 9.2). If a rounded nodule can be halved, the broken face of one half makes an excellent platform, and it is not too difficult to strike a long, thin flake off some surface to make the first blade, as in the first example below (Figure 9.7). Sometimes a bifacial edge can be flaked and then used as a ridge that the first blade will follow, as in the second example (Figure 9.13). This is referred to as a *lame à crête*, or crested blade (Bordes and Crabtree 1969), and is in effect burinating a thick biface. You can even make a thick biface and break it in half, using the fracture surface as a platform for a crested blade that removes the biface edge (Biagi and Cremaschi 1991).

There are a number of common ways of striking blades. Direct percussion by hard or soft hammer is of course one. The English gunflint knappers used a metal hammer and got very good results. A good deal of precision is needed in making blades, and direct percussion is not necessarily the best way to be very accurate. Indirect percussion or some form of pressure flaking is more often used by modern knappers, and is described in the ethnographic literature.

Indirect percussion involves striking a punch set on the platform. This allows very precise placement of the force and control of the angle of force as well. The punch can be antler, but because antler is soft, it wears rapidly and makes detachment difficult if strong platforms are used. Most modern knappers use copper-tipped punches.

Blades can also be made by pressure flaking. Blades are much larger than ordinary pressure flakes and require some kind of specialized pressure tool such as a chest crutch (Figure 9.3, see also Figure 3.26). The chest crutch, tipped with antler or copper, allows body weight to be applied in a controlled way to a core held in some sort of vice, and very long, fine blades can be made. Don Crabtree made the chest crutch popular in his experiments replicating Mesoamerican obsidian blades (Crabtree 1968) and Folsom fluted points (Crabtree 1966), although others had experimented with them earlier, including Ellis (1939), with whom Crabtree had worked.

In making Mesoamerican blades, Crabtree was attempting to repli-

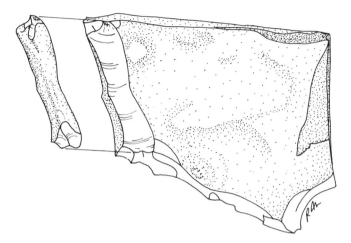

9.2
Beginning a blade core on
the corner and edge of a
tabular piece of chert.

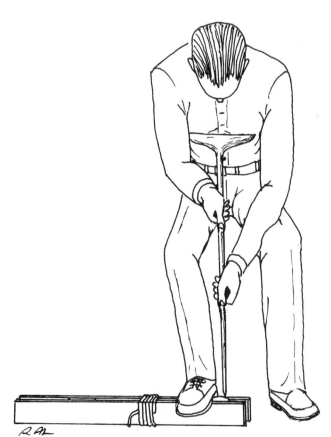

9.3
Using a chest crutch to
make microblades.

cate an old Spanish account, and his work shows the difficulty of using old accounts of stone tool manufacture written by nonknappers. Crabtree came up with a plausible and successful method of blade making that conformed to his reading of the Spanish account. More recently, others have disagreed on how the Spanish should be interpreted (Fletcher 1970), and John Clark (1982, 1984, 1985) has developed a completely different pressure device that he feels better fits the archaeological evidence and historical accounts. Clark's method involves a sort of hooked tool that is used while sitting with the core held between the feet. Without going into details, I bring this up only to point out that old accounts have more than one possible interpretation and that different methods can produce similar results. To decide which technique was actually used at a particular Mesoamerican site is very difficult and requires evaluation of the historical accounts, replicative experiments, and careful examination of the archaeological material in comparison with the replicated tools and the debris from making them. Even then, there is lots of room for argument.

Various mechanical lever devices can be used to apply pressure. A number of modern knappers use these with good results, and one form will be described in the section on fluting. They were almost certainly not available to prehistoric knappers.

PLATFORMS

As in everything else, platform preparation is crucial. Many blades are made with very steep platform angles. Remember the mechanical flaking experiment which showed that, all else being equal, the closer the platform angle is to 90 degrees, the longer the flake. High platform angles also mean that more force is needed to detach a flake as well as more precision in the application of the force. This is why direct percussion is often not the best way to make blades. The blades in Figure 9.4 are from a small Bronze Age site called Tell el Hayyat in Jordan (Falconer and Magness-Gardiner 1989). Although some bronze tools were becoming available, they are rarely found, but flint blades are one of the most common artifacts. Many of them were used in sickles (see also Figures 3.12, 3.13, 11.14). The specimens shown represent different stages in the reduction of a blade core and different platform preparation techniques. The first (Figure 9.4a) is rather uneven and probably resulted from the early stages of a blade core, before the beautifully parallel ridge system was well established. The exterior platform angle is close to 90 degrees, and the edge of the platform has been trimmed to reduce the overhang above the negative bulb left by the previous blade. A next stage is represented by Figure 9.4c and is much straighter, with a platform angle around 70 degrees and relatively little trimming.

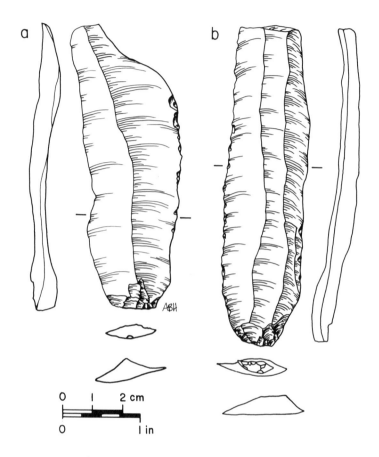

Figure 9.4b is very straight, and its platform has been trimmed and facetted to obtain a high angle (ca. 90 degrees). This is the ideal form produced by this industry. Compare the platform of this blade to the Levallois platforms we have discussed earlier (Figure 6.41). The relatively large bulbs of percussion and distinct points of percussion suggest that direct percussion or a pointed punch was used in making the three Bronze Age blades. The fourth blade (Figure 9.4d) is an earlier one, probably Neolithic. It is less regular and has been patinated and dulled by river action.

As the examples show, platform angle can be controlled by trimming and facetting, just as in ordinary hard-hammer flaking, but good platforms are even more important in blade making. Many knappers also grind the platform surface in blade making. This increases the friction and helps keep a punch or pressure tool from slipping off as force is applied. Some suggest that the scratches also weaken the surface and make it easier to begin the crack that detaches the blade, just as a scratched line guides a break in modern glass cutting.

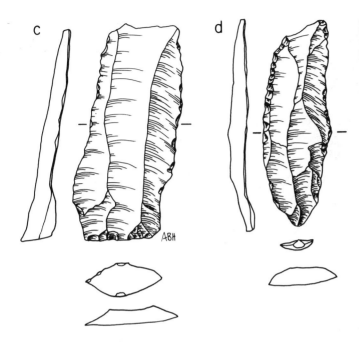

9.4
Blades from Tell el Hayyat, Jordan: (a, b, c) Bronze Age, (d) Neolithic. The platform of each is shown between the exterior surface view and the cross-section.

HOLDING

Because great force must be used to detach a large flake, it is important to immobilize a blade core. If it rotates, you will get curved blades and a tendency to overshoot the end of the core. If you are using a punch or pressure device that requires both hands, you will need to hold the core with something else. A friend makes a great vice. Another knapper is best since they not only hold as ordered, but point out problems ("Your punch slipped when you straightened it up"). It is sometimes hard to see what you are doing at the far end of a long tool, and if precision is necessary, the little shifts and twitches of your body as you get set and strike a blow can spoil your aim. François Bordes and some other knappers have favored holding the core between their feet (see Figure 3.27), and Jacques Tixier used a *sous le pied* method, pinning a core down under one foot and striking blades off sideways like a croquet player "sending" an opponent. Most of us modern folk have rather weak and soft-skinned feet, and I do not recommend a barefoot grip, but sturdy rubber soles are ideal for holding a core firmly.

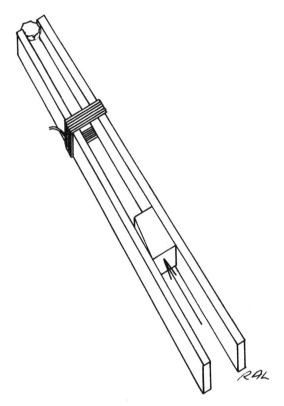

9.5
A primitive vice. Pushing the wedge in toward the binding tightens the jaws holding the core.

You can also use some kind of vice. Unpadded metal will crush the sides of a core, but a properly protected modern vice will work. You can make a more primitive vice with a couple of boards or branches and some cord (Crabtree 1968). Tie the two pieces of wood loosely together to form a pincer that will hold the core. Forcing a wedge between the poles at the other end will close the pincer end tightly on the core (Figure 9.5). You may find it hard to tighten such a vice enough, and the core must still be pinned firmly against the ground with pressure on the top and bottom to keep it from rotating.

PUNCHES

Two punches for making blades or fluting Paleo-Indian points are shown in Figure 9.6. Whether you use antler or copper, you need to keep the tip sharp. The smaller the area in contact with the platform, the easier it is to start a flake. The problem is that the sharper the tool tip, the greater the stress on it and the more likely it is to crush. Antler

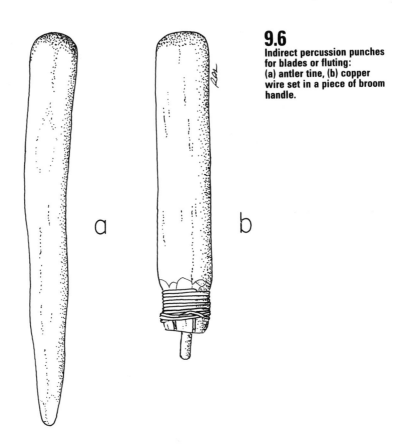

9.6
Indirect percussion punches
for blades or fluting:
(a) antler tine, (b) copper
wire set in a piece of broom
handle.

is especially difficult to maintain and use, and most modern knappers use copper tips for making blades. It is also important that the rest of the tool not strike or crush the edge of the platform after the tip detaches the blade, so the whole tool must be rather narrow to give clearance.

THE BLOW

A large flake requires more force. However, blades are long and thin and thus rather weak. As described earlier, the application of force, either by percussion or pressure, results in a crack going down into the material and the flake or blade being pulled away from the core. The longer the blade is, the more danger there is of pulling it away from the core too much, flexing it and snapping it. If it snaps before coming off, you are left with a step on the core that is very difficult to remove and may spoil the core for further blades. This can also happen if the blade is not struck with enough force. Excessive force can shatter the blade

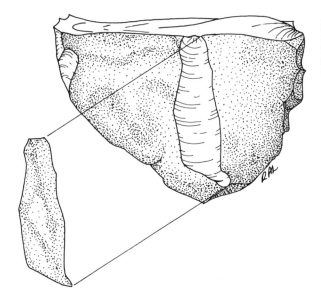

9.7
**Percussion blades: the core
is begun on a split nodule by
striking a blade that follows
a natural ridge.**

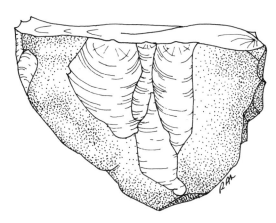

9.8
**Percussion blades: three
more direct percussion
blades were struck off the
core, leaving a prominent
ridge in the center.**

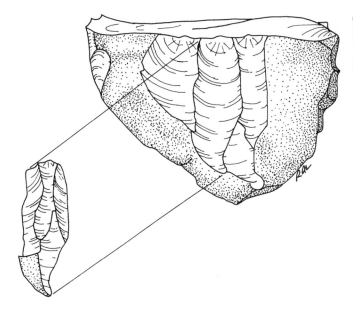

9.9
Percussion blades: the first indirect percussion blade removed from the core follows the ridge left by previous removals.

and get the same result, and increases the risk of overshooting. To avoid ill temper, it is necessary to judge the force of the blow very carefully, and this comes only with practice.

I have avoided discussing every detail of blade making here because most of it has already been said earlier. Most of blade making is just a more careful application of what you learned in basic hard-hammer percussion. The addition of special tools like punches and chest pressors makes it a little more mechanically complex, but the principles are the same. There are quite a number of variations used by different knappers that you can find if you look (e.g., Arnold 1985; Bordes and Crabtree 1969; Crabtree and Swanson 1968; Kelterborn 1981; Newcomer 1975; Sollberger and Patterson 1976b). A couple of examples will give you more ideas, and the best way to learn is to try it.

Example 1: Indirect Percussion Blades

Starting with half of a round obsidian nodule, I used the flat fracture surface as a platform (Figure 9.7). The first blade was struck by percussion, using a large, soft hammerstone. I struck an oblique, almost glancing blow with the edge of the hammerstone, tearing the blade away from the core rather than striking it off with a more direct blow to the platform surface. Crabtree and Swanson (1968) call this the *edge-ground cobble technique*, as it produces characteristic wear on the striking edge of the hammerstone. I struck three more flakes using the hammerstone (Figure 9.8). The two larger were on either side of the

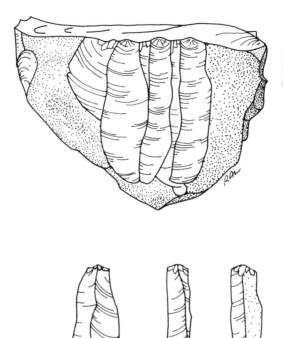

9.10
Percussion blades: three indirect percussion blades have been removed, becoming straighter and more regular.

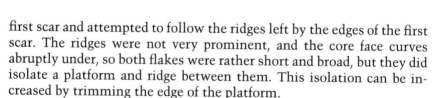

first scar and attempted to follow the ridges left by the edges of the first scar. The ridges were not very prominent, and the core face curves abruptly under, so both flakes were rather short and broad, but they did isolate a platform and ridge between them. This isolation can be increased by trimming the edge of the platform.

The percussion blades were struck holding the core on my left thigh with the blade falling onto a piece of leather between my legs. A hammer blow is relatively fast, and the core is not likely to be moved by it. A soft punch, however, is more likely to allow the core to shift at the blow, and indirect percussion requires a hand to hold the punch and one to strike the blow, so I sit on the ground and hold the core between my feet, as in Figure 9.18 or Figure 3.27. It is difficult to hold the core completely still, which is why the next blade, struck with an antler punch, is more curved (Figure 9.9). Note that it follows a straight path

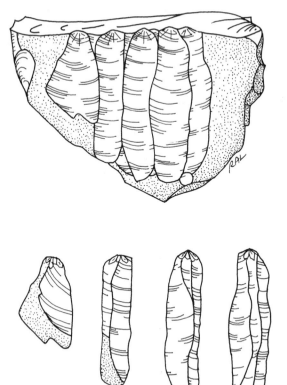

9.11
Percussion blades: the final
set of blades and their core.

on the face of the core because of the ridge formed by the previous removals. The platform for this blade was isolated by trimming and then ground. It is also important that the bottom and face of the core where the blade is to come off should not be touching anything. If the core rests on the ground where the blade ends, the tendency to overshoot is increased. As in the case of the percussion blades above, the angle of force was quite low, with the punch held to an angle of about 45 degrees to the platform surface.

As additional blades are removed, the core becomes more angular—that is, the ridge systems formed by flake scars become more prominent. Platform angles get higher, and the blades become increasingly straighter and more regular (Figure 9.10, 9.11). The last flake removed was short and broad, and merely helped maintain the ridge system for any later series of blades.

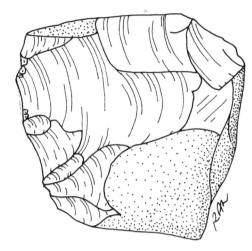

9.12
Pressure microblades: a
thick flake is prepared with
a bifacial edge to the left.

Example 2: Pressure Microblades

I began this core with a large, angular obsidian flake, on which I flaked a bifacial edge (Figure 9.12). I burinated the edge, as shown in Figure 9.13. This first "crested blade" left a face with ridges for the next blades to follow.

Platform preparation was a bit tricky on this piece. The platform was narrow, and slanted so that the platform angles were usually too low on one side of the biface and too steep on the other. This sort of problem is solved by facetting the platform. Even if the platform angle is slightly above 90 degrees, you can usually pressure-flake a small, short flake off it. The bulb of this flake leaves a depression in which you can seat the tip of the pressure tool (Figure 9.13), in this case a version of Crabtree's chest crutch. The platform should also be ground. I grind such a small platform by rubbing it with the edge of a chert flake, which scratches the softer obsidian easily.

The next problem is in holding the core steady while considerable force is applied. I used the vice shown in Figures 9.5 and 9.3. A friend stood on the end of the vice, and I kept one foot on top of the back end of the core to keep it from rotating when I applied pressure to the platform at the front end. I pressed with the chest crutch at an angle slightly less than 90 degrees to the platform, applying the force as rapidly as possible with a sort of lunge. Some knappers who are more skillful at this than I am recommend a steady buildup of pressure without lunging, but I have trouble getting a blade to start without some rapid change in the force, much the way a slight downward motion in pressure flaking helps initiate a flake. Figures 9.14 and 9.15 show two results from this core.

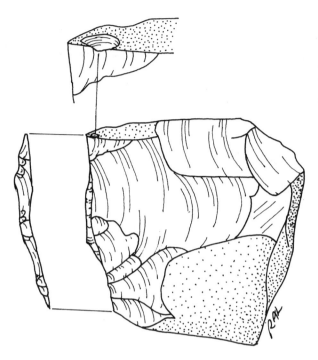

9.13
Pressure microblades: the bifacial edge is burinated to produce a "crested blade." The platform is prepared for the next blade by removing a small flake to provide a seat for the pressure tool.

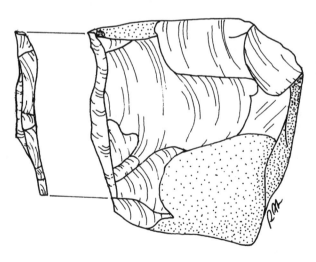

9.14
Pressure microblades: a first microblade is pressed off and the platform prepared again.

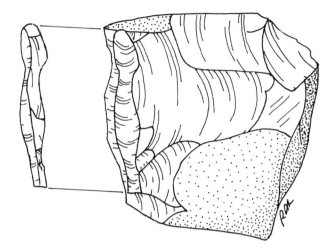

9.15
Pressure microblades: a second microblade is removed.

FLUTING

Clovis and Folsom fluted points were used in much of North America from about 11,500 to 10,500 years ago. Probably more has been written about fluting than about any other single technique in flintknapping, despite the fact that it was an unusual technique used for a relatively short period in a limited geographic area (Akerman and Fagan 1986; Boldurian, Fitzgibbons, and Shelley 1985; Boldurian et al. 1986, 1987; Callahan 1979a, 1979b; Crabtree 1966; Flenniken 1978; Frison and Bradley 1980, 1981; Gryba 1988; Ibarra and Wellman 1988; Imel 1988; Neill 1952; Patten 1979a, 1979b, 1980; Sollberger 1977b, 1985; Sollberger and Patterson 1980, 1986). The preceding list of citations is by no means complete, but shows what I mean. I chose to cite mostly works that are of some use in trying to learn how to flute a point. A surprising number contain claims that the author's technique is the only one that properly reproduces the features seen on prehistoric points. As others point out, this is nonsense—different techniques often produce the same results, and besides, there is no reason to assume that only one technique was used in the past. I expect the prehistoric hunters debated the merits of their favorite fluting technique the way modern computer buffs argue about whether IBM or Tandy computers are more "powerful." From the tone of the modern knappers' arguments you would think they had almost as much at stake as the Folsom knapper whose points brought him dinner.

In any case, the stone work of the Paleo-Indian cultures of the Americas attracts attention by its excellence and great age. Fluting probably had a practical use in thinning the points for easier hafting, but it is certainly not necessary and in some points was carried to extremes of perfection and fragility. Fluting appeals to modern knappers as a statement of confidence, a kind of bravado. Having worked hard on a complex piece, the knapper, in trying to flute it, is risking all for the sake of one or two final flakes that set the stamp of a particular time and culture and display the knapper's mastery of the craft. We cannot know that prehistoric knappers felt this way, but we do know that some fluted points are far finer than they needed to be, probably even to the point where they were less useful, and we see many specimens that were broken in the process of fluting (e.g., Frison and Bradley 1980).

Ease of hafting was probably the reason for fluting, but unfluted points of similar size and shape can be hafted just as well. There are a number of other ideas about fluting. Display of skill is one. Others have suggested that flutes are "blood grooves" that would allow a wounded animal to bleed more freely, but this makes little sense since the flutes would be covered by the haft. Another idea is that the flutes allowed the spear to be pulled out of the wound and re-armed with another point, while the first point stayed in the wound and kept it open. One of my professors speculated incautiously about this as the "repeated thrust" style of hunting that may have been possible when human hunters first encountered slow, stupid Pleistocene animals that were not wary of human predators. This idea did not find favor in the irreverent minds of his graduate students, and a cartoon circulated in the department showing a mammoth under attack by Paleo-Indian hunters. The slow, stupid mammoth was saying, "Ooh, ah, do it again." In any case, a loosely hafted point would be wobbly and unlikely to penetrate well, so it is more likely that flutes were intended to provide a firmer, more stable hafting (Titmus and Woods 1991). On most fluted points the basal edges are ground dull. This probably indicates that they were tightly lashed onto a haft; dulling the edges prevented them from cutting the sinew binding. This may indicate that points hafted in a short foreshaft (see Chapter 10) were also used as knives. Dulled edges on a point would only be necessary to protect the lashing if the tool was used hard and repeatedly, and dulled basal edges are common on later Archaic points that were resharpened during use as knives.

Although others had speculated about fluting and even tried to replicate it (Neill 1952), Don Crabtree (1966) was the first to experiment extensively and describe his replications in detail. His article is well worth reading today, not merely for ideas about fluting but because it is still a model for replicative experiments. Crabtree tried a number of techniques, comparing the resulting points and the waste flakes to archaeological examples. He felt that pressure with a chest crutch produced the most accurate replications, but recognized that other techniques could not be ruled out.

Crabtree favored his chest crutch for fluting, but other knappers have

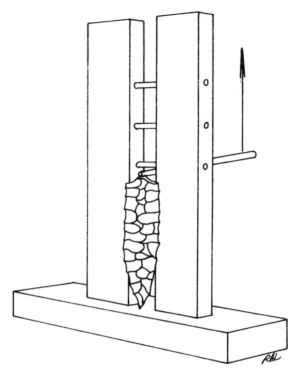

9.16
A lever device for fluting or other pressure flaking. Further bars or shims can be used to adjust for points of different sizes. Pulling upward on the lever applies pressure downward on the platform.

used hand pressure, direct percussion, indirect percussion, and mechanical lever devices. Removing a pressure flake large enough to flute a biface by normal pressure-flaking methods requires expert preparation and more strength than most of us have. Not many people have reported success. Direct percussion is very risky. It is hard to remove a large flute from a small biface without breaking it, even if it is supported very well. You can try wrapping the point in leather or even clay to support it and lessen the shock, but if you hold it in your hand, it is very difficult to keep it from moving while striking a forceful blow.

Mechanical devices have received a lot of attention lately, especially from the commercial and amateur knappers who are not as concerned with replicating the prehistoric techniques as they are with producing fine stone work. Various kinds of lever systems can be used to apply powerful controlled pressure to a point held in some kind of a vice. I have not experimented with these, so I will not discuss them in detail. Figure 9.16 shows an idealized version of one possible device (see also Sollberger 1978, 1985). Although several people (Frison and Bradley 1981; Ibarra and Wellman 1988; Sollberger and Patterson 1980) have argued that such mechanical lever systems may well have been used prehistorically, most archaeologists are not convinced. It is possible, but contrivances like this are simply not characteristic of early stone-using technologies, at least as far as we can tell from historic records, ethnography, and archaeological evidence. As the same results can be reached with simpler equipment, there is no good reason to expect relatively complicated lever devices in Paleo-Indian times.

Indirect percussion has been used to flute points by a number of knappers (e.g., Flenniken 1978; Akerman and Fagan 1986). This is the technique I favor, so I will use it in the example. Indirect percussion is probably the easiest to learn and use successfully of all the methods of fluting, but it is difficult to use for really long flutes or very fine points.

Fluting embodies the principles of blade making discussed above with some slight differences. Instead of being flat, as in most blade cores, the platform for fluting is a biface platform on an edge, as in pressure flaking or soft-hammer percussion. The ridge followed by the fluting flake is formed by pressure flaking the face of a projectile point. It is thus relatively flat, and the fluting flake is relatively wide and thin. The easiest way to discuss the details of fluting is by following an example step by step.

EXAMPLE: FLUTED POINT

Figures 9.17 to 9.20 summarize the fluting and finishing of a Clovislike point made of black obsidian from Arizona. High-quality, easily flaked material like obsidian is best to learn on. It is also best to start with large points, especially in fluting by indirect percussion, which many knappers find too risky for fine, thin Folsom points. I began by making a medium-sized biface, using an antler billet. When I had a regular biconvex cross-section and even faces without major flaws (Stage 3 or even 4 in Chapter 8), I carefully refined the form and faces by pressure flaking. Figure 9.17 shows the pressure-flaked biface ready for its first flute. Both faces are evenly flaked, but not flat, as the end view shows. A convex surface is necessary to provide a ridge that the fluting flake can follow. The other key to success is the platform. It is well isolated by flakes removed from both faces and well below the centerplane, very close to the surface from which the flute will be removed. On this face (Face I), medium flakes on each side of the fluting platform isolate it so that the flute will not spread out too soon. The small isolated platform is ground very heavily, to strike a nice balance between a small platform that will detach easily and strength for a large flake. The edge view of the biface shows how the platform is beveled, and the punch as drawn indicates the angle of the blow. The tip end of the biface is left rounded and dull and is heavily ground. This prevents it from flaking or crushing when the force of the blow drives it into the padded wood it rests on.

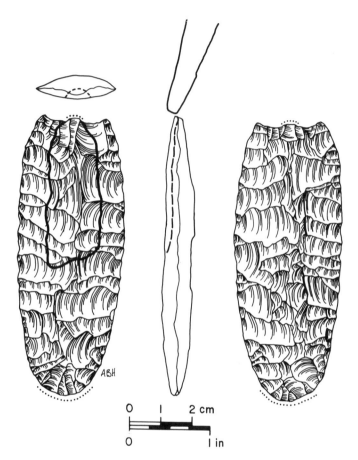

9.17
Fluting a Clovis point: both faces evenly flaked, platform prepared for first flute. The angle of the punch is shown and heavy line indicates subsequent flute. Dots indicate ground edges.

0 | 2 cm

0 | 1 in

I like to sit on the ground and hold points between my feet (Figure 9.18). The point is pressed between my heels, with the face to be fluted facing me. Hiking boots with soft cleated soles work well; the point fits into the grooves between cleats. If you want to be more primitive, leather pads would work, too. The tip of the point is rested on a piece of wood padded with leather. It is important to immobilize the point completely. If, for instance, the tip is not pressed against the wood, it will be driven down on it by the blow and may fracture. If the point is loosely held, it will shift with the blow and the flake will come off short, or the point may be twisted and broken. My sitting position is a little clumsy, especially because it is difficult to see the angle and placement of the punch as well as one should and because swinging the hammer to strike the punch may shift your whole body if you are not careful. I also usually lay a piece of leather over my heels to keep the flake from bouncing up at me. An assistant to watch or to hold the

9.18
Fluting a Clovis point: the point is held between the feet to strike the fluting flake.

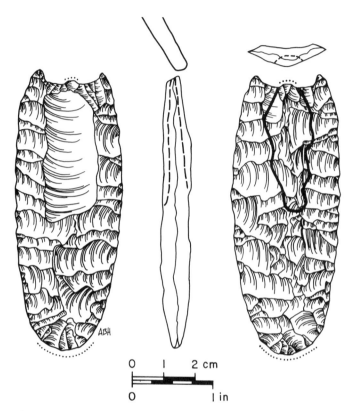

9.19
Fluting a Clovis point: Face I was successfully fluted, and a platform has been prepared on Face II for the second flute. Punch position and subsequent flake are indicated.

0 | 2 cm

0 | in

point makes life easier, but with practice one can place the punch by feel and move only the hammer arm during the blow. You might find it easier to flake away from yourself, but I have never been able to do this as well.

Having successfully fluted the first face, the base of the point is prepared for the second flute by beveling and isolating the platform in the opposite direction (Figure 9.19). The new platform is carefully prepared and ground. Note that the base of the point becomes increasingly concave as you do this. The flute is struck as for the first face (shown in outline on the point, Figure 9.19). As the outline of the second flute and the cross-section show, the second flute was a bit too narrow. This is because Face II was a little too convex, so the fluting flake did not spread out as it did on Face I. It might be possible to enlarge the flute by removing other fluting flakes parallel to this one, as was done on some prehistoric examples (see Figure 3.14). Having invested a lot of time in drawing and redrawing this point, I am content that I did not break it and I will quit while I am ahead.

The point is finished by pressure flaking to give it a sharp tip and final form (Figure 9.20). I removed only a few flakes from the edges

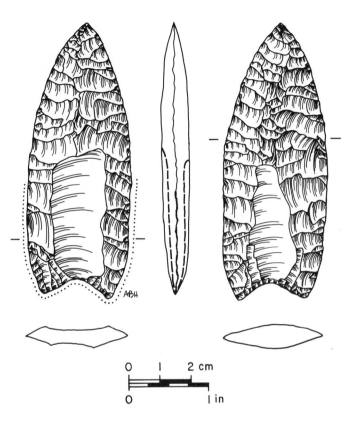

9.20
Fluted Clovis point completed. Both faces were fluted, and final pressure flaking has finished the tip and edges. Dots indicate where the basal edges have been ground to dull them for hafting.

near the base to avoid running them into the flute. Most prehistoric fluted points were also fluted when the lower edges were close to their final form, but there are examples showing that at least some retouch was done after fluting. A fluted point from the Lamb Site in New York (Figure 9.21) shows where the ends of several of the final retouch flakes invaded the flute. This can be prevented in part by flaking on a hard, padded surface like the hand anvil mentioned in Chapter 7. The edges of the flute are held in contact with the anvil and flakes from the edges of the point usually terminate at the flute without going into it. On my point the more extensive retouch to finish the tip was not a problem. I removed two complete series of flakes from each face toward the tip before getting the shape and finish I wanted.

Do not be discouraged if you break your first few fluted points. Fluting is a risky technique. For your encouragement, excellent archaeological examples of fluting disasters are shown by Frison and Bradley (1980) from the Hanson Folsom site in Wyoming. I made several kinds of errors when I began. The punch must be held at the right angle. If the punch (and thus the angle of the blow) is too close to 90 degrees, the force may smash the point or the fluting flake may plunge and

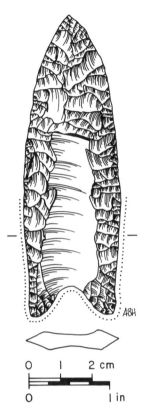

9.21
Fluted point 74/87 from the Lamb Site, Genesee County, New York. The point is made of fine gray chert, probably from Ohio. Note the ground basal edges and the final pressure flakes invading the flute, especially on the left. Drawn from Lithic Casting Lab Cast P-49, information from R. M. Gramly in catalogue description.

cut the tip off the point. This also happens if the point bends or moves at the blow. If the angle of the blow is too acute, only a short flake will be removed. If the point is squeezed too tightly from the edges, it may bend lengthwise and split. If the platform is too strong or too close to the centerplane, the point may be damaged; if it is too weak or too close to the face of the point, only a small flake will result. I made one piece too complicated to draw. It must have been loosely held, because when I struck it, a fine, large flute went halfway to the tip and then plunged. At the same time, the tip was driven against the wood and a large but shallower flute started at the tip and ran back toward the base, and actually passed above the real flute going the other way! Needless to say, I have never been able to duplicate this, nor do I want to.

If you can make a decent fluted point, you have achieved a fairly high degree of knapping competence. With the information in Chapter 10, you could haft this weapon and take on a mammoth. However, big-game hunting with stone-tipped spears is even less safe than knapping without gloves, so I must advise against it. I like pasta better anyway.

10
USING STONE TOOLS

Damn! That's sharp!
—All knappers, sooner or later

I once made a set of simple stone tools as a Christmas present for my wife's cousin's children. They opened the rest of their presents with them, ignoring the Swiss Army knives their grandmother had given them. Then they proceeded to their parents' room, where one of them accidentally demonstrated the efficiency of a flint edge by slicing his finger. With a little care, you can do more controlled and less painful experiments, as many archaeologists have done. If you are interested in making stone tools, you will want to have at least a little experience with their use.

STONE VS. STEEL

By the time you have flaked a little bit, you are well aware that stone tools can be very sharp. In fact, a fresh, unretouched feather edge on a glass or obsidian flake is considerably sharper than a surgical scalpel. Don Crabtree was the first of several archaeologists to have sensitive surgery performed on himself (by surgeons, not archaeologists) with obsidian blades (Crabtree and Callahan 1979; McIlrath 1984; Buck 1982). Several knappers have recently been trying to market obsidian blades to the medical profession, and there seems to be some potential for such tools (Buck 1982).

The only major disadvantage of stone tools as compared with metal ones is that they are relatively fragile and rapidly become dull. If you cut or scrape a piece of wood and listen carefully, you will hear the edge of the stone tool crunching a bit, and if you look at it with a lens, you will see that tiny flakes have been detached. Sometimes the edge damage or *use-wear* can be interpreted to give information about how the tool was used, a subject discussed in the next chapter. For now, we are merely concerned with the fact that if one cuts wood, scrapes a gritty hide, or slices meat and hits a bone, the edge of a stone tool will be dulled much faster than that of a metal tool used for the same task.

EDGES AND CUTTING

In spite of this, stone tools can be used very effectively. Try cutting something soft with a simple flake first. If you have nothing better,

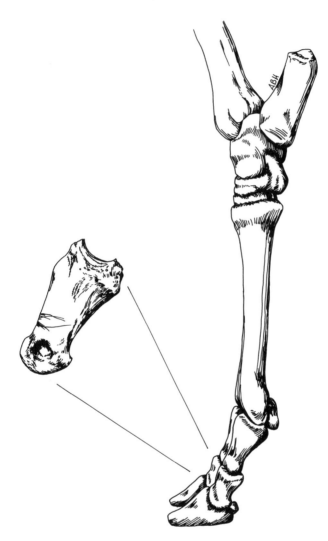

10.1
Cut marks left on the
exterior surface of a sheep
phalanx (toe bone) while
cutting hide to detach it at
the foot.

cutting up your steak or a chicken from the grocery store makes a good experiment, but try it some night when you don't have your in-laws over for dinner. I frequently use an apple or orange and a piece of leather in demonstrations. Cutting up a larger animal will give you some useful insights into the way stone tools could have been used, how efficient they really are, and some of their limitations.

When I was learning to knap at the University of Arizona, I participated in a number of butchering experiments. The photos in this chapter are from the first of these, in which Phil Chase and I were mostly interested in gaining some practical experience in cutting up a

10.2
Sheep and numbered tools laid out for butchering.

medium-sized animal with stone tools. Phil works with Mousterian faunal remains (Chase 1986), so we also wanted to see what kinds of cut marks stone tools made on the bones, to improve his ability to recognize and interpret butchering marks on ancient specimens (Figure 10.1). Figure 10.2 shows our sheep and numbered stone tools laid out for recording. We kept track of what each tool was used for, how long it was used, and what bones it contacted. The sheep was killed humanely, not hacked to death, and we roasted and ate it at the end of the experiment. Although I have since butchered a variety of animals, this was our first experiment of this sort. We learned several things the hard way, and no doubt a Neanderthal would have been disgusted at our inefficiency.

We were soon reminded that many flakes have more than one sharp edge. Don't press a sharp back edge into your hand while cutting with the other edge. If you hold a flake between your fingertips and use a slicing motion, the sharp edge of the tool will do all the work and you will not even have to exert much force. You can also protect your hand by dulling one edge or wrapping the tool in a piece of hide or a bundle of leaves, especially for heavy cutting such as disjointing a large animal.

A simple flake is adequate for butchering any animal up to the size of a deer, and more efficient for some tasks than a biface. If you are just cutting meat, a sharp, unretouched edge cuts more cleanly and faster

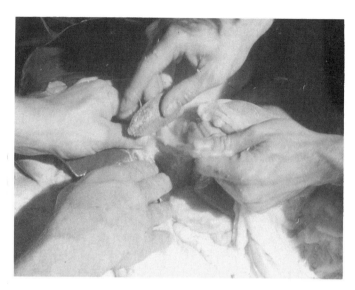

10.3
Removing internal organs: cutting with a sharp flake.

(Figure 10.3). A retouched edge is usually not as sharp as an unretouched flake, but the retouched edge works like a serrated steak knife. A medium-sized biface is a good all-purpose butchering tool. It endures heavy cutting around joints, where you will strike bone often. In detaching hides, the sharp but controllable edge of a biface is less likely to cut the hide than an irregularly shaped razor-sharp flake (Figure 10.4). Bifaces can also be more easily shaped and hafted, dull less easily, and can be resharpened and used again and again. Steeply retouched edges, like those on scrapers, can also be used for cutting but are better for scraping, as in Figure 10.5, in which a scraper is being used to remove flesh and fat from the sheep's hide.

By the time we finished butchering that first sheep, we were enthusiastic, if not expert, stone tool users (Figure 10.6). Our experiences, and those of many others, show that stone tools are extremely effective, especially when you understand their advantages and limitations.

Working hard materials needs a strong edge. You can whittle wood with a sharp flake, especially if it is of a tough material, but hard materials like wood, bone, and antler are often better worked by scraping and planing if you use stone tools. Steep edge angles (45 to 90 degrees or even obtuse angles) work well for scraping and planing. You can use a fresh flake or retouch it steeply to make a scraper edge. Unifacially retouched tools are best used for scraping and planing. You can also use the burin you made in Chapter 6. The right-angle edge formed by a bending fracture is also a very good tool, and in fact, when I was a boy, my uncle showed me how to scrape and smooth wood with a broken piece of window glass. Your snapped bifaces can be used the same way,

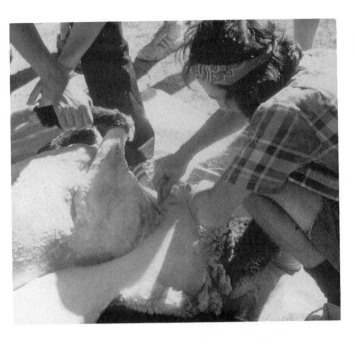

10.4
Skinning sheep with a biface.

10.5
Scraping hide with a steeply retouched scraper.

10.6
The knapper triumphant: Phil Chase with sheep leg and stone tool.

and there are even archaeological examples showing similar use (Frison and Bradley 1980).

Many stone tools, even most in some cultures, were simple unretouched flakes, made as needed, used once, and discarded with the same disregard that smokers show toward their matches. Other stone tools, usually more complex ones, were made easier to use by attaching them to some kind of handle. The handles were often of perishable material, but enough have survived in different sites to give us a good idea of the range of hafting techniques. One basic and common form is the slotted wooden handle or haft, commonly used on knives and arrows. These are easily made with basic stone tools and serve as a good example of the kinds of tasks you can perform with them.

MAKING A PROJECTILE FORESHAFT

In the dry caves of the Southwest, slotted foreshafts for arrows or atlatl darts are occasionally found, sometimes with the stone point still attached (e.g. Cosgrove 1947; Gifford 1980). These foreshafts would fit into the socket of a main shaft, which was usually made of cane or other light material and which was often feathered (Figure 10.7). There are a number of reasons why projectiles would be made this way. The most breakable part of a stone-tipped projectile is the stone point, but as you will see if you try, it is often the easiest part to make. The

10.7
Schematic of compound arrow: (a) point, (b) foreshaft, (c) mainshaft, (d) fletching, (e) nock. The prehistoric waste piece (f) is from foreshaft making, Boynton Canyon, Arizona. Not to same scale.

e

d

c

b

a

f

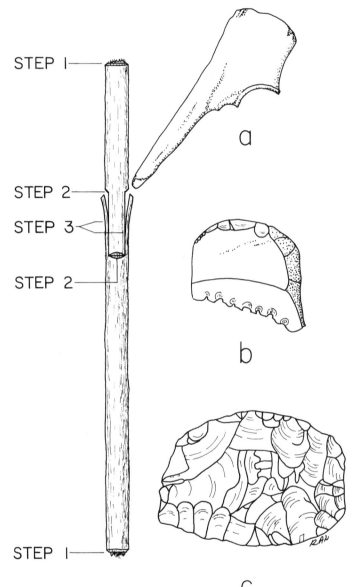

STEP 1

STEP 2

STEP 3

STEP 2

STEP 1

a

b

c

10.8
Making a foreshaft. Step 1: detach blank from limb at both ends. Step 2: saw shallow cuts to mark piece removed for slot. Step 3: split out waste piece from upper to lower cuts. Examples of woodworking tools: (a) bone chisel used for splitting; (b) serrated flake saw—this one is prehistoric, from a site in Colorado, and was not actually used; (c) biface used to saw foreshaft.

foreshaft adds to the work, but if you smash the point and foreshaft against a rock or watch it vanish into the woods in a wounded animal, you have still saved yourself a lot of work if the main shaft drops off and can be recovered and reused. The foreshaft and point also makes a handy knife, and before bows and arrows a hunter with thrusting spears or an atlatl and darts could have reduced the weight he had to carry by carrying several foreshafts and only a couple of main shafts that he counted on recovering and re-arming (Frison 1978). However, although a foreshaft system has advantages, it is not the only way of doing things, and in many areas, arrows and darts were made in a single piece.

In any case, I will illustrate the making of a typical atlatl dart foreshaft (Figures 10.8–10.11). The process is essentially the same for an arrow foreshaft or for a knife.

1. Select your tools. You will develop your own preferences. I like to use a medium-sized thin biface with a straight edge and a couple of large flakes with sharp, steep, unretouched edges for scraping and planing (Figure 10.8c; 10.11a, c). A couple of small, sharp flakes for cutting sinew or hide will be useful, and I use a slab of sandstone to smooth the shaft at the end. A small wedge or awl of bone that you have ground to a chisel shape is often handy (Figure 10.8a). I sometimes like to wear a leather glove while working—it allows me to use more force and feel happier about my valuable flesh. Other materials you will need include adhesive and lashing. Some points were glued into the foreshaft, others lashed, and many used both a lashing and an adhesive. These will be discussed in their place.

2. Select a suitable piece of wood. Almost any kind of wood will do. Green wood is much easier to work than seasoned wood, and this is an important consideration if you are using stone tools. The harder the wood is, the more work it will be to carve, but if you intend to use the dart, the foreshaft should be tough. To reduce the amount of work, use a piece of a branch that is not much thicker than you intend to make the foreshaft. The finished foreshaft shown in Figure 10.11 is .9 centimeter thick (⅓ in.) and 9.2 centimeters (3.5 in.) long. The finished foreshaft should be slightly narrower than the stem of the point that will go in it. Depending on the weight and style of your projectile, the foreshaft should be anywhere from a few inches to a foot or more long. I generally make them rather short.

3. Cut your wood to a handy length (Figure 10.8, step 1). I like to begin with a branch 15 to 30 centimeters (6–12 in.) long. I sometimes don't detach short foreshafts from the branch until they are almost complete, because they are much easier to hold that way. Branches are cut by the *groove-and-snap* technique. A wide groove is sawn around the branch with the biface, and when the groove is deep enough, the

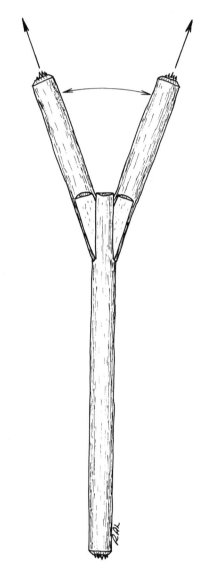

10.9
Making a foreshaft. The slot in the foreshaft is formed by pulling and bending until the waste piece breaks out.

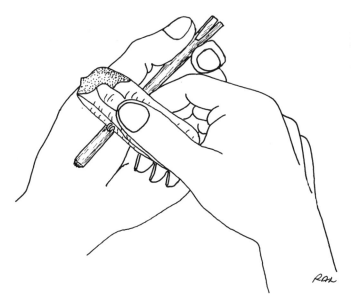

10.10
Shaving the proximal end of the foreshaft with a flake. Note the pinching hold on the flake to avoid being cut by the sharp back edge.

branch can be bent back and forth to break through the remaining thickness. This is a common prehistoric technique in working wood or bone, and saves a lot of time over sawing completely through. Rough ends can be smoothed later.

4. Decide how long your foreshaft will be, and where on the branch. I prefer short foreshafts, 10 to 15 centimeters (4–6 in.) long, but many prehistoric foreshafts were longer. Pick a straight length, with few twigs, knots, or flaws. Scrape off the bark with one of the flakes, using a planing or scraping motion.

5. Make the slot for the point—this is easier than you might expect. The first few hafts I made, I tried cutting the slot, as recommended by some others (Sollberger 1969). You can begin by sawing with the biface, but this soon becomes difficult. The deeper you get, the thicker your biface edge is and the more it rubs against the sides of the cut. Another problem is that lithic tools can withstand some pressure, but very little bending. As you struggle to saw back and forth, you will twist the tool, and small flakes will be broken out of the edge, or you may even snap it. This is why it is difficult to use a thinner flake for deeper sawing. For deep slots, I despaired and used either steel tools or a bone chisel. Bone chisels are surprisingly effective and are easy to make by grinding a sharp edge on a splinter of bone. I chiseled and pried out splinters, trying to shape the inside of the slot to fit the worst irregularities on the stone point that was to go in it, sometimes shaping the point base a bit to fit the foreshaft. All this was a lot of hard, frustrating work, but

I describe it here because it shows some of the limitations of stone tools, which I learned by trial and error. Having said that, I'll tell you about a better way, which was described by Cosgrove (1947:52–54) from finished and unfinished arrows found in caves in New Mexico and Texas.

The best way to slot a haft is by using a groove-and-snap technique to split out a strip from the center of the haft to form the slot. Cut two grooves on opposite sides of the branch, wherever you want the end of the foreshaft to be. They should go only deep enough to leave between them the thickness of wood that will be split out for the slot. Farther down, at the desired depth of the slot, cut two shallower grooves, 90 degrees around the foreshaft from the others (Figure 10.8, step 2). Then hold the branch firmly below the grooves and bend it gently back and forth to split the forward end loose, with two splits running down from the first two grooves to the second pair. The bone chisel can be used to help start the splits (Figure 10.8, step 3). Then rotate the branch 90 degrees and bend it back and forth in the opposite direction at the second grooves, at the same time pulling on the ends slightly (Figure 10.9). This will break out the tab of wood in the slot, detaching it at the second set of grooves. With practice, all this can be done in a couple of minutes, a great improvement over sawing and chiseling.

An alternative to this kind of slotted foreshaft is a socketed one. You can split the foreshaft, carve a socket, and lash and glue the foreshaft together again.

6. Cut another groove all the way around the shaft some distance below the slot. This is to form a shoulder that will butt up against the socket in the main shaft. If the foreshaft is still attached to the branch, cut another groove around the shaft at the point where you intend to detach the foreshaft from the rest of the branch. These grooves should go all the way around the branch and will serve as stops for planing and scraping. Now scrape and plane the foreshaft to narrow the butt end and shape the distal end (Figure 10.10), using steep-edged flakes or scrapers (Figure 10.11a, c). The butt end should be narrow enough to fit into whatever main shaft you use, and the distal end should be flattened. With a sharp flake you should be able to plane off small curls of wood without too much effort, if you don't try to cut too deeply on each stroke.

7. When the foreshaft is mostly shaped, if you work with it attached to the branch, cut it off the rest of the branch with the groove-and-snap technique. Do any final shaping and smoothing by scraping and sanding with a piece of sandstone. A sidewalk works if nothing else is available and you don't mind the neighbors' staring. If you want to go to a bit more effort, you can make a shaft smoother of two flat pieces of abrasive stone with matching grooves in each (see Flenniken and Oz-

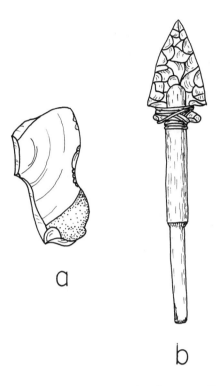

10.11
Finished foreshaft fitted with an obsidian point, flanked by scraping tools: (a) notched flake, (b) foreshaft with point held in place by sinew and resin, (c) unretouched flake with steep edge.

a

c

b

bun 1988). On a knife I usually leave the area rough around the slot that will be covered by lashing, or I even cut grooves in it to make the lashing hold better.

8. Fix the point in the foreshaft (Figure 10.11). I usually use both glue and lashing, but for many purposes one is enough. A variety of plant resins can be used as glue. The most familiar and easiest to find is pine resin. To apply it, you should warm it until it is runny, but avoid heating it too much or it will be brittle when hardened. You can glue a point into a shaft with resin and also use a thin coat to waterproof a sinew lashing.

Sinew is the usual material for lashing. The best sinew runs in a long, thin sheet along the spine of large animals like deer. Leg tendons are very stout but shorter. The sinew fibers can be separated to make threads of any size, and can be rolled or woven to make stronger cords. You can dry sinew and keep it indefinitely. Soaking it in water for a half hour before using it will restore its flexibility. Sinew dries stiff and hard, and shrinks by several percent of its length as it dries. This helps tighten a lashing. If you want a lashing that is really strong, use rawhide—that is, untanned skin. Leather is not much good. Like sinew, a piece of rawhide can be dried and stored until needed. Even if you live in a city, you should be able to pick up a dead squirrel or cat from the road, if you don't mind being considered a bit odd. Scrape the hair off a piece of skin, and to make a long rawhide for lashing, cut around and around in a spiral. You can't cut hide as thin as you can split sinew fibers, so I use rawhide on knives and other heavy-duty tools, where I don't mind a coarser lashing and where the tightening effect adds strength.

Vegetable fibers were used for hafting by some aboriginal groups, including the Lacandon Maya (Lewenstein 1987:50). The modern stone-tipped Lacandon arrows I bought in Mexico (Figure 3.21) were lashed with heavy, waxed commercial thread, which is of course an option if you can't get sinew. You can also try various natural fibers like milkweed or yucca, depending on where you live. Some of the books cited in the next section will give you information on plant fibers and other resources.

GOING ON

I don't intend to describe making the rest of the shaft, but you can use the same basic techniques if you use stone tools. Useful information on primitive projectiles and related crafts can be found in a number of places. The most enjoyable is Ernest Thompson Seton's novel *Two Little Savages* (Seton 1903), which, besides being a delightful story, contains a lot of excellent woodcraft. Some of the many books oriented toward wilderness survival have good instructions for crafts that can be adapted to stone tool use (e.g., Angier 1962; Olsen 1990). The *Bulletin of Primitive Technology* is a current publication that emphasizes experiments and practical applications.

Good information on aboriginal bows and arrows and how to make them can be found in several works (e.g., Hamilton 1972; Laubin and Laubin 1980; McPherson 1987; Waldorf and Waldorf 1985). Saxton Pope wrote two excellent studies inspired by his friendship with Ishi, one (1974) an account of Ishi's hunting and archery and the other (1923) a classic series of experiments with bows and arrows. A large literature has developed describing experiments with replicating and using atlatls (e.g., Browne 1940; Butler 1975, 1977; Cole 1972; Davenport 1943; Howard 1974, 1976; Hunter 1992; Peets 1960; Raymond 1986). Spencer (1974) discusses using stone tools to replicate an atlatl.

Various experiments with stone projectile points provide information on hafting, penetration, efficiency, and damage patterns (Barton and Bergman 1982; Bergman and Newcomer 1983; Browne 1940; Fischer, Hausen, and Rasmussen 1984; Flenniken 1985; Flenniken and Raymond 1986; Friis-Hansen 1990; Frison 1978, 1989; Huckell 1982; Odell and Cowan 1986; Titmus and Woods 1986; Woods 1987).

Woodworking with stone tools is discussed by Crabtree (1973b), Crabtree and Davis (1968), Sollberger (1968, 1969), and Spencer (1974).

A good many people have butchered animals with stone tools, including Frison (1989), Huckell (1979), Robicsek and Hales (1984), and Walker (1978). One of the most complete experimental studies of the use of a whole stone tool industry is that of Lewenstein (1987). She used replicas of Mayan tools from Cerros for heavy and light woodworking, butchering, hide preparation, cutting plant fiber, digging, shaping stone, shell, and potsherds, and other tasks. She also examined the use-wear resulting from all of these experiments.

John Coles has written two excellent and readable books on experimental archaeology (1973, 1979) that contain lots of ideas and information on experiments with all sorts of prehistoric technologies. The bibliographies by Hester and Heizer (1973) and Honea (1983) provide numerous references to additional experiments.

11
ARCHAEOLOGICAL ANALYSIS
OF STONE TOOLS

Behavior is the first thing to go when you're dead.

—Larry Martin (Paleontologist,
in Monastersky 1990:41)

The results of history lie strewn around us, but we cannot, in principle, directly observe the processes that produced them. How then can we be scientific about the past? As a general answer, we must develop criteria for inferring the processes we cannot see from the results that have been preserved.

—Stephen Jay Gould (1982:16)

If you have learned how to make stone tools, you have also learned how to look at them. You should be able to read any individual piece of stone for information on how it was made, the quality of the material, problems the knapper found or errors he or she made, how they were overcome, and why the piece was finally discarded. Much of the delight of understanding a stone tool comes from the ability to make contact with a person who has been dead for centuries, recognizing that individual's struggle and skill, and comparing it with your own. However, while each stone tool may be fun to look at and have a story to tell to the experienced knapper, individual pieces do not tell us all that much about the person who made them. To understand another person, you must know something about the world he or she lived in. In trying to read the faint message of the past, sentences and paragraphs are much more useful than single words—any individual tool does not tell us nearly as much as the same tool in its archaeological context, as part of a group of tools and other remains that were once part of human lives. In this chapter, I will discuss some aspects of archaeological analysis of stone tools. I do not intend to give a thorough discussion with detailed methodologies for different problems; that deserves another entire book. Instead, I want to expand on one of the themes I have used throughout—that stone tools are most interesting if we see them in the context of the cultures that produced them. How we do so should be of interest to any knapper, and the ideas and examples that follow can be further explored in the references given here and in earlier chapters.

Archaeologists look at stone tools as a group of artifacts that make up a part, and sometimes a particularly informative part, of the record of the past. Two themes that run through all of archaeology should be emphasized. First, as mentioned above, we are ultimately interested in people and their lives; artifacts are more interesting as documents of other lives than as objects to be fondled and displayed. As such, they are most meaningful when studied in context and in association with the other objects that all belonged together in a living culture. We are thus usually examining stone tools as groups of artifacts, and also trying to bring in information from many other kinds of artifacts and non-artifactual remains. Accordingly, archaeologists should be interested in anything that yields information about the vanished people. We study things in convenient categories like stone tools, but stone tools alone do not tell us everything we want to know, even about the stone tools themselves.

Ideally we want to study everything and know everything, but a second theme underlying all archaeology is the incompleteness of the remains we study. It is impossible to ask the dead about themselves (unless you share the egotistical delusions of "psychics"), so we study the less perishable traces of their lives. Stone tools have the advantage of being almost indestructible, but even so, what we see is never more than a part of the picture. The tools themselves are usually only fragments—the broken tool that was thrown away, the debitage left while the tool was kept, the stone point that was only a part of a complicated tool of wood, sinew, feathers, and stone. An archaeologist's life is balanced between regret that we cannot know more, cannot reach out to shake that prehistoric hand, and the pleasure of finding ways to learn more and more as we attempt to bring part of prehistory back from oblivion.

TYPOLOGY

Archaeologists are occasionally accused, even today, of a pathological desire to classify everything into neat little pigeonholes. While classification can be carried to absurd extremes, there are a number of good reasons why we are interested in *typology*, studying and establishing schemes for classifying objects and phenomena (see, for instance, Jelinek 1976; Sackett 1973, 1982).

In fact, classification is part of everyone's life. You cannot even think without forming and using categories for people, objects, and events.

One purpose of a typology is to condense information so that we can talk, for instance, about the 80 blades and 375 flakes from a site without describing each one individually.

A typology, a classification system, also provides a common vocabulary for communication. When I describe the lithic assemblage at a site as consisting of 80 blades and 375 flakes, if you know what I mean by blades and flakes, then you have a rough idea of what the assemblage is like.

There has been a good deal of argument about what typologies should do, beyond condensing and communicating basic concepts (Brew 1946; Burling 1964; Clarke 1968; Deetz 1967; Dunnell 1978; Ford 1954a, 1954b; Gifford 1960; Jelinek 1976; Krieger 1944; Rouse 1960; Sackett 1973, 1982; Spaulding 1953, 1954; Swartz 1967; Hill and Evans 1972 is a good summary). Should typologies be universal? Do they reflect an underlying "reality" or are they arbitrary figments of the archaeologist's mind? Should they agree with the categories used by the people who made the tools, and is it possible to discover these categories? The reasonable view adopted by most archaeologists is that typologies serve a number of purposes. There should be some widely used and understood classifications that allow archaeologists to speak to each other and compare their work, but it is also frequently necessary to produce more detailed classification systems that can be used to study particular problems. For instance, you can compare the assemblage of 80 blades and 375 flakes above to that from a nearby site where no blades are found and begin to suspect that something different was going on at the two sites. In order to pin down the differences more closely, you might begin by classifying flakes into different groups by size, materials, manufacturing techniques, and so on, and then comparing the sites in these terms. We cannot cover all the uses of typology, but some of the common kinds of information studied through them should be mentioned.

STONE TOOL TYPES AND CHANGE THROUGH TIME

One of the most important uses of typology is to provide temporal information. In the 1840s the Danish archaeologists Thomsen and Worsaae recognized that dividing artifacts into stone, bronze, and iron groups not only made for tidy display cases, but also formed groups of artifacts that were consistently found together and represented change through time. Subsequent workers classified much of prehistory as the Stone Age and subdivided it into Old, Middle, and New (Paleolithic, Mesolithic, Neolithic) on the basis of changes in the characteristic stone tools. Certain stone tools became recognized as "index fossils" that indicated a particular period—for instance, handaxes belonged to the Paleolithic, ground stone axes to the Neolithic. We discussed the major changes in stone tool technology in Chapter 3. Considerably refined by data from other dating techniques, the use of stone tool types as dating aids continues.

In the Americas, projectile point types are often the best clue to a site's date. Some point types were used over a large area for a long time and are therefore not very useful in dating, but others have been closely dated to a short span by stratigraphy or associated carbon-14, tree-ring, or other dates. Types are often named for a site in which they are found, sometimes with a descriptive term like "side-notched" added to the name. For example, the Clovis point (see Figures 3.14, 9.21) is a variable but distinctive type that occurs consistently in sites where bone or charcoal can be dated by carbon-14 to between 9000 and 9500 B.C. (Bonnichsen and Turnmire 1991; Frison 1978; Howard 1990; Willig 1991). In some sites, layers with Clovis material are covered by layers with Folsom points and later dates between 8500 and 9000 B.C. Accordingly, a site with Clovis points but no other datable material can be expected to date between 9000 and 9500 B.C. There are now a great number of published typologies of North American projectile points with information on the date ranges of different types (e.g., Bell 1960; Fogelman 1988; Harwood 1986; Heizer and Hester 1978; Justice 1987; Morrow 1984; Richie 1961; Suhm and Jelks 1962; Turner and Hester 1985; Waldorf and Waldorf 1987).

Point types in some areas are not well defined or consistently named. In the southwestern United States, where I work, there are consistent point forms that change through time and are recognized as belonging to different periods (Figure 11.1). However, decorated pottery types are even more useful, and very precise dates can often be obtained from tree-ring dating and other means, so no one has established any widely used point typology, although some localized typologies have been proposed (e.g., Holmer and Weder 1980), and a few distinctive early types are named and widely recognized.

In other parts of the world, there are few individual stone tool types as precisely dated as are some North American projectile points. Comparable information is available for British points (Green 1980; Figures 11.2, 11.3) and could doubtless be found for other areas.

Other kinds of stone tools could be used as chronological markers, but few are as complex, distinctive, common, and rapidly changing as American projectile points. Even with these there are some problems. Figure 11.4 shows a sequence of point types found in different levels of a stratified site at Gatecliff Shelter, Nevada (Thomas 1981, 1983). The different strata represent unknown amounts of use within the rather broad time limits established by radioactive carbon dates and other information. All the point types shown are well-known named types with consistent dates at other sites as well (Baumhoff and Byrne 1958;

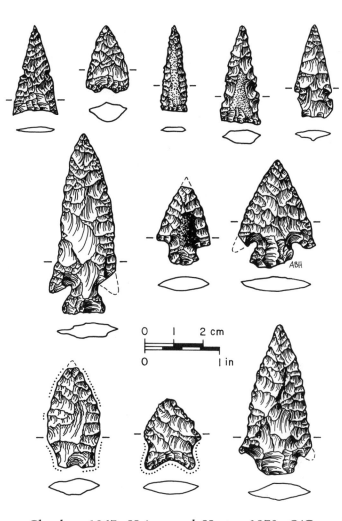

11.1
Sequence of points in Sinagua region, represented by specimens from Lizard Man Village, Arizona. *Bottom,* Archaic. *Middle,* Late Archaic to early Sinagua. *Top,* Late Sinagua. Dots indicate ground edges or heavy wear.

Clewlow 1967; Heizer and Hester 1978; O'Connell 1967; Thomas 1970). As you can see, the different point types overlap quite a bit in time, at least as defined by their positions in Gatecliff Shelter. There are several reasons for this.

Styles often change slowly, by gradual modification, so types of points in any area often overlap or grade into one another. More than one distinctly different point form may be in use at any given time, and we will consider reasons for this later.

In any archaeological site, there is mixing and disturbance of old material as people dig storage pits, bury the dead, scoop out fill for building material, and so on. The stratigraphic levels in an archaeological site represent a series of constantly changing surfaces where people live, dropping their trash, trampling it in, and digging it up. If

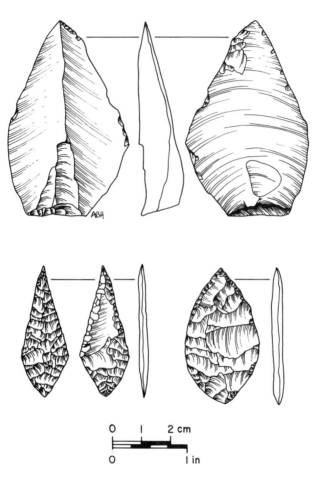

11.2
Sequence of points in
Ireland. *Top,* Mesolithic
flake point. *Bottom,* two
forms of Neolithic bifacial
leaf point. Royal Ontario
Museum specimens.

you were to camp in a rockshelter today, you would be sleeping on a modern surface where the stone tools of ancient hunters might rub shoulders with the beer cans left by modern slobs. Your grandchild, visiting the same shelter in fifty years, might walk on a surface half a foot higher, built up of windblown sand and covering both the cans and the points.

People also save, collect, and reuse old artifacts. As a result, old objects often occur in later contexts. The antique vase on Grandma's coffee table is a good example, as are the prehistoric artifacts in my laboratory. There are a number of ethnographic accounts of old points being used for magic or other symbolic purposes by later people (Ellis 1968; Hill 1982; Holland and Weitlaner 1960; Thomas 1976; Weigand 1970, 1989), and there is every reason to believe that this practice is very ancient. Old flakes and stone tools were also seen by some folks as raw material to be reworked (Jolly 1970; McDonald 1991).

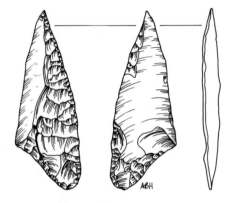

11.3
Sequence of points in
Ireland. *Top,* later Neolithic
transverse point. Royal
Ontario Museum specimen.
Bottom, two forms of late
Neolithic–Bronze Age
barbed-and-tanged point
(after Raftery 1951 : 135).

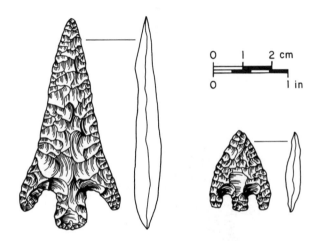

Any individual stone tool may also change its form as it is dulled and
resharpened or broken and reshaped (Ahler 1971; Frison 1968; Luchterhand 1970). What the archaeologist sees is only the last form, which
represents the last uses of a tool and is often further confused by damage in use or by natural forces after it has been discarded. Flenniken
and Raymond (Flenniken 1985; Flenniken and Raymond 1986) argue
that because points may be reworked after breakage into quite different
forms, point types are unreliable for dating. They performed a series of
experiments with replicated Elko points, hafting them on atlatl darts,
throwing the darts at various targets until the points were damaged,
and then reworking them to make functional points with the least effort. In the process, a number of points became much smaller, or lost
corners or bases and had to be reworked in such a way that an archaeologist would have classified them as different types with different
time ranges. Although interesting in other ways, this experiment is

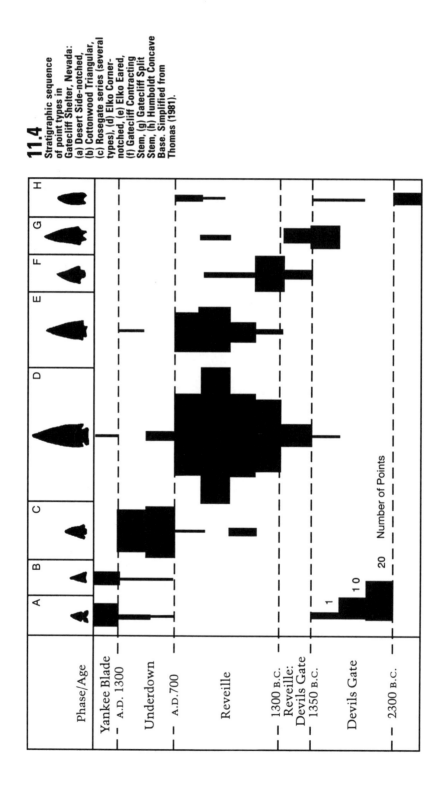

11.4
Stratigraphic sequence of point types in Gatecliff Shelter, Nevada: (a) Desert Side-notched, (b) Cottonwood Triangular, (c) Rosegate series (several types), (d) Elko Corner-notched, (e) Elko Eared, (f) Gatecliff Contracting Stem, (g) Gatecliff Split Stem, (h) Humboldt Concave Base. Simplified from Thomas (1981).

largely irrelevant to the problem of using point types to date sites, and illustrates what Thomas (1986) calls a "fundamental conceit" of flintknapping.

If particular point forms are consistently associated with dates obtained from other sources, then those point forms are useful chronological indicators. The possibility that some specimens may have had a different shape when first made makes no difference. The date still applies to the final form. For us as knappers, it is even more important to recognize that just because a modern knapper can rework a damaged point to a different form and finds that this procedure is an efficient use of time and material, we cannot assume that this is what a prehistoric knapper would choose to do. If a prehistoric knapper did rework a point, it might change form, but only to a type considered suitable in the knapper's time and culture. Flintknapping gives us great insights into what could have been done, but we must be very careful to consider this information as a source of useful ideas to be tested against evidence, not as confirmation that prehistoric knappers must have done the same things. Flintknapping is only one source of information about stone tools, and we should not let the thrill of being able to make a stone tool blind us to other sources of different information.

The Gatecliff Shelter point sequence in Figure 11.4 also shows the tendency for artifacts to rise and fall in popularity, and to overlap with other artifacts that are replacing them. If I look around my classroom today, I see that perhaps 90 percent of my students are wearing "casual" shoes (sneakers, sandals, hiking boots) and only 10 percent have "formal" shoes (patent leather, high heels, Oxfords, etc.). Fifty years ago the percentages would have been reversed; most students dressed much more formally. In between, there was a shift in American footwear preferences, and the percentages of "formal" and "casual" shoes would have gradually changed, producing the same kind of "battleship-shaped" graph (Deetz 1967) of popularity as the Elko points at Gatecliff Shelter.

Patterns like this are useful because if you find one Elko Corner-notched point in a site, you can expect the point, and thus the site, to date between roughly 1350 B.C. and A.D. 700. But that is a 2,000-year span, which may not be precise enough to be useful. Moreover, a single point may have arrived at the site anytime in that span, or may even be an early point dropped on a late site or dug up from early layers, in which case the date of the point does not apply to the human activities you are interested in dating. If, however, you have a larger assemblage of points and almost all of them are Elko Corner-notched, but a few can be called Elko Eared, then you have a consistent pattern that is not likely to be accidental, and which provides a much tighter date. The proportions of the two point types are good evidence that the site was occupied during the early part of the Elko Corner-notched time span, after the Elko Eared form had appeared, but before it became popular.

In the many areas where there are few individual stone tool types that are as tightly dated as some American points, the frequencies of different tool types are as important as their presence and absence in describing and dating assemblages. In Europe, François Bordes was a pioneer in this, defining an elaborate typology for the Lower and Middle Paleolithic (Bordes 1961). Others developed similar systems for other periods and geographical areas (e.g., Brézillon 1968; Tixier 1974). Some of the tool types used by Bordes and others are restricted in space and time and therefore make good "index fossils," but more often European typologists consider changes in the relative percentages of different tools. Some of these changes represent trends through time, but other factors must also be considered.

WHAT PEOPLE DID WITH STONES

When François Bordes developed his typology of Paleolithic tool types, he was able to classify different Mousterian assemblages according to differing frequencies of tool types, thus defining several kinds of Mousterian industries (Bordes 1972 is a readable summary). Quina Mousterian, for instance, has many scrapers (up to 80 percent of the tools). Many of the scrapers are Quina scrapers—thick, usually transverse, with heavy, steep retouch with many step terminations. Handaxes, backed knives, and denticulates are absent or rare. Only a few tools are made on Levallois flakes. In contrast, Mousterian of Acheulean Tradition has fewer scrapers and very few Quina scrapers, a fair number of denticulates, backed knives, and especially handaxes. A variable but higher percentage of tools are made on Levallois flakes. Denticulate Mousterian is characterized by high percentages of denticulates and notches and relatively few scrapers.

Bordes had recognized that changes in tool frequency might be as good as "index fossil" tools for dating sites, but the different Mousterian industries defined by Bordes did not appear to represent change through time. They were often interstratified—that is, one might find a level of Quina Mousterian covered by a layer of Denticulate Mousterian, but with another Quina Mousterian level on top of that. Bordes felt that the different Mousterians could best be interpreted as different cultures, or tribes perhaps, that lived at the same time, moving around in the valleys of France and occupying and abandoning the same caves time and again over thousands of years. Other archaeologists were skeptical about the implication that different groups of people could live so closely together for over 50,000 years without mixing together and losing their distinctive stone tool traditions. The strongest challenge to Bordes's interpretation came from Lewis and Sally Binford

(1969). They used Bordes's typology to examine several Mousterian assemblages from the Levant. Using computerized clustering techniques, they defined groups of tools that tended to occur together at site after site and reflected in part Bordes's different Mousterian assemblages. However, they argued that the consistent groupings of tools represented tool kits that were used for different activities at different times by the same people. There were a number of problems with their analysis. Bordes pointed out, for instance, that layers containing Mousterian industries in most caves represent the accumulated rubbish of hundreds, even thousands, of years of visits and occupations, and it is rarely possible to sort out a group of individual tools that were used at one short period of time. In other words, no actual tool kits, in the everyday sense of the word, can be identified. The Binfords were suggesting that different Mousterian assemblages were largely repeated accumulations of many examples of a consistent group of tools. However, that implied that certain caves were set aside for particular activities for long periods of time and then used exclusively for something else for another long span. An equally serious problem is the way the Binfords assigned functions to their presumed tool kits. These were interpreted as butchering kits, hunting kits, and so forth mostly by speculation, with very little real knowledge of how any of the tools were actually used.

Further work on the Mousterian has included closer examinations of the functions of tools (Anderson 1979), searches for consistent relationships between tool types or industries and climatic conditions (Laville, Rigaud, and Sackett 1980), and attempts to correlate different tool assemblages to the hunting of particular big-game species (Chase 1986). Recently, it has been argued that Mousterian tools and industries are not discrete units, but grade continuously from one type to another. For instance, the different types of scrapers may not represent different forms made intentionally by Neanderthals for specific purposes, but a general-purpose tool that varies in shape, size, and number of retouched edges largely because some pieces have been used longer and resharpened more frequently than others (Dibble 1987). The variation between Mousterian assemblages can be interpreted similarly in terms of the intensity of use, reuse, and resharpening of tools (Rolland and Dibble 1990). Intense use of tools reflects difficulty in obtaining raw material, which in turn reflects local climate and geology, human mobility, and other factors. The availability and quality of material also affects the size and shape of some tools, which contributes to the diversity of assemblages. This view of Mousterian assemblages implies that the Neanderthals adapted rather mechanically to local environmental conditions and that human cultures were pretty much the same over huge spans of time and distance.

None of the interpretations of the Mousterian is completely satisfactory. There is probably some truth in many of them, and we have certainly not heard the last word in this debate. As an influential problem in lithic studies, it serves to introduce some of the kinds of interpretations that can be made by looking at stone tool assemblages and using different kinds of typologies and different interpretations of the variation in stone tools.

SOURCES OF VARIATION: WHY STONE TOOLS ARE NOT ALL ALIKE

If we consider the factors that should influence the shape of a stone tool, we can see four categories. Each exerts a limiting influence on what can be done with a piece of stone.

1. *Material.* The first limitation on a stone tool is the material of which it is made. Some stone is entirely unsuited for knapping, and different kinds of stone are good for different purposes. Obsidian can be used for extremely sharp edges and fine pressure flaking, but is rather fragile. Basalt is tough, hard to flake, and rather grainy, so basalt edges are not as sharp, and fine pressure flaking usually cannot be done. It is not uncommon to find different materials used for different kinds of tools (Beck and Jones 1990). For instance, at Lizard Man Village in Arizona (Kamp and Whittaker 1990), basalt was used for choppers, scrapers, and a few flake tools, while most of the projectile points were of obsidian.

2. *Technology.* The available technology limits the kind of tools that can be made. Technology, as I use the term, also includes knowledge and the ability to use techniques and tools. When you first begin knapping, you cannot make a flat biface, even if the material would allow it. Different cultures use different technologies to solve their problems, and differing technology serves as a marker through time, also distinguishing different groups of people at the same time.

3. *Function.* The intended use of a stone tool will influence its shape. A projectile point must penetrate skin and flesh, so it will be sharp. It will need to be hafted to the spear or arrow, so the base may be notched or narrowed. Functional needs limit the form of a tool. A square wheel may look cute in a cartoon, but it won't work.

4. *Style.* Even given the limitations of material, technology, and function, there are usually a number of different ways to make a tool that will do the same thing. You can make your projectile point triangular or oval, notched or unnotched, roughly shaped or carefully finished, wide or narrow, and still bring down the game. Style is usually considered by archaeologists to be the variation that is not explainable by material, technology, or function (Close 1978; Stiles 1979). For instance, it is assumed that the projectile points from two different areas or two different times differ largely because each culture used its own

style, learned by knappers, and passed on to those they taught. Within a culture, there is variation because each individual differs in his or her ability and preferences.

Given these four major influences on the form of stone tools, let us discuss in more detail how archaeologists can examine material, technology, function, and style in stone tools to tell us about the life of prehistoric people.

ANALYZING STONE TOOL MATERIALS

We have discussed the qualities of different materials and some other considerations at length in Chapters 2 and 4. The practical concerns of material quality and availability were important to prehistoric people as well, and they took considerable pains to obtain suitable stone. If the archaeologist can identify prehistoric stone sources and their products, it is possible to say something about patterns of trade or movement.

In some cases identifying material sources is easy. Some materials are so distinctive in color, pattern, or other qualities that they can be readily recognized. For instance, a number of large bifaces made of a distinctive banded brown chert were found in several widely separated sites in Arizona and one in New Mexico. No local sources of the chert could be found, and it eventually proved to be "Tiger Chert" from southern Wyoming. The presence of large bifaces of Wyoming chert in Arizona suggests that they were part of the widespread exchange of exotic goods typical of the Puebloan Southwest, and documents some kind of contact with an area far to the north of most Pueblo interaction (Whittaker, Ferg, and Speth 1988).

Most often, material sources are not so easy to identify by sight because there is a great range of variation in the stone at any one source and because many widely exchanged materials come from a number of sources whose materials look quite similar. The classic example is obsidian. In many parts of the world the demand for high-quality obsidian spread the material for hundreds of miles around its sources. Although some obsidian is visually distinctive, often there are a number of volcanic sources in a region that produced very similar obsidians, yet were used at different times and in different ways. However, obsidians that look alike but come from different volcanic flows usually differ in their chemical composition. This is usually a matter of differences in trace elements, which can be detected by a number of sophisticated techniques such as optical emission spectroscopy, X-ray fluorescence spectrometry, and neutron activation analysis. Information on the physics and chemistry of trace-element analyses and their archaeological uses can be found in general texts (e.g., Renfrew and Bahn 1991; Thomas 1989) and more specific sources (e.g., Goffer 1980; Harbottle 1982;

Henderson 1989; Parkes 1987; Taylor 1976). For our purposes, it is enough to know that by comparing archaeological specimens to samples from known obsidian sources, it is possible to tell where the material of a flake or point originated.

One of the first important trace-element studies of lithic sources dealt with obsidian exchange in the Aegean and Mediterranean regions (Cann, Dixon, and Renfrew 1970; Dixon, Cann, and Renfrew 1968; Renfrew, Cann, and Dixon 1968; Shelford et al. 1982; Torrence 1986). In the Aegean, almost all of the obsidian used by the Neolithic and Bronze Age cultures of Greece, Crete, and western Asia Minor (the region of Troy) came from outcrops on the island of Melos, between Greece and Crete. This finding was important for a number of reasons. It showed that people throughout this wide region were interacting and involved in large regional economic networks. Obsidian preserves well and is easily recognized by archaeologists, and widespread occurrences of imported obsidian in sites implies that other, more perishable goods were being traded in the other direction. The exploitation and exchange of obsidian from Melos began early and persisted for thousands of years, despite probable periodic disruptions as cities rose and fell, populations moved, and volcanic eruptions, wars, famines, and other catastrophes affected the region.

Renfrew's work with obsidian in the Mediterranean and Anatolia ultimately led him to formulate useful mathematical models of exchange (Renfrew 1977; Renfrew and Bahn 1991). If one plots the percentages of obsidian in stone tool assemblages, there is a zone of sites close to the source that have very high percentages of obsidian, but beyond a certain point, obsidian percentages decrease very rapidly as you get farther from the source, forming an exponential curve. What this seems to show is that the sites closest to the source had easy access to obsidian and probably obtained their own obsidian in large quantities. Sites outside this zone had to get their obsidian by exchange.

There are a number of ways exchange could take place. A good American capitalist might expect some sort of market system, with barter of one good for another, and prices set by supply and demand and by haggling between buyer and seller. In many ethnographic societies, much exchange takes place in the form of gifts and reciprocal obligations. For instance, a knapper from a source area might visit a friend, relative, or trading partner in a distant village and give that person a number of obsidian cores. Some time in the future, he expects that the friend will visit him, with a gift of more or less equal value, perhaps some resource to which the friend has access but the knapper does not, or perhaps an item obtained by exchange from a third, more distant connection. This kind of exchange is often in the context of some social event such as a feast, a religious celebration, a marriage, or the formalization of an alliance. Elite members of societies frequently exchanged valuable, exotic, and traceable goods that are of great archaeological interest, but small-scale exchange of ordinary goods was probably even more common.

Obsidian in the Aegean and Mediterranean was exchanged both as a basic flaked-tool material and as finely worked exotic valuables, carved as well as flaked. Whether it was exchanged by gift or barter, the expectation of Renfrew's model is that at each step in a chain of connections, some of the obsidian would be kept, used up, discarded, or otherwise taken out of the system. At the next most distant site, it would be worth more, less would be available, and less would enter the archaeological record.

Sometimes this ideal "fall-off" pattern, representing "down-the-line" exchange, is not found, alerting the archaeologist that the system might have been different. For instance, a large site at a distance from a source may have much higher percentages of obsidian than sites closer in. Here we expect some different mode of exchange—for instance, control of the source by the distant center or a special trade relationship with sites at the source that bypasses those in between.

Trace-element analyses and interpretations based on them are now common for archaeological obsidian. There are innumerable Mesoamerican examples from Teotihuacan (Charlton 1978; Clark 1986, 1987; Nelson et al. 1977; Spence 1967, 1981) and many other areas (e.g., Boksenbaum et al. 1987; Gaxiola and Clark 1989; Hammond 1976; Hester, Heizer, and Jack 1971; Johnson 1976; Moholy-Nagy and Nelson 1987; Pires-Ferreira 1976; Sheets et al. 1990; Stark et al. 1992). There are extensive literatures for the American Southwest (e.g., Baugh and Nelson 1987; Findlow and Bolognese 1980, 1982; Harry 1989; Schreiber and Breed 1971; Stevenson and Klimkiewicz 1990) and California (e.g., Ericson 1977a, 1977b, 1981; Ericson, Hagan, and Chesterman 1976; Hughes 1986; Jack 1976), to cite only a few. Trace-element source identifications have been useful with many other materials that are not used for flaked tools such as metals, turquoise, and pigments. They have even been tried for cherts and flints. There is so much variation within any one source of these sedimentary rocks, however, that source identifications of cherts and related rocks have been less successful, although occasionally useful (Griffiths and Woodman 1987; Luedtke 1978, 1979; Tobey 1986).

Obsidian is also one of a few nonorganic materials that can be directly dated (Ericson 1978, 1981; Ericson, MacKenzie and Berger 1976; Friedman and Long 1976; Friedman, Smith, and Clark 1970; Michels and Tsong 1980; Taylor 1976). Obsidian *hydrates*—that is, it absorbs water in minute amounts at a measurable rate. As water works into the obsidian, there are chemical changes, and a hydration rind forms at the surface of the obsidian. When a flake is removed, a fresh surface is exposed, and hydration begins again. If you cut a small section out of an obsidian tool or flake, grind it thin, and examine it microscopically, the depth of the hydration (usually only a few microns) can be measured. The rate of hydration is controlled by the chemical composition of the obsidian and the climatic conditions around it, primarily temperature. Tools made of obsidian from the same source and found in the same site can be put in temporal order by measuring the hydration rinds—all else being equal, the older pieces will have thicker hydration rinds. If you can correlate a sequence of hydration measurements with absolute dates from carbon-14, for instance, you can measure the rate of hydration—let us say one micron per 1,000 years—and date obsidian tools directly. Hydration rates have also been calculated in the laboratory by inducing hydration under artificially high temperature and pressure.

When obsidian hydration dating was developed in the 1960s, it was expected to become a fantastic new tool that would allow dating of the many sites that have obsidian tools but lack other datable material. As is often the case, further research showed that the factors influencing obsidian hydration, such as temperature, chemical composition, and so on, complicate matters considerably. As a result, obsidian hydration, in combination with trace-element sourcing, is useful but not the cure-all originally hoped. Attempts have been made to date chert artifacts by weathering rinds, but as in source determination, the variation even within a single nodule of chert is so great that there has been little success.

TECHNOLOGY AND WHAT IT TELLS US

So far, technology has been the focus of this book. Many of the works cited are experiments or other studies intended to help archaeologists interpret the technology used in stone tool production. Ideally, our understanding of stone tool technology can be used to interpret the artifacts we find as one small part of the human world of the past. I will use a simple example typical of some of the work done by myself and many others to illustrate several points.

In 1981 I conducted a small excavation project for the National Park Service in Wawona, the southern part of Yosemite National Park (Whittaker 1981). Like much of American archaeology these days, the project was made necessary by plans for development—in this case, a new sewage system for Wawona. I tested a number of sites in alternate sewage development locations, trying to disturb the sites as little as possible while recovering enough data to determine which ones should be avoided by development or excavated if need be to save the information. In addition, although some work had been done in the main

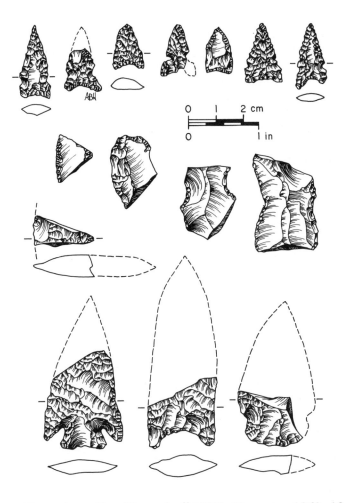

11.5
Obsidian tools from Wawona. *Top,* late arrow points. *Middle,* four small scrapers and a wedge-shaped fragment of a large biface. *Bottom,* three fragmentary early points.

Yosemite valley (Bennyhoff 1956; Fitzwater 1962, 1968a, 1968b; Moratto 1984:309–311), little was known about the Wawona valley, so I wanted to see if a similar cultural sequence was followed in both and to develop some preliminary ideas about what the prehistoric people were doing in Yosemite.

The sites in Wawona mostly consist of a *midden*—that is, an area of trash deposits, often with a few bedrock mortars. The mortars are simple cups pounded into boulders and bedrock, and were used for processing the staple food of the area, acorns. With a crew of four Miwok teenagers (who happen to be descendants of the prehistoric inhabitants), I excavated small test pits in a number of sites, screening all the deposits through ⅛-inch mesh to recover small artifacts and collecting samples of soil to be analyzed for pollen and charred plant remains that could provide information about the past climate and human diet.

Bone was not preserved in the Wawona sites, and with few exceptions, only stone artifacts were recovered.

Four 1-by-2-meter excavation units produced over 10,000 flakes, of which all but 53 were obsidian. Of 190 retouched tools, most were small obsidian flake scrapers, with a few projectile points and fragments (Figure 11.5). Most of the points were the small triangular forms known as Desert Side-notched and Cottonwood Triangular (unnotched) points. From other work we know that these would have been in use in the Wawona area from about A.D. 1350 until the Miwok were driven out in the mid-1800s. They appear earlier to the east, in Great Basin sites like Gatecliff Shelter (see Figure 11.4). The larger points in lower levels of the sites can be related to earlier occupations of the Sierra Nevada and also have Great Basin affinities.

Analyzing 10,000 flakes is a laborious job, but necessary to confirm or deny the vague impressions formed by casual observation. The flakes were sorted into size categories of less than 1 centimeter, 1–2 centimeters, and greater than 2 centimeters. Within these categories they were sorted again by material (almost all obsidian), whether or not they had cortex, and technological category (biface thinning flake, hard-hammer flake, or unidentifiable flake). Most of the flakes were small, none larger than 5 centimeters (2 in.) in maximum dimension. Only 25 percent were larger than 1 centimeter, and only 1.6 percent were larger than 2 centimeters. Less than 4 percent of the flakes had cortex on the exterior surface. None of this is surprising when we consider the source of the material. There are no obsidian sources in Yosemite, and although we were unable in this study to pinpoint specific sources, we know that most of the obsidian was being carried over the Sierra Nevada mountains from several sources in the Great Basin to the east of Yosemite. If you are going to carry stones over mountains on your back, you want to reduce the weight, and the prehistoric knappers were flaking off the useless cortex at the quarry area. Quarries in the Great Basin sources do in fact contain lots of large flakes, cores, and cortical material (Singer and Ericson 1977).

Of the flakes larger than 1 centimeter, 79 percent were biface thinning flakes. We have discussed the difference between biface thinning flakes and flakes struck off an ordinary core in Chapter 8. A number of formal experiments as well as knapping experience allow us to distinguish them with a fair degree of confidence, and it was readily apparent that the people in Wawona were making lots of bifaces. As a standard of comparison to illustrate my interpretations, I flaked three bifacial points using obsidian from the source and antler tools. One was a Desert Side-notched point made by pressure flaking a biface thinning flake, the second a large point made entirely by pressure flaking, and the third a large point flaked with an antler hammer and finished by pressure. Figure 11.6 shows the results of replicating the Desert Side-notched point. On the left is a handful of representative obsidian debitage from site 4-MRP-343. On the right is a Desert Side-notched point from the same site. In the center is the replicated point and its debitage. The lower flakes did not pass through a ⅛-inch screen and would have been recovered archaeologically. The small box contains the rest—dust and tiny flakes.

Although the prehistoric flakes from Wawona were small, they were still too large to be just the waste from pressure flaking. Only percussion-flaked points, like my third point, produced the right kind of flakes. Some of the biface thinning flakes in Wawona sites could thus have come from the production of the larger earlier points, but they were just as common in the later levels, when small triangular points had replaced the earlier forms. The Wawona people had to have been making something larger too. In addition to the flakes, the only evidence of larger bifaces were a few tiny pieces like the wedge-shaped fragment illustrated in Figure 11.5.

Analyzing the debitage at Wawona thus showed that relatively large bifaces, which were not being found in the excavation, were being worked there. Large, rough bifaces (Stage 1 or 2 in Chapter 8) are a common product at prehistoric stone quarries and are in fact sometimes called "quarry blanks." They are an ideal form for transporting material, because by the time material has been worked into thick bifaces, most of the cortical waste has been removed and flawed pieces discarded, but the rough biface can still be worked into a number of forms, and the flakes that are removed in doing so are still large enough to use as tools or to make into smaller bifaces such as Desert Side-notched points. If the Wawona people were receiving large bifaces from the quarries across the mountains and working them in Wawona, we ought to see these bifaces elsewhere, even if they did not turn up in Wawona. In fact we do. Beside the evidence for the beginning stages of biface manufacture at the quarries (Figure 11.7), caches of bifaces are occasionally found in the mountain passes of Yosemite, over which the traders or knappers would have passed to and from the quarries. A few of them put down their load of bifaces and never returned. Their reasons are lost to us, although we can imagine hazards such as early blizzards, bears, and accidents along the trail. Other bifaces, usually more refined, are sometimes found in sites in the foothills below Wawona, where bifaces 10 to 20 centimeters long sometimes appear in burials (Moratto 1972). We know that in historic times some California Indians used large bifaces as objects of wealth, prestige, and ceremonial display (Kroeber 1905, 1925; Rust 1905).

The Wawona sites are probably a middle point along a route that took obsidian in the form of bifaces from the sources to distant con-

11.6
Archaeological and experimental points and debitage from Wawona.

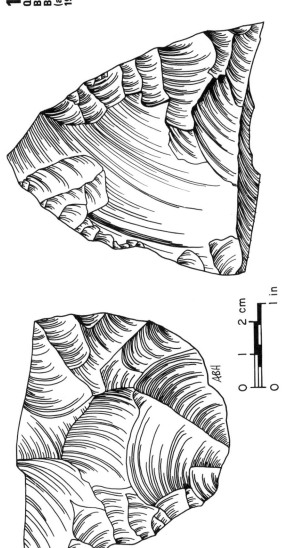

11.7
Quarry blanks from Mono Basin obsidian source at Bodie Hills, California (after Singer and Ericson 1977:179).

2 cm

1 in

sumers. Wawona is at an elevation too cold for comfort in winter, and the historic Miwok spent only summers there. In Wawona and other mountain villages they could hunt deer while avoiding the heat of the foothills where their main villages and acorn resources were. Wawona was also closer to the mountain passes and the Mono and Paiute groups who controlled the area around the obsidian sources. In historic times, there was a flourishing trade across the mountains, and Great Basin resources like obsidian and pinyon nuts moved west in exchange for Miwok products like acorns, as well as soapstone and shell which had been obtained from the coast (Barrett and Gifford 1933; Davis 1961; Heizer and Treganza 1944). This was surely the case in prehistory as well, so why did we not find any bifaces, only the waste flakes? Even the most skillful knappers are bound to break a biface now and again. Obsidian west of the mountains was an import, and expensive. Even broken bifaces could be worked down, and only the smallest pieces like the wedge illustrated were discarded. Even in the more important foothill villages, whole bifaces are usually found only when they were intentionally buried in graves, and most obsidian debitage is consistently small.

As this example shows, the technological analysis of stone tools, which is based on knowledge gained through knapping experiments, can be combined with other information to add a great deal to our picture of prehistoric folk. In this case, I relied heavily on waste flakes, a category of artifact that was usually ignored by most archaeologists until the 1960s and is still despised by some.

FIGURING OUT FUNCTION

Many of the type names used by Bordes and others have found their way into American archaeology. A large number of them imply some interpretation of the tool's use: scraper, handaxe, point, chopper, and so forth. In many cases these names were assigned a long time ago by prehistorians who had little real idea of what the tools were used for, but made a guess based on shape and context. Sometimes these are not bad guesses, but type names should be treated as convenient labels, not interpretations. To understand stone tools and the human lives they reflect, we would like to know how they were actually used, and there are four basic ways archaeologists approach this problem.

Analogy

If I show you the stone tools in Figure 11.8, you will immediately identify them as arrowheads. If you are inclined to be cautious, you may prefer to call them projectile points, which lets you be less specific about how you think they were hafted and used. In either case, your identification is based on *analogy,* comparing the new stone tool to

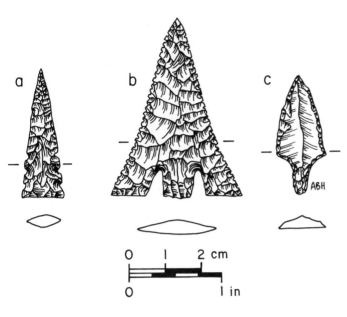

11.8
Typical "arrowheads" from three continents:
(a) Sinagua, Fortress Hills Pueblo, Arizona, ca. A.D. 1200, obsidian; (b) Early Bronze Age, France, John Whittaker replica; (c) Neolithic Palestine, chert.

something you have seen before. All archaeological interpretation, and indeed most human understanding of anything new, is based on interpreting it by comparison to what we have already experienced (Ascher 1961). In the case of a stone projectile point, most people are familiar with arrowheads from such sources as books, museums, and movies. These in turn probably used ethnographic observations as a source for their illustrations, identifications, or imitations. There was a time when American Indians still used stone-tipped arrows, and there are eyewitness accounts and specimens in collections. A modern steel arrow point is a somewhat more distant analogy, but it is still very similar, and some "common sense" analogy based on experience of what sharp edges and points are good for may also be involved.

The most direct kind of analogy for identifying the functions of archaeological stone tools is of course seeing similar tools in use by native peoples today. Unfortunately, our opportunities to do so are limited and decreasing all the time. There are now very few people who actually make and use stone tools as part of their technological systems, and none who rely wholly on them. Accordingly, we have to depend largely on historic accounts and museum collections for ethnographic analogies and turn to other means of interpreting archaeological materials.

Context
The context in which it is found is one of the most important sources of information about any artifact. If we find one of the arrow points in

Figure 11.8 jutting out of an animal bone, we consider that a good indication of its function. This too is an analogical interpretation; our past experience shows that stone tools do not grow out of bones but an arrow may penetrate a bone and remain in it. Contextual information is usually less dramatic and is built up by finding repeated patterns. The frequent association of handaxes with the bones of large mammals suggests that some handaxes were butchering tools. Artifacts may have multiple uses, which can be seen in different contexts. Arrow points found among the bones of bison trapped in a dry wash were used to kill the animals. The same stone tools may also be found with waste from making them, allowing us to interpret that context as a work area. Or a group of points may be included in a burial, where they can suggest offerings at the funeral of an important individual or personal possessions needed in the afterlife, a reflection of a culture's beliefs.

The need to interpret artifacts by contexts, and contexts and their human meanings by the artifacts in them, explains the archaeologist's feelings about looters. Once an artifact is removed from its context, it is little more than an object, and the chance of interpreting the context itself and thus learning something about people in the past is lost. Collectors have a place in archaeology if they preserve what would otherwise be destroyed, collect only from already disturbed contexts, and record the circumstances of their finds. Looters who dig into sites, destroying them to find objects for sale or collection, are thieves who steal from all of us our chance to learn about the past. Archaeological excavation of course also destroys the contexts it works with; excavation is only acceptable when it is done correctly and when the information is recorded, interpreted, and made available to others.

Experiment

Another way to look at the use of a stone tool is to try it yourself. Experimentation has an important limit. It does not tell you how a particular prehistoric tool *was* used; it tells you only how it *could have been* used and identifies situations in which it will not work. If you take a handaxe and try to chop down a tree, your fingers will probably come off before the tree falls, and you will conclude that a handaxe was not for felling trees, at least not when held in the hand. You can, however, cut up a large animal with it and demonstrate one possible use for such tools. If you do many experiments, in the end you will have a list of things you can do with a handaxe and a list of things that do not work, but there will be other things you have not tried and ways to use a handaxe that you did not test adequately, perhaps because you were not strong enough or held it incorrectly. After all, few of us have as many years of experience using stone tools as some of our ancestors.

None of this tells you precisely how a particular handaxe excavated from your most recent site was actually used. What you have done is produced a set of analogies; you can now say that tools like the one you have excavated work for cutting up elephants, but not for cutting down trees.

Too many flintknappers fail to understand the limits of experiments. Our knapping gives us a body of information that is very important in understanding how stone tools were made and used, but it never proves anything except negatives—for example, that dripping cold water on hot chert is not the way to make arrowheads. Occasionally a flintknapper will appear to claim that since he or she has duplicated a stone tool with a particular technique, that is how all similar stone tools were made. As many of the discussions throughout this book and your own experience will show, this is not correct. There are usually many ways of making the same tool, and it is often difficult if not impossible to decide which one was really used in a particular case.

Use-Wear

If you have tried using any of your stone tools, you have certainly created and probably noticed use-wear. When a stone tool cuts something hard, you can sometimes even see and hear small flakes being removed from the edge, but any use of a tool, even a steel tool, will eventually leave marks on it. In recent years archaeologists have realized that the marks on stone tools can be interpreted to shed light on how a particular tool was actually used. Shea (1992) gives a good recent overview.

Some forms of use-wear are fairly obvious and dramatic: we have already mentioned impact damage to projectile points (Figures 7.38, 7.41). Severe wear or damage may lead to visible changes to the form of an artifact, as discussed earlier. Projectile points damaged by impact may be reworked and end up much shorter than when they were first used. Dulled knives may be resharpened (Figure 11.9), and since the way to resharpen a flint tool is to flake a new edge, the tool is whittled down and gets smaller with each resharpening (Frison 1968; Luchterhand 1970).

Most use-wear is much less dramatic. Much of the damage to an edge is in the form of microflaking and scratches. These are sometimes visible to the naked eye, but more often a microscope is necessary to see and analyze them. Scratches and microflaking are visible at relatively low magnifications, and the early use-wear studies focused on such marks (Semenov 1973; Tringham et al. 1974). Scratches and microflaking sometimes indicate the direction in which a tool was moved while it was in contact with the material it was cutting. For instance, scratches parallel to the edge of a blade indicate a sawing motion,

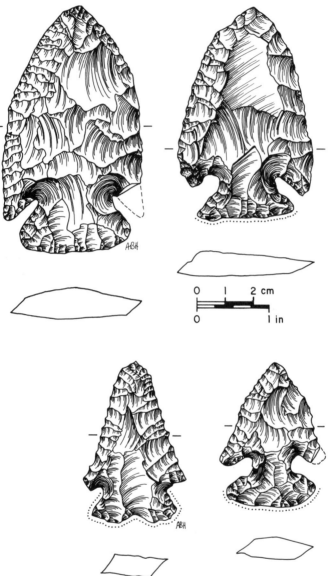

11.9
Four Early Archaic points from the Midwest. Edges beveled by unifacial resharpening are typical of tools used as knives. The four points show how repeated resharpening can change the size and shape of a tool. The two lower examples probably started out looking much like the upper pair. All are the same thickness, and the bases are all about the same size; only the blades were changed by resharpening. Dots indicate grinding on edges.

0   1   2 cm

0   1 in

while scratches perpendicular to the edge indicate a whittling or scraping motion (Figures 11.10–11.13).

The edge of a stone tool is also polished by use. *Sickle sheen,* a form of polish that is visible to the naked eye (Figures 11.12a, 11.14; see also Figure 3.13), has been recognized for a long time, and the earliest experimental studies of use-wear involved sickles (Curwen 1930, 1935; Spurrell 1892; Steensberg 1943). Sickle sheen results from the friction of the stone tool against the stalks of grasses like wheat and barley, which also contain silica. Exactly how it is produced is still a matter of debate; it appears to be both by abrasion of the stone tool and the addition of silica from the grain stalks (Anderson 1980; Unger-Hamilton 1989). Other polishes are visible only at high magnification, but they often differ according to the material being worked. For instance, wood is said to leave a bright polish on the high spots of the tool, while meat takes much longer to form a polish, which looks softer and duller. Because the meat is soft, polish appears in the depressions on the tool's surface as well as on the high spots (Keeley 1977, 1980). Polishes may also develop where a tool rubs against a haft or the hand that holds it (Figure 11.10).

Most recent use-wear studies follow Keeley in concentrating on polishes visible at high magnification, using either light or electron microscopes. This is often combined with information from more readily visible use damage and microscopic residues on tool edges (e.g., Anderson 1980; Cook and Dumont 1987; Hayden 1979; Vaughan 1985). Residues such as blood (Gurfinkel and Franklin 1988; Hyland and Anderson 1990; Hyland et al. 1990), which are detectable by chemical tests, are not really use-wear, but are a related kind of evidence and seem likely to be increasingly useful as new techniques for analyzing them are developed.

Although use-wear studies promise to give exact information on the use of tools, they are not without problems (Shea 1992). In the first place, they too rely on building up a body of analogy through experiment; we can only recognize sickle sheen for what it is because we have reproduced it by harvesting wheat with a stone sickle. Trampling, frost, chemical action in the soil, and other processes after deposition can destroy or obscure traces of wear. Some feel that there is a good deal of subjectivity and observer error in use-wear studies (McGuire et al. 1982; Newcomer, Grace, and Unger-Hamilton 1986, 1987), but the same can probably be said of any analysis of stone tools. More important, microscopic studies are not always practical. They often require complex and expensive equipment and experience in its use. Worse, they are extremely time-consuming. You have seen how much waste is produced by a few minutes of flaking. Imagine the plight of an ar-

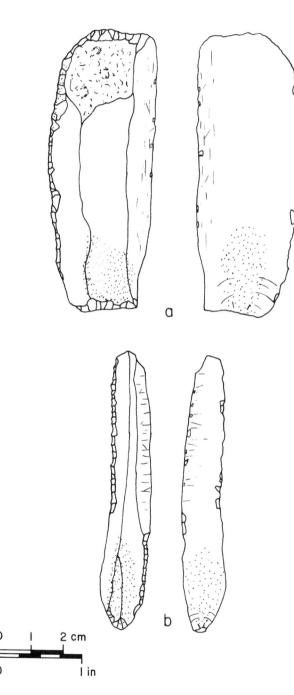

11.10
Idealized use-wear on a blade: (a) scratches parallel to edge and small irregular flakes off both faces indicate use with a sawing motion; (b) scratches perpendicular to edge and tiny stepped flakes off interior face indicate use as a knife—that is, slicing or whittling. The steep retouch along one edge forms a dull back, and the stippling indicates where polish from the finger grip would develop. All the use-wear shown here would be microscopic except some of the flakes.

a

b

0   1   2 cm

0   1 in

11.11

Sawing at leather held
between the teeth might
produce the striations
and polish shown in
Figure 11.10a. Drawing by
Carl Whittaker.

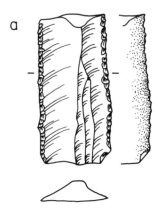

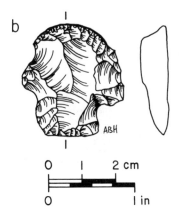

11.12

Idealized use-wear that
would be visible to the
naked eye: (a) sickle sheen
on a Bronze Age blade
(indicated by stippling);
(b) wear on a Woodland
hafted scraper from Iowa.
The edge has been rounded
and dulled, and tiny flakes
with step terminations have
been pulled off the upper
face of the edge.

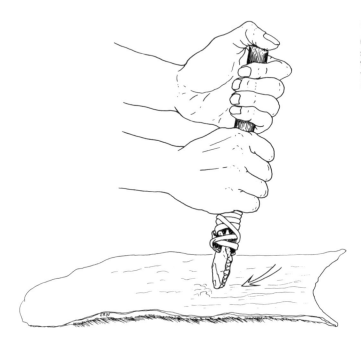

11.13
One way of using the scraper in Figure 11.12b that would produce the wear shown. Drawing by Carl Whittaker.

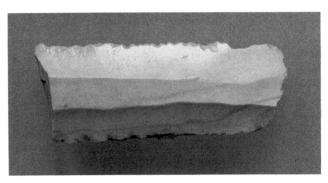

11.14
Sickle sheen on toothed edge of a flint blade, Tell el Hayyat, Jordan. Blade segment is 65 millimeters (2.6 in.) long.

chaeologist who wants to study the use-wear on stone tools from a site where there may be thousands of pieces. If microscopic examination takes fifteen to thirty minutes per tool, it is probably not possible to examine every flake. Should you look only at the retouched pieces, which were obviously modified for use, and ignore pieces where the naked eye can see nothing, knowing that many unmodified flakes were also tools? If you want to look at flakes, too, how many must you examine to get a good idea of what people were doing at the site? An intelligent and extensive sampling scheme is necessary. For these reasons, use-wear studies, although extremely useful for some purposes, are not as widely attempted as they might be.

QUESTIONS OF STYLE

Very few objects in the world around us are just objects without meaning. Humans cannot help assigning meanings to objects. These can be personal or shared throughout a culture. A monkey wrench is not just a lifeless tool. The particular monkey wrench in my tool box has a battered edge that always reminds me of the time I used it to crack open a promising nodule, only to find that it was almost unbreakable quartzite. It also resembles the trademark on a brand of oil, and the word "monkey wrench" is a widely used metaphor for destructive interference or, among environmental activists, for creative harassment of those who are destroying our natural environment. I do not mean to say that I enjoy deep philosophical reflections each time I open my tool box, but any object from a paper clip to a Clovis point, pens, swords, flags, books, buildings, cars, and wedding rings—all are part of a world of ideas and symbols as well as objects. We use them to mean things as well as to do things.

In ethnographic societies stone materials and tools made from them are also meaningful. In Australia a particular kind of stone may be preferred for points because the stone is associated with the spiritual power of the Ancestors, and this spiritual power is what makes the point deadly, as much as its sharp edges (Taçon 1991). Hard, sharp, cutting, penetrating stone tools may also be symbols of maleness, male powers, and male activities, and thus their possession and use can reflect a man's position in his society (Jones 1990; Jones and White 1988; Sharp 1952). If we reflect on the modern knapping world, dominated by men, we may suspect that American culture, as well as native Australian, considers stone and stone tools to be symbolically more male than female. It is the loss of this intangible world of meanings that saddens me when I examine stone tools as an archaeologist. Much of what was most important to the user of a tool is lost when he or she dies or a culture disappears. Nevertheless, some shreds of the meanings of artifacts are sometimes recoverable. The concept of style, as used by archaeologists, is usually involved in attempts to recover some of the simpler aspects of meaning from artifacts (see, for instance, Conkey and Hastorf 1990; Hodder 1987, 1989).

Often there are several ways to do the same task, and we make a choice between different tools or variations on the same tool that are functionally equivalent. A Volkswagen will get you to work as well as a Cadillac. If you are Amish, you may use a horse and buggy instead of a car. This kind of choice between different solutions to a problem is what archaeologists call style. Style in this sense reflects both personal decisions and the expectations of the culture around you, and stylistic choices are often very meaningful to the people who made them.

Returning to stone tools, we expect that each culture will define the "correct" tool for a job, and this makes possible the use of stone tools as cultural and temporal markers. The proper spear point for a hunter on the high plains 11,000 years ago was long and fluted, and someone who tried triangular notched points would probably have been considered odd. Nevertheless, people do experiment and eventually change established ways, and even within a norm there is often lots of room for individual variation, as we have seen with the small triangular points from Grasshopper (Figures 7.43, 7.44). Different ways of doing the same thing are also stylistic decisions. The unifacial resharpening of knives shown in Figure 11.9 also represents a choice: it would have been equally possible, although slightly less efficient, to resharpen the knives bifacially.

In recent years, archaeological examinations of style have increasingly focused on style as a message, a way of expressing social and individual identity (e.g., Hodder 1982; Weissner 1983; Wobst 1977). At my college, if you wear a suit and necktie every day, you are probably an older faculty member, or would like to be. You are expressing a particular identity, membership in a certain group of people. If you prefer more casual dress, you are associating yourself with a different part of your social world, including more of the younger faculty. Similarly, the southwestern Pueblos have always had distinctive styles of pottery decoration. They are well aware of each other's styles, and there is some copying and exchange of designs as well as trade of pots, but you can usually tell an Acoma pot from a Hopi pot, for instance.

Stylistic variation in artifacts such as pots and clothes can be intentionally manipulated to express social differences and group membership, but it is also a product of habit, learning from and imitating those around you. By the time you have achieved some skill in knapping, you will also have developed a personal style. When I knap with others, there are usually distinct differences in the areas of the debitage pile where different people sit. You can see the differences in what each knapper likes to make, average size of flakes, choice of materials, preference for soft hammer, hard hammer, or pressure, types of platform preparation, and so on. Some of your personal style will be copied from people you have learned from, such as whether you do percussion flaking on your leg or freehand. Harold Dibble and I, for instance, both worked with François Bordes before we had learned much knapping, and some of our techniques developed from what we learned from him. In spite of this and in spite of learning by working together, we prefer to make different kinds of artifacts and have slightly different approaches when we make the same things.

Stylistic differences that distinguish individuals and small social groups are very hard to deal with archaeologically, but a number of people have been trying (see Hill and Gunn 1977). The most common and successful archaeological studies have looked at small communities and tried to sort out social groups like families or clans on the basis of particular kinds of artifacts and pottery designs that cluster in different residential areas of the community (e.g., Hill 1970, 1977; Longacre 1970). As prehistoric artifacts go, stone tools are often rather simple. There is usually less room for decoration, elaboration, and stylistic choice than on a pot. This is why in regions with pretty painted pottery, like the American Southwest where I work, archaeologists have usually neglected the study of stone tools. Moreover, you rarely find archaeological sites with all the possessions of a family neatly preserved in the family's living quarters. In most sites, the bulk of the material is jumbled together, often having been discarded in trash areas, broken, poorly preserved, and separated from the places where artifacts were made, owned, and used.

If sorting out the artifacts of families and other small social groups is hard, distinguishing individuals is even harder. I could see the individual knapping areas in my debitage pile because I knew who sat where and what they usually did, but imagine trying to identify individuals from the same debitage after 700 years, with all the knappers dead and gone, and the pile disturbed and mixed by repeated uses, trampling, salvage, burial, rodent tunnels, and archaeological excavation. In spite of the difficulties, if we can identify individuals and recognize their work, we can sometimes trace patterns of exchange and learn how craft work was organized and controlled.

Again, I will use an example from Grasshopper Pueblo (Whittaker 1987a) to illustrate some of the problems involved in interpreting stone tools. If you are a glutton for punishment and want all the details, see my dissertation (Whittaker 1984). You are now familiar with the common small triangular projectile points made at Grasshopper, as was I after a summer on the field school staff. The arrow points looked like a good bet for trying to identify individual variation in stone tool manufacture. They are nicely made, with a considerable range of variability within the basic small triangular form. Material and technology are pretty much the same for all, and so is function since they were all probably arrow points, as there is not much else you can do with such small fragile bifaces. Accordingly, the differences in the points should be largely within the realm of style. It was of course possible that different kinds of points were used for different kinds of game—notched points for hunting deer and unnotched points for hunting bear, to make up an example. There could have been changes in preference through the one hundred years or so that the pueblo was occupied. It was never possible to answer these questions fully, but in the end it did not matter much, as I was able to work with sets of points that had been sorted out into groups by the prehistoric people themselves, groups that could be reasonably expected to be the work of different individuals.

More than six hundred burials have been excavated at Grasshopper (Whittlesey 1978). Of these, eleven have sets of 3 to 13 points. The points in each of these burials are all alike, and different from the points in any other burial. In addition, there was a single burial with 128 points that seemed to make a number of sets, a cache of 8 points, and two rooms with lots of points and debris from their manufacture.

Following others who have worked with individual variation in artifacts (e.g., Hardin 1977; Hill 1977; Muller 1977; Weissner 1983), I expected two sources of variation. One was intentional—expressions of individual preferences and identity, perhaps as a way of marking who made or owned an arrow. Knapper A might prefer red chert, Knapper B long narrow points, Knapper C points with no notches, and so on. These are the kind of descriptive characteristics that archaeologists often measure and discuss for projectile points anyway.

There is also a good deal of variability among individuals that they do not control and may not even notice. We all know that some knappers are skilled and others less so, some lazy and some careful. We also develop habits of holding tools and working that are likely to affect details of the final product. In particular, the way you hold a point and apply your pressure tool to it affects the angles and shape of the flake scars. If you flake as in Figure 11.15a, a right-handed knapper will tend to get a pattern with scars on the left edge running up toward the tip and scars on the right slanted down toward the base. This was the common pattern at Grasshopper. You can change your holding position (Figure 11.15b) and get the opposite pattern, but most knappers have consistent habits. Several people have worked with flake scar patterns and had some success in distinguishing work by modern knappers (Gunn 1975, 1977; Young and Bonnichsen 1984), so flake scar patterns seemed a good bet for distinguishing prehistoric knappers as well.

I used some fancy statistical techniques (it was a dissertation, after all) to confirm what my eyes told me—that the points in each set were very similar, and different from the points in other sets. The statistics worked equally well whether I used variation visible in things like length, width, thickness, and height and depth of the notches, or unconscious variation reflected in the angles of flake scars.

I then needed to show that known individuals would be distinguishable using the same kinds of data, so I found four knapper friends who would make points with me, and we each made several points using chert from Grasshopper and trying to copy a single point from one burial (Figure 11.16). In spite of the fact that we all tried to copy the same point, all our sets were distinctively different, and the same

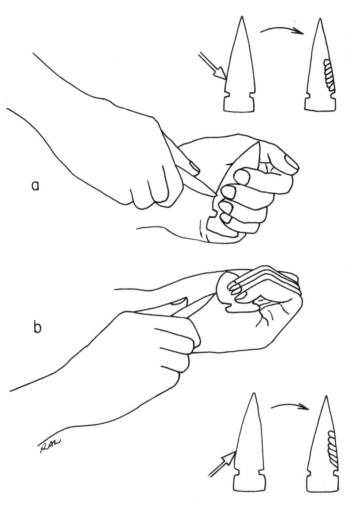

11.15
Two alternate holding positions for pressure flaking that produce opposite flake scar patterns: (a) my usual position, with wrist rotated and pressure applied downward; (b) alternate position with hand held flat and pressure applied horizontally across palm (base-to-tip on point), producing opposite pattern of scars.

statistics that I used on the prehistoric sets worked on the modern ones. Evidently, there is variation not just in habits of knapping, but in how we see artifacts and what feels "right" to us when we attempt to copy something. As a result, even the features like length and notch size that we think we control are often varied unconsciously. In any case, my ability to separate modern knappers by the same means as prehistoric point sets supported my argument that each set was the work of a different knapper.

What can we do with that information? Ideally, it would be possible to identify the work of a particular knapper in a burial and also in a room where points were made, or at least in the trash from one area of the pueblo. This did not prove possible, but I was able to look at three contexts with many points. One was a very rich burial (Burial 140),

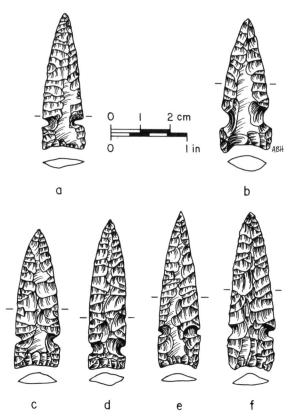

11.16
Individual variation in replicating a point: prehistoric model (a) and representative points by Caroline Wickham-Jones (b), John Whittaker (c), Peter McCartney (d), Bruce Huckell (e), and Harold Dibble (f).

0   1   2 cm

0   1 in

a

b

c   d   e   f

with several pots, shell jewelry, carved bone hairpins, and other goods, including 128 arrow points. Among the points in this burial I was able to distinguish eleven sets that tested statistically as well as the sets from individual burials. In addition there were six sets of only two or three points each (too few points for statistical tests), and some 45 points that could not be assigned to sets. This probably means that at least seventeen (and probably more like twenty-five to thirty) knappers contributed points to the grave of one very important individual. This is the closest we can come to a "census" of knappers at any one time. There is no way to say whether or not all the knappers in the pueblo contributed, but it provides a minimum estimate at least.

Burial 140 brings up another important question. What do the points in burials mean? All the point sets are with adult males who have lots of other goods buried with them. If they were just personal equipment, we would expect most of the men of the pueblo to have bows and arrows, but only a few men were buried with arrow sets. This is consistent with Grasshopper burial ritual; there are very few things that seem to be tool kits or utilitarian personal or household equipment. The most common burial offering by far was pottery, but even these were usually decorated wares, often special types, and almost never storage jars or used cooking pots. Other acceptable burial goods were mostly jewelry, ornaments, and small objects that appear to have ritual or social meaning. The points in burials are rarely broken or damaged by use, and most (although not all) are larger and more carefully flaked than most points from the site. This again suggests that they are not just part of a man's equipment. Some items of personal adornment like bone hairpins, shell bracelets, and turquoise earbobs may have been marks of rank or badges of membership in a social or ceremonial group (Reid and Whittlesey 1990). In modern pueblo burial ritual, things included with a burial usually symbolize the person's social position in some way (Ellis 1968). This is probably the best way to interpret the point sets—they were the equivalent of the sword owned by some modern Knights of Columbus, a sign of membership or status rather than a weapon.

Were they made by the man they were buried with? It is impossible to be sure, but probably not. Again, we can only look at the ethnographic pueblos and suggest that things may have been similar in prehistoric Grasshopper. Among the Hopi, it is not uncommon to hire someone with special skills to make goods for ceremonial or other occasions where extra quality is important (Beaglehole 1937). It is likely that the sets of points in Grasshopper burials were mostly made for burial, to symbolize something about the deceased.

Two other places in the site contained concentrations of points. Both were dumps of lithic debris and other trash in rooms, probably abandoned rooms where someone worked on the roof and dropped trash in through the entry hatch. Points from Room 28 have already been illustrated (Figures 7.34–7.37). Room 246 had a huge dump of lithic debris, including the bifaces shown earlier (Figures 8.31–8.34) and about 88 points. I tried the same kind of analysis on the points from these two rooms as on the burial sets. The 23 finished points (out of 93 points) from Room 28 are variable, but formed a consistent set in the statistical analyses and were probably made by one knapper. The 20 finished points from Room 246, however, were very diverse in shape and workmanship. This room was very large, with some special features and also a lot of ceremonial and ornamental items. It is probably best interpreted as a clan room, which in modern pueblos is a sort of headquarters for a group of related families where the senior woman of the clan often resides and where men perform some ceremonial activities and make and store the clan's ceremonial paraphernalia and other artifacts.

The fiercest arguments in Southwestern archaeology lately have been over what level of organization the large late pueblos reached. They may have been like historic pueblos with a relatively loose structure, a head chief and council drawn from the leading clans with many ceremonial and some leadership responsibilities, but little real authority and little control of wealth and power for their own benefit. This is the most usual opinion, but there have been many arguments lately that prehistoric pueblos were more complex, with more centralized political control and more powerful authorities who controlled large populations and were able to divert some of the wealth of the society for their own aggrandizement (e.g., Cordell and Plog 1979; Upham 1982). If this were the case, one of the things we would expect to see is centralized control of trade and manufacture and the development of craft specialists, which is why the ability to trace individual craftsmen may be useful.

At Grasshopper and other large prehistoric pueblos, there is little evidence of centralized economic control. We do not see much that can be interpreted as centralized storage areas, or large workshops for the production of trade goods, nor much evidence of specialized craftsmen.

My projectile point data do not help us look directly at the political structure, but we can begin to evaluate the possibility of specialists in stone tool manufacture. Being near unusually good chert sources, Grasshopper would be in a good position to export stone work, and of course a central authority could control the production of stone tools for local use as well. If there were specialist knappers, perhaps full-time craftsmen, we would expect relatively few knappers at any time, heavy use of a few workshop rooms but little lithic work elsewhere, and some degree of standardization of the stone tools being made (Becker 1973; Clark 1986, 1987; Evans 1978; Gibson 1982; Shafer and Hester 1983, 1986; Spence 1981; Torrence 1986). There is some subjective interpretation involved in all of this (how few is few?), and specialists can be full-time craftsmen who make their whole living through their craft or part-time experts like most of today's knappers.

If we look at Grasshopper Pueblo, the two rooms with evidence of point manufacture (out of over one hundred excavated) suggest special workshops. On the other hand, projectile points, both finished and unfinished, occur everywhere in the site. Rooms 28 and 246 simply happen to be the only two rooms so far with good evidence of knapping preserved in a single deposit. This is not surprising—most knapping debris would have been dumped away from living areas, as ethnographic knappers often do (Clark 1989, 1991; Clark and Kurashina 1981).

Room 246 contained the work of several individuals, making points of different forms and qualities. The knapper in Room 28 could be a specialist, but his points are only average in quality, and there is no sign of standardization, except in the use of a consistent sequence of work and a fairly consistent form. If points were made by specialists, we might expect high quality, although I can think of lots of exceptions to that in the modern world. Throughout the site there is lots of variation in form and quality of work—from points of amazing delicacy that represent an hour or more of careful labor, to the usual mediocre points like those in Room 28, to those made by klutzes or beginners. It is very difficult to rate the quality of artifacts when we do not know the motivations of the maker—a knapper capable of superb work may make a mediocre point instead of a work of art if he just wants something to bring down a deer. Nevertheless, at Grasshopper it looks as if there were many knappers, at many levels of skill, rather than a few skilled specialists. There is no reason to think that things were different from the modern pueblos, where everyone could be described as a competent generalist (Beaglehole 1937), with a few people whose outstanding talents could be called on for special occasions such as burials.

I want to make one other point while on this subject. The individuals buried with point sets at Grasshopper were all males, but I do not want to imply that all the knappers there were men. Points are consistently associated with male burials, and in most ethnographic societies, men do most of the hunting and maintain the equipment for it. Points at Grasshopper were probably made by men and may have had a symbolic connection to maleness and male activity. However, archaeologists have a strong tendency to see all stone tools and knapping as male craft, although there is usually little or no direct evidence one way or another. This is partly because the most complex and interesting stone tools are often used in hunting and processing game and partly because most ethnographic accounts of knapping are of male knappers. However, much of all early ethnography, and the accounts of knapping in particular, are by male observers, who often had better access to male informants and more interest in what men did in another culture. The fact that modern knapping, both as experiment and as craft, is almost completely dominated by men probably also biases our views.

There are in fact good reasons to expect that women in many societies made stone tools (Gero 1991). Modern female knappers and a few ethnographic accounts show that women are as capable as men. At Grasshopper, as elsewhere, women (and children, too) surely prepared food, butchered animals, scraped hides, cut leather, cleaned fibers, carved wood, and performed a thousand other activities that required stone tools. Most of the stone tools used at Grasshopper and all over the world were simple flakes. It makes little sense to have to go to a specialist when anyone can be taught to make flakes in a couple of hours. Even relatively complex tools like bifaces can be made by any normal person with a little training. Until we see large populations and complex social systems, it is unlikely that stone tools were the domain of specialists. A few common tools like prismatic blades (Clark 1987) or later metal knives may be most economically produced and distributed by specialists, but even then many simpler stone tools continued to be made and used by much of the population.

CONCLUSIONS

Many lines of evidence must be pulled together to understand stone tools and ultimately the past lives of the people who made and used them. This brief discussion only introduces a complex subject, and there are almost as many approaches as there are archaeologists. I have tried to give a few typical examples with which I am familiar to demonstrate some of the kinds of things that can be learned from stone tools.

Unfortunately many of the reports of lithic analyses are technical and difficult, not much fun for even the most dedicated lithic lover. Some are given to jargon like "If flake manufacture was operative, remnants of this behavioral activity should be evident . . ." (Stafford 1980:264). In such reports stone tools appear to create themselves in a vacuum from which the people have vanished, leaving only disembodied abstracts of what they did, like the pure energy entities of Star Trek.

The other side of the coin exists, too, although it is rarer. For instance, Emma Lou Davis and Carol Panlaqui (1978:34) write, "Contents of the A bags from a stake were spread on the table and slowly inspected, turning each piece to all angles and holding it obliquely to the sunlight. It was a rapt study in which we established a mystical bond with these worn fragments. We used to talk to them like an Eskimo carver holding a block of ivory and searching for its *inua*, its spirit. 'Who are you who dwells in there?' Through such absorbed, complete immersion, we began to see a host of new qualities so that the stone, a surrogate for a person, a Spirit, became a living entity in itself. In this way we participated in an experience far transcending mere sterile detail—a deeply enjoyable experience." This at least acknowledges that people were involved, but it does not leave you feeling that the real evidence of people was intelligently examined.

The archaeologists quoted above have done good work, and I have pulled passages out of context to make a point about what I think archaeology can and should be. We should be able to avoid the boring and inhuman abstractions of the first quote and still look carefully and scientifically at the evidence. We should also avoid the silly romanticism of "vibrational archaeology" and use real evidence to learn something about how people lived, worked, ate, thought, suffered, and rejoiced. Flintknapping and experiments with stone tools give us some of the knowledge necessary to interpret prehistoric artifacts and use them as evidence to see past ways of life. Knapping also provides insights through personal experience with an important craft. In the process of knapping we can feel our bonds with all people and by learning to use artifacts to understand the people who left them, we can explore both the world of the past and our own world and lives.

APPENDIX
RESOURCES FOR KNAPPERS

The following list was assembled from a number of sources and includes only some of the resources available in 1992. I have not included the many individuals who make and sell replicas and lithic art or primarily raw materials. They and much else can be found in advertisements in the newsletters listed below. I have included sources of instructional materials. Avoid the occasional ads that offer genuine prehistoric artifacts—buying from these people encourages the destruction of archaeological sites.

This list is intended to be helpful to the beginning knapper, and I have made a few comments on some entries, but this is not advertising, and I accept no responsibility for any results of contacting the people and organizations listed. The knap-ins listed are those advertised in 1991–1992 and may not all be continued.

COMMERCIAL SOURCES
OF KNAPPING MATERIAL

H and R Castings
Milford Hanson and
Richard Roemmich
P.O. Box 3076
Cody, Wyoming 82414
(casts of stone tools, mostly High
Plains and Paleo-Indian)

Lithic Casting Lab
Route 1, Box 102
Troy, Illinois 62294
(casts of Old and New World stone
tools, very high-quality, informative
catalog)

Mound Builder Arts and Trading
Company
D. C. Waldorf
P.O. Box 702
Branson, Missouri 65616
(replications, instructional materials,
edits the newsletter *Chips*)

Native Way
P.O. Box 159
Washington, Mississippi 39190
(replications, tools, raw materials,
bows and atlatls, instructional
materials)

Piltdown Productions
Errett Callahan
2 Fredonia Avenue
Lynchburg, Virginia 24503
(replicas and modern flintknapped
art, tools and raw material, instructional materials)

Jim Regan
23107 Erskin N.E.
Bethel, Minnesota 55005
(copper knapping tools)

NEWSLETTERS AND JOURNALS

Archaeology
Archaeological Institute of America
Subscription Service
P.O. Box 420423
Palm Coast, Florida 32142-0423
(readable archaeology by
professionals)

The Atlatl
World Atlatl Association
8800 State Hwy. 133
Carbondale, Colorado 81623

Bulletin of Primitive Technology
Society of Primitive Technology
P.O. Box 3226
Flagstaff, Arizona 86003
(good articles and illustrations of variety of early crafts, advertising, best
of the current periodicals)

Chips
D. C. and Val Waldorf, editors
P.O. Box 702
Branson, Missouri 65616
(flintknapping tips, news, advertis-
ing, announcements)

The Flint Knapper's Exchange
Chas. Spear
278 W. 8th St.
Peru, IN 46970
(very informal newsletter, advertising, announcements, tips, directory
of knappers)

Lithic Technology
Dr. George Odell, editor
Department of Anthropology
University of Tulsa`
Tulsa, Oklahoma 74104-3189
(lithic archaeology, published from
1972 to 1988, to be revived 1993)

The Platform
Gene Altiere, editor
712 Medical Arts Building
Duluth, Minnesota 55802
(regional newsletter, articles, and
tips)

EVENTS

Colorado Front Range Flintknapping
Workshop (June)
Fall Campout/Knap-in at Folsom
(September)
Contact: Bob Patten
888 Owens Ct.
Lakewood, Colorado 80226

Flint Ridge Knap-in (September)
Contact: Bob Geyer
8893 Raiders Run Rd.
Cincinnati, Ohio 45236
Contact: Mark Heisey
314 South Main St.
West Milton, Ohio 45383

Fort Osage, Missouri, Knap-in
(May, September)
Contact: Bob Hunt
2013 Stephanie Court
Blue Springs, Missouri 64014
Contact: Don Dreisoerner
2701 N.E. Owens School Rd.
Independence, Missouri 64050

Fort Robinson, Nebraska, Knap-in
(August)
Contact: Larry Waldron
52 Westview Ct.
Chadron, Nebraska 69337

Midwest Knap-in (June)
Contact: Larry Kinsella
Pleasant Ridge Park
Fairview Heights, Illinois 62208

Minnesota Knappers Guild Knap-in
(June)
Contact: Jim Regan
23107 Erskin N.E.
Bethel, Minnesota 55005

Northern Indiana Knap-in (April)
Contact: Larry Schieber
225 Colombia St.
Huntington, Indiana 46750
Contact: Dan Lincoln
1100E 3535S
Upland, Indiana 46989
Contact: Jeff Pigg
Rt. 3, Box 99A
Peru, Indiana 46970

Old Stone Fort, Tennessee, Knap-in (May)
Contact: Ward Weems, Superintendent
Old Stone Fort Archaeological Area
Rt. 7, Box 7400
Manchester, Tennessee 37355

Rabbitstick Rendezvous (September)
Contact: Boulder Outdoor Survival School
P.O. Box 3226
Flagstaff, Arizona 86003

Rocky Hollow/Killeen/Maxdale, Texas, Knap-in (March, August)
Contact: Dave Crawford
P.O. Box 10235
Killeen, Texas 76547

Scheile Museum Knap-in (August)
Contact: Steve Watts
Gastonia, North Carolina

REFERENCES

Addington, Lucile R.
   1986   *Lithic Illustration: Drawing Flaked Stone Artifacts for Publication.*
   Chicago: University of Chicago Press.
Ahler, Stanley
   1971   *Projectile Point Form and Function at Rodgers Shelter, Missouri.*
   Missouri Archaeological Society Research Series no. 8. Columbia: Missouri Archaeological Society.
   1983   Heat Treatment of Knife River Flint. *Lithic Technology* 12(1):1−8.
Akerman, Kim, and John L. Fagan
   1986   Fluting the Lindenmeier Folsom: A Simple and Economical Solution
   to the Problem, and Its Implications for Other Fluted Point Technologies.
   Lithic Technology 15(1):1−8.
Aldred, Cyril
   1965   *Egypt to the End of the Old Kingdom.* New York: McGraw-Hill.
Anderson, Patricia C.
   1979   A Microwear Analysis of Selected Flint Artifacts from the Mousterian of Southern France. *Lithic Technology* 9:32.
   1980   A Testimony of Prehistoric Tasks: Diagnostic Residues on Stone
   Tool Working Edges. *World Archaeology* 12(2):181−194.
Andrefsky, William, Jr.
   1986   A Consideration of Blade and Flake Curvature. *Lithic Technology*
   15(2):48−54.
Angier, Bradford
   1962   *How To Stay Alive in the Woods.* New York: Macmillan.
Ardrey, Robert
   1961   *African Genesis.* New York: Atheneum.
Arnold, Jeanne E.
   1985   The Santa Barbara Channel Islands Bladelet Industry. *Lithic Tech-
   nology* 14(2):71−80.
   1987   Technology and Economy: Microblade Core Production from the
   Channel Islands. In *The Organization of Core Technology,* edited by
   J. K. Johnson and C. A. Morrow, pp. 207−238. Boulder: Westview Press.
Ascher, Robert
   1961   Analogy in Archaeological Interpretation. *Southwestern Journal of
   Anthropology* 17:317−325.
Austin, Robert J.
   1986   The Experimental Reproduction and Archaeological Occurrence of
   Biface Notching Flakes. *Lithic Technology* 15(3):96−101.
Avery, B. P.
   1873   Chips from an Indian Workshop. *Overland Monthly* 2(6):489−493.
   Reprinted in R. F. Heizer and A. B. Elsasser, *Some Archaeological Sites
   and Cultures of the Central Sierra Nevada,* Appendix C. *University of
   California Archaeological Survey Reports* 21. Berkeley: University of
   California, 1953.

Balfour, Henry
  1903   On the Methods Employed by the Natives of N.W. Australia in the
          Manufacture of Glass Spear-heads. *Man* 3(35):65, Plate E.
Banks, Larry D.
  1990   *From Mountain Peaks to Alligator Stomachs: A Review of Lithic
          Sources in the Trans-Mississippi South, the Southern Plains, and Adja-
          cent Southwest.* Norman: University of Oklahoma.
Barbieri, Joseph A.
  1937   Technique of the Implements from Lake Mohave. *Southwest Mu-
          seum Papers* 11:99–107.
Barrett, S. A., and E. W. Gifford
  1933   Miwok Material Culture. *Milwaukee Public Museum Bulletin*
          2(4):119–377. Reprint. Yosemite National Park: Yosemite National His-
          tory Association [1978].
Barton, R. N. E., and C. A. Bergman
  1982   Hunters at Hengistbury: Some Evidence from Experimental Archae-
          ology. *World Archaeology* 14(2):237–248.
Baugh, Timothy G., and Fred W. Nelson, Jr.
  1987   New Mexico Obsidian Sources and Exchange on the Southern
          Plains. *Journal of Field Archaeology* 14(3):313–329.
Baumhoff, Martin A., and J. S. Byrne
  1958   *Desert Side-Notched Points as a Time Marker in California.* Uni-
          versity of California Archaeological Survey Reports 42. Berkeley: Uni-
          versity of California.
Beaglehole, Ernest
  1937   *Notes on Hopi Economic Life.* Yale University Publications in An-
          thropology, no. 15. New Haven: Yale University Press.
Beck, Charlotte, and George T. Jones
  1990   Toolstone Selection and Lithic Technology in Early Great Basin Pre-
          history. *Journal of Field Archaeology* 17(3):283–299.
Becker, Marshall J.
  1973   Archaeological Evidence for Occupational Specialization among
          Classic Period Maya at Tikal, Guatemala. *American Antiquity* 38(4):
          396–406.
Bell, Robert E.
  1960   *Guide to the Identification of Certain American Indian Projectile
          Points.* Special Bulletin no. 2. Oklahoma City: Oklahoma Anthropologi-
          cal Society.
Bennyhoff, James A.
  1956   *An Appraisal of the Archaeological Resources of Yosemite National
          Park.* University of California Archaeological Survey Reports 34. Berke-
          ley: University of California.
Benson, Michael P.
  1980   A Prehistoric Subsistence Kit from Castle Valley, Utah. *Flintknap-
          pers' Exchange* 3(1):6–15.
Bergman, C. A., and M. H. Newcomer
  1983   Flint Arrowhead Breakage: Examples from Ksar Akil, Lebanon. *Jour-
          nal of Field Archaeology* 10(2):238–243.
Biagi, Paulo, and Mauro Cremaschi
  1991   The Harappan Flint Quarries of the Rohri Hills (Sind-Pakistan). *An-
          tiquity* 65(246):97–102.

Binford, Lewis R.
　1981　*Bones: Ancient Men and Modern Myths.* New York: Academic Press.
　1983　*In Pursuit of the Past: Decoding the Archaeological Record.* London: Thames and Hudson.
　1986　An Alyawara Day: Making Men's Knives and Beyond. *American Antiquity* 51(3):547–562.
Binford, Lewis R., and Sally R. Binford
　1969　Stone Tools and Human Behavior. *Scientific American* 220(4): 70–84.
Blacking, John
　1953　Edward Simpson, alias 'Flint Jack': A Victorian Craftsman. *Antiquity* 27:207–211.
Blackman, E. E.
　1932　A Study in Chipping a Nebraska Flint Knife. *Nebraska History Magazine* 13(1):36–41.
Blinkenberg, Christopher
　1911　*The Thunderweapon in Religion and Folklore: A Study in Comparative Archaeology.* Cambridge: Cambridge University Press. Reprint. New Rochelle: Caratzas Publishing Co., 1987.
Blumenschine, Robert J., and John A. Cavallo
　1992　Scavenging and Human Evolution. *Scientific American* 267(4): 90–96.
Boksenbaum, Martin W., Paul Tolstoy, Garman Harbottle, Jerome Kimberlin, and Mary Neivens
　1987　Obsidian Industries and Cultural Evolution in the Basin of Mexico before 500 B.C. *Journal of Field Archaeology* 14(1):65–76.
Boldurian, Anthony T., George Agogino, Phillip H. Shelley, and Mark Slaughter
　1987　Folsom Biface Manufacture, Retooling, and Site Function at the Mitchell Locality of Blackwater Draw. *Plains Anthropologist* 32(117): 299–311.
Boldurian, Anthony T., Philip T. Fitzgibbons, and Phillip H. Shelley
　1985　Fluting Devices in the Folsom Tradition: Patterning in Debitage Formation and Projectile Point Basal Configuration. *Plains Anthropologist* 30(110pt1):293–303.
Boldurian, Anthony T., Philip T. Fitzgibbons, Phillip H. Shelley, and John L. Montgomery
　1986　A Reply to Sollberger and Patterson on Experimental Folsom Biface Manufacture. *Plains Anthropologist* 31(113):245–248.
Bonnichsen, Robson, and Karen L. Turnmire (editors)
　1991　*Clovis: Origins and Adaptations.* Corvallis: Center for the Study of the First Americans.
Bordaz, Jacques
　1965　The Threshing Sledge. *Natural History* 74(4):26–29.
　1969　Flint Flaking in Turkey. *Natural History* 78(2):73–77.
　1970　*Tools of the Old and New Stone Age.* Garden City: Natural History Press.
Bordes, François
　1947　Étude Comparative des Differentes Techniques de Taille du Silex et des Roches Dures. *L'Anthropologie* 51:1–29.

1961   *Typologie du Paléolithique Ancien et Moyen.* Publications de l'Institut de Prehistoire de l'Université de Bordeaux. Memoire 1. Bordeaux: Imprimeries Delmas.

1972   *A Tale of Two Caves.* New York: Harper and Row.

Bordes, François, and Don Crabtree
  1969   The Corbiac Blade Technique and Other Experiments. *Tebiwa* 12(2):1–21.

Bosch, P. W.
  1979   A Neolithic Flint Mine. *Scientific American* 240(4):126–132.

Bourke, John G.
  1890   Vesper Hours of the Stone Age. *American Anthropologist,* o.s. 3:55–63.
  1891   Remarks, on Arrows and Arrow-makers. *American Anthropologist,* o.s. 4:71–74.

Bradley, Bruce A.
  1972   Predynastic Egyptian Flint Implements—An Inductive Technological Sequence. *Newsletter of Lithic Technology* 1(3):2–5.
  1974   Comments on the Lithic Technology of the Casper Site Materials. In *The Casper Site,* edited by G. Frison, pp. 191–197. New York: Academic Press.
  1975   Lithic Reduction Sequences: A Glossary and Discussion. In *Lithic Technology: Making and Using Stone Tools,* edited by Earl Swanson, pp. 5–14. The Hague: Mouton.
  1978   Hard Hammer—Soft Hammer: An Alternate Explanation. *Flintknappers' Exchange* 1(2):8–10.

Brew, J. O.
  1946   The Use and Abuse of Taxonomy. In *Archaeology of Alkali Ridge, Southeastern Utah. Papers of the Peabody Museum of American Archaeology and Ethnology* 21:44–66. Cambridge: Harvard University Press.

Brézillon, M.
  1968   *La Dénomination des Objets de Pierre Taillée: Matériaux pour un Vocabulaire des Préhistoriens de Langue Française. Gallia Préhistoire,* suppl. 4. Paris: Centre National de la Recherche Scientifique.

Browne, Jim
  1940   Projectile Points. *American Antiquity* 5(3):209–213.

Brundage, Burr Cartwright
  1979   *The Fifth Sun: Aztec Gods, Aztec World.* Austin: University of Texas Press.

Buck, Bruce A.
  1982   Ancient Technology in Contemporary Surgery. *Western Journal of Medicine* 136:265–269.

Burling, Robbins
  1964   Cognition and Componential Analysis: God's Truth or Hocus-Pocus? *American Anthropologist* 66:20–28.

Butler, B. M., and E. E. May (editors)
  1984   *Prehistoric Chert Exploitation: Studies from the Midcontinent.* Occasional Papers no. 2. Carbondale: Center for Archaeological Investigations, Southern Illinois University.

Butler, William B.
  1975   The Atlatl: The Physics of Function and Performance. *Plains Anthropologist* 20(68):105–110.

1977   Atlatl Functions, Fancy, Flex, and Fun: A Reply to Howard. *Plains Anthropologist* 22(76pt1):161–162.

Cabrol, A., and L. Coutier
1931   L'utilisation du Bois en Guise de Percuteur pour Tailler la Pierre. *Bulletin de la Société Préhistorique Française* 28:170.

Callahan, Errett
1979a   The Basics of Biface Knapping in the Eastern Fluted Point Tradition: A Manual for Flintknappers and Lithic Analysts. *Archaeology of Eastern North America* 7(1):1–180.
1979b   Comments on Patten's Analysis of the Clovis from Clovis. *Flintknappers' Exchange* 2(3):17.
1981   Danish Dagger A-10198. *Flintknappers' Exchange* 4(2):11–14.
1985   *Flintknapping Flash Cards: Pressure Flaking of Flakes.* Lynchburg: Piltdown Productions.

Campbell, Bernard G.
1985   *Humankind Emerging.* 4th ed. Boston: Little, Brown, and Company.

Cann, J. R., J. E. Dixon, and Colin Renfrew
1970   Obsidian Analysis and the Obsidian Trade. In *Science in Archaeology,* edited by D. Brothwell and E. Higgs, pp. 578–591. New York: Praeger.

Caton-Thompson, G., and E. W. Gardner
1934   *The Desert Fayum.* London: Royal Anthropological Institute of Great Britain and Ireland.

Charlton, T. H.
1978   Teotihuacan, Tepeapulco, and Obsidian Exploitation. *Science* 200:1227–1236.

Chase, Philip G.
1985   Illustrating Lithic Artifacts: Information for Scientific Illustration. *Lithic Technology* 14(2):57–70.
1986   Relationships between Mousterian Lithic and Faunal Assemblages at Combe-Grenal. *Current Anthropology* 27:69–71.

Clark, Grahame
1975   *The Earlier Stone Age Settlement of Scandinavia.* Cambridge: Cambridge University Press.

Clark, J. Desmond, and Hiro Kurashina
1981   A Study of the Work of a Modern Tanner in Ethiopia and Its Relevance for Archaeological Interpretation. In *Modern Material Culture: The Archaeology of Us,* edited by R. Gould and M. Schiffer, pp. 303–321. New York: Academic Press.

Clark, John E.
1982   Manufacture of Mesoamerican Prismatic Blades: An Alternative Technique. *American Antiquity* 47(2):355–375.
1984   Counterflaking and the Manufacture of Mesoamerican Prismatic Blades. *Lithic Technology* 13(2):52–61.
1985   Platforms, Bits, Punches, and Vises: A Potpourri of Mesoamerican Blade Technology. *Lithic Technology* 14(1):1–15.
1986   From Mountains to Molehills: A Critical Review of Teotihuacan's Obsidian Industry. *Research in Economic Anthropology,* Supplement 2:23–74.
1987   Politics, Prismatic Blades, and Mesoamerican Civilization. In *The Organization of Core Technology,* edited by J. K. Johnson and C. A. Morrow, pp. 259–284. Boulder: Westview Press.

1989 La Technica de Talla de los Lacandones de Chiapas. In *La Obsidiana en Mesoamerica*, edited by M. Gaxiola and J. E. Clark, pp. 443–448. Mexico City: Instituto Nacional de Antropologia e Historia.

1991 Flintknapping and Debitage Disposal among the Lacandon Maya of Chiapas, Mexico. In *The Ethnoarchaeology of Refuse Disposal*, edited by E. Staski and L. D. Sutro, pp. 63–78. Arizona State University Anthropological Research Papers 42. Tempe: Arizona State University.

Clarke, David L.
1968 *Analytical Archaeology*. London: Methuen.

Clarke, Rainbird
1935 The Flint-Knapping Industry at Brandon. *Antiquity* 9:38–56.

Clewlow, C. William, Jr.
1967 Time and Space Relations of Some Great Basin Projectile Point Types. *University of California Archaeological Survey Reports* 70, pp. 141–149. Berkeley: University of California.

Close, Angela E.
1978 The Identification of Style in Lithic Artifacts. *World Archaeology* 10(2):223–236.

Coggins, Clemency Chase, and Orrin C. Shane III
1984 *Cenote of Sacrifice: Maya Treasures from the Sacred Well at Chichén Itzá*. Austin: University of Texas Press.

Cole, George S.
1972 The Bannerstone as a Spear Weight. *Michigan Archaeologist* 18(1):1–7.

Cole, Sonia
1970 *The Neolithic Revolution*. 5th ed. London: British Museum.

Coles, John
1973 *Archaeology by Experiment*. New York: Charles Scribner's Sons.
1979 *Experimental Archaeology*. New York: Academic Press.

Collins, Michael B.
1975 Lithic Technology as a Means of Processual Inference. In *Lithic Technology: Making and Using Stone Tools*, edited by E. Swanson, pp. 15–34. The Hague: Mouton.

Collins, Michael B., and Jason M. Fenwick
1974 Heat Treating of Chert: Methods of Interpretation and Their Application. *Plains Anthropologist* 19(64):134–144.

Conkey, Margaret, and Christine Hastorf (editors)
1990 *The Uses of Style in Archaeology*. Cambridge: Cambridge University Press.

Cook, Jill, and John Dumont
1987 The Development and Application of Microwear Analysis Since 1964. In *The Human Uses of Flint and Chert*, edited by G. Sieveking and M. Newcomer, pp. 53–62. Cambridge: Cambridge University Press.

Cordell, Linda S., and Fred Plog
1979 Escaping the Confines of Normative Thought: A Reevaluation of Puebloan Prehistory. *American Antiquity* 44(3):405–429.

Cosgrove, C. B.
1947 *Caves of the Upper Gila and Hueco Areas in New Mexico and Texas*. Papers of the Peabody Museum of American Archaeology and Ethnology 24(2). Cambridge: Harvard University Press.

Cotterell, B., B. Hayden, J. Kamminga, M. Kleindienst, R. Knudson, and

R. Lawrence
1979 The Ho Ho Classification and Nomenclature Committee Report. In *Lithic Use-Wear Analysis*, edited by B. Hayden, pp. 133–135. New York: Academic Press.

Cotterell, Brian, and Johan Kamminga
1979 The Mechanics of Flaking. In *Lithic Use-Wear Analysis*, edited by Brian Hayden, pp. 97–112. New York: Academic Press.
1987 The Formation of Flakes. *American Antiquity* 52(4):675–708.

Coutier, L.
1929 Experiences de Taille pour Rechercher les Anciennes Techniques Paléolithiques. *Bulletin de la Société Préhistorique Française* 26:172–174.

Crabtree, Don E.
1966 A Stoneworker's Approach to Analyzing and Replicating the Lindenmeier Folsom. *Tebiwa* 9(1):3–39.
1967a Notes on Experiments in Flintknapping: 3—The Flintknapper's Raw Materials. *Tebiwa* 10(1):8–24.
1967b Notes on Experiments in Flintknapping: 4—Tools Used for Making Flaked Stone Artifacts. *Tebiwa* 10(1):60–73.
1968 Mesoamerican Polyhedral Cores and Prismatic Blades. *American Antiquity* 33(4):446–478.
1970 Flaking Stone with Wooden Implements. *Science* 169:146–153.
1972a *An Introduction to Flintworking*. Occasional Papers no. 28. Pocatello: Idaho State University Museum.
1972b The Cone Fracture Principle and the Manufacture of Lithic Materials. *Tebiwa* 15(2):29–42.
1973a Experiments in Replicating Hohokam Points. *Tebiwa* 16(1):10–45.
1973b The Obtuse Angle as a Functional Edge. *Tebiwa* 16(1):46–53.
1974 Grinding and Smoothing of Stone Artifacts. *Tebiwa* 17(1):1–6.

Crabtree, Don E., and B. Robert Butler
1964 Notes on Experiments in Flint Knapping: 1—Heat Treatment of Silica Materials. *Tebiwa* 7(1):1–6.

Crabtree, Don, and Errett Callahan
1979 Craftsman: Don Crabtree. *Flintknappers' Exchange* 2(1):27–34; 2(2):8–13; 2(3):22–26.

Crabtree, Don E., and E. L. Davis
1968 Experimental Manufacture of Wooden Implements with Tools of Flaked Stone. *Science* 159:426–428.

Crabtree, Don, and Earl H. Swanson
1968 Edge-Ground Cobbles and Blade-Making in the Northwest. *Tebiwa* 11(2):50–54.

Curwen, E. Cecil
1930 Prehistoric Flint Sickles. *Antiquity* 4:179–186.
1935 Agriculture and the Flint Sickle in Palestine. *Antiquity* 9(33):62–66.

Cushing, Frank H.
1895 The Arrow. *American Anthropologist* 8(4):307–349.

Daniel, Glynn
1981 *A Short History of Archaeology*. London: Thames and Hudson.

Dart, Raymond A.
1967 *Adventures with the Missing Link*. Philadelphia: Institutes Press.

Davenport, J. Walker
1943 Some Experiments in the Use of the Atlatl. *Bulletin of the Texas Archaeological and Paleontological Society* 15:30–37.

Davis, Emma Lou, and Carol Panlaqui
  1978   Stone Tools, The Action Units. In *The Ancient Californians: Ran-cholabrean Hunters of the Mohave Lakes Country*, edited by Emma Lou Davis, pp. 30–75. Los Angeles: Natural History Museum of Los Angeles County.
Davis, James
  1961   *Trade Routes and Economic Exchange among the Indians of California. University of California Archaeological Survey Reports 54.* Berkeley: University of California.
Deetz, James D.
  1967   *Invitation to Archaeology.* New York: Natural History Press.
de Lumley, Henry
  1969   A Paleolithic Camp at Nice. *Scientific American* 220(5):42–56.
de Morgan, Jacques
  1926   *La Préhistoire Orientale: Tome II: L'Égypte et L'Afrique Du Nord.* Paris: Paul Geuthner.
Dibble, Harold L.
  1981   Technological Strategies of Stone Tool Production at Tabun Cave, Israel. Ph.D. diss., University of Arizona.
  1985   Technological Aspects of Flake Variation. *American Archaeology* 5(3):236–240.
  1987   The Interpretation of Middle Paleolithic Scraper Morphology. *American Antiquity* 52(1):109–117.
Dibble, Harold L., and John C. Whittaker
  1981   New Experimental Evidence on the Relation between Percussion Flaking and Flake Variation. *Journal of Archaeological Science* 8:283–298.
Dixon, J. E., J. R. Cann, and Colin Renfrew
  1968   Obsidian and the Origins of Trade. *Scientific American* 218(3): 38–46. Reprinted in *Old World Archaeology: Foundations of Civilization: Readings from* Scientific American, edited by C. Lamberg-Karlovsky, pp. 80–88. San Francisco: W. H. Freeman and Company, 1972.
Dunnell, Robert C.
  1978   Style and Function: A Fundamental Dichotomy. *American Antiquity* 43:192–202.
Eames, Frank
  1915   *The Fashioning of Flint.* Twenty-seventh Annual Report of the Ontario Provincial Museum, pp. 63–70. Toronto: A. T. Wilgress.
Eiseley, Loren C.
  1954   Man the Fire-Maker. *Scientific American* 191(3):52–57.
Elkin, A. P.
  1948   Pressure Flaking in the Northern Kimberley, Australia. *Man* 48(130):110.
Ellis, Florence Hawley
  1968   An Interpretation of Prehistoric Death Customs in Terms of Modern Southwestern Parallels. In *Collected Papers in Honor of Lyndon Lane Hargrave*, edited by A. Schroeder, pp. 57–76. Papers of the Archaeological Society of New Mexico, no. 1. Albuquerque: Archaeological Society of New Mexico.
Ellis, H. Holmes
  1939   *Flint-Working Techniques of the American Indians: An Experimental Study.* Reprint. Columbus: Ohio Historical Society, 1965.

Ericson, Jonathan E.
  1977a   Prehistoric Exchange Systems in California: The Results of Ob-
          sidian Dating and Tracing. Ph.D. diss., University of California, Los
          Angeles.
  1977b   Egalitarian Exchange Systems in California: A Preliminary View. In
          Exchange Systems in Prehistory, edited by Timothy Earle and J. E. Eric-
          son, pp. 109–126. New York: Academic Press.
  1978   Obsidian Hydration Dating in California. *Society for California Ar-
          chaeology Occasional Papers in Method and Theory in California Ar-
          chaeology* 2, pp. 44–52. Oxford: British Archaeological Reports.
  1981   *Exchange and Production Systems in Californian Prehistory: The
          Results of Hydration Dating and Chemical Characterization of Ob-
          sidian Sources.* British Archaeological Reports, International Series 110.
          Oxford: British Archaeological Reports.
Ericson, J. E., T. A. Hagan, and C. W. Chesterman
  1976   Prehistoric Obsidian in California II: Geologic and Geographic As-
          pects. In *Advances in Obsidian Glass Studies*, edited by R. E. Taylor,
          pp. 218–240. Park Ridge: Noyes Press.
Ericson, J. E., J. D. MacKenzie, and R. Berger
  1976   Physics and Chemistry of the Hydration Process in Obsidians I:
          Theoretical Implications. In *Advances in Obsidian Glass Studies*, edited
          by R. E. Taylor, pp. 25–45. Park Ridge: Noyes Press.
Ericson, Jonathan E., and Barbara A. Purdy (editors)
  1984   *Prehistoric Quarries and Lithic Production.* Cambridge: Cambridge
          University Press.
Ericson, Jonathan E., R. E. Taylor, and Rainer Berger (editors)
  1982   *Peopling of the New World.* Los Altos: Ballena Press.
Evans, Robert K.
  1978   Early Craft Specialization: An Example from the Balkan Chalco-
          lithic. In *Social Archeology: Beyond Subsistence and Dating*, edited by
          C. Redman et al., pp. 113–129. New York: Academic Press.
Fagan, Brian M.
  1983   *People of the Earth: An Introduction to World Prehistory.* 4th ed.
          Boston: Little, Brown, and Company.
Falconer, Steven F., and Bonnie Magness-Gardiner
  1989   Bronze Age Village Life in the Jordan Valley: Archaeological Investi-
          gations at Tell el-Hayyat and Tell Abu en-Ni'aj. *National Geographic Re-
          search* 5(3):335–347.
Faulkner, Alaric
  1972   Mechanical Principles of Flintworking. Ph.D. diss., Washington
          State University.
Findlow, Frank J., and Marisa Bolognese
  1980   An Initial Examination of Prehistoric Obsidian Exchange in Hidalgo
          County, New Mexico. *Kiva* 45(3):227–252.
  1982   Regional Modeling of Obsidian Procurement in the American South-
          west. In *Contexts for Prehistoric Exchange*, edited by J. E. Ericson and
          T. K. Earle, pp. 53–81. New York: Academic Press.
Fischer, Anders, Peter Vemming Hansen, and Peter Rasmussen
  1984   Macro and Micro Wear Traces on Lithic Projectile Points: Experi-
          mental Results and Prehistoric Examples. *Journal of Danish Archaeology*
          3:19–46.

Fitzwater, Robert J.
   1962   Final Report on Two Seasons' Excavations at El Portal, Mariposa County, California. *University of California, Los Angeles, Archaeological Survey Annual Reports 1961–62*, pp. 235–282. Los Angeles: University of California.
   1968a   Big Oak Flat; Two Archaeological Sites in Yosemite National Park: Excavations at Crane Flat. *University of California, Los Angeles, Archaeological Survey Annual Reports* 10, pp. 276–300. Los Angeles: University of California.
   1968b   Big Oak Flat; Two Archaeological Sites in Yosemite National Park: Excavations at the Hogdon Ranch Site (Tuo 236). *University of California, Los Angeles, Archaeological Survey Annual Reports* 10, pp. 303–311. Los Angeles: University of California.
Flenniken, J. Jeffrey
   1978   Reevaluation of the Lindenmeier Folsom: A Replication Experiment in Lithic Technology. *American Antiquity* 43(3):473–479.
   1981   *Replicative Systems Analysis: A Model Applied to the Vein Quartz Artifacts from the Hoko River Site.* Reports of Investigations, no. 59. Pullman: Washington State University Laboratory of Anthropology.
   1984   The Past, Present, and Future of Flintknapping: An Anthropological Perspective. *Annual Review of Anthropology* 13:187–203.
   1985   Stone Tool Reduction Techniques as Cultural Markers. In *Stone Tool Analysis: Essays in Honor of Don E. Crabtree,* edited by M. G. Plew, J. C. Woods, and M. G. Pavesic, pp. 265–276. Albuquerque: University of New Mexico Press.
Flenniken, J. Jeffrey, and Terry L. Ozbun
   1988   Experimental Analysis of Plains Grooved Abraders. *Plains Anthropologist* 33(119):37–52.
Flenniken, Jeff, L. W. Patterson, and Brian Hayden
   1979   More on Staging. *Flintknappers' Exchange* 2(1):26.
Flenniken, J. Jeffrey, and Anan W. Raymond
   1986   Morphological Projectile Point Typology: Replication, Experimentation, and Technological Analysis. *American Antiquity* 51(3):603–614.
Fletcher, Charles S.
   1970   Escapable Errors in Employing Ethnohistory in Archaeology. *American Antiquity* 35(2):209–213.
Flood, Josephine
   1983   *Archaeology of the Dreamtime: The Story of Prehistoric Australia and Her People.* Sydney: Collins.
Fogelman, Gary L.
   1988   *Projectile Point Typology for Pennsylvania and the Northeast.* Turbotville: Fogelman Publishing Company.
Ford, James A.
   1954a   Comment on A. C. Spaulding, "Statistical Techniques for the Discovery of Artifact Types." *American Antiquity* 19:390–391.
   1954b   The Type Concept Revisited. *American Anthropologist* 56(1):42–54.
Fox, Daniel E.
   1979   *The Lithic Artifacts of Indians at the Spanish Colonial Missions, San Antonio, Texas.* Special Report no. 8. San Antonio: Center for Archaeological Research, University of Texas at San Antonio.
Fox, William A.
   1984   Dhoukani Flake Blade Production in Cyprus. *Lithic Technology* 13(2):62–68.

Frank, Ted
1992 Flintknapping Indirect Percussion. *Chips* 4(2):8–9.
Fraser, Thomas H.
1908 Touching Aboriginal History. *Sports Afield* 40:67–69.
Frere, John
1800 Account of Flint Weapons Discovered at Hoxne in Suffolk. *Archaeologia* 13:204–205. Reprinted in *The Archaeologist at Work: A Source Book in Archaeological Method and Interpretation*, edited by R. Heizer, pp. 216–218. New York: Harper and Row, 1959.
Friedman, Irving, and William Long
1976 Hydration Rate of Obsidian. *Science* 191:347–352.
Friedman, Irving, Robert C. Smith, and Donovan Clark
1970 Obsidian Dating. In *Science in Archaeology*, edited by D. Brothwell and E. Higgs, pp. 62–75. New York: Praeger.
Friis-Hansen, Jan
1990 Mesolithic Cutting Arrows: Functional Analysis of Arrows Used in the Hunting of Large Game. *Antiquity* 64(244):494–504.
Frison, George C.
1968 A Functional Analysis of Certain Chipped Stone Tools. *American Antiquity* 33:149–155.
1978 *Prehistoric Hunters of the High Plains.* New York: Academic Press.
1982 A Probable Paleo-Indian Flint Knapping Kit from the Medicine Lodge Creek Site 48BH499, Wyoming. *Lithic Technology* 11(1):3–5.
1989 Experimental Use of Clovis Weaponry and Tools on African Elephants. *American Antiquity* 54(4):766–783.
Frison, George C., and Bruce A. Bradley
1980 *Folsom Tools and Technology at the Hanson Site, Wyoming.* Albuquerque: University of New Mexico Press.
1981 Fluting Folsom Projectile Points: Archeological Evidence. *Lithic Technology* 10(1):13–16.
Gallagher, James P.
1977 Contemporary Stone Tools in Ethiopia: Implications for Archaeology. *Journal of Field Archaeology* 4(4):407–414.
Gaxiola, Margarita, and John E. Clark (editors)
1989 *La Obsidiana en Mesoamérica.* Mexico City: Instituto Nacional de Antropologia e Historia.
Gero, Joan M.
1991 Genderlithics: Women's Roles in Stone Tool Production. In *Engendering Archaeology*, edited by J. M. Gero and M. W. Conkey, pp. 163–193. Cambridge: Basil Blackwell.
Geyer, Bob
1988 Heat Treating in a Roaster Oven (or Lithics in the Kitchen). *20th Century Lithics* 1:82–83.
Gibson, Eric C.
1982 Upper Paleolithic Flintknapping Specialists? The Evidence from Corbiac, France. *Lithic Technology* 11(3):41–49.
Gifford, E. W.
1936 Northeastern and Western Yavapai. *University of California Publications in American Archaeology and Ethnology* 34(4):247–354.
Gifford, James C.
1960 The Type-Variety Method of Ceramic Classification as an Indicator of Cultural Phenomena. *American Antiquity* 25:341–347.
1980 *Archaeological Explorations in Caves of the Point of Pines Region,*

Arizona. Anthropological Papers of the University of Arizona, no. 36. Tucson: University of Arizona Press.

Goddard, Pliny Earl
  1903–1904   Life and Culture of the Hupa. *University of California Publications in American Archaeology and Ethnology* 1(1):1–88.

Goffer, Zui
  1980   *Archaeological Chemistry: A Sourcebook on the Applications of Chemistry to Archaeology*. New York: Wiley.

Goldschmidt, Walter
  1951   Nomlaki Ethnography. *University of California Publications in American Archaeology and Ethnology* 42(4):303–443.

Gould, Richard A.
  1980   *Living Archaeology*. Cambridge: Cambridge University Press.
  1981   Brandon Revisited: A New Look at an Old Technology. In *Modern Material Culture: The Archaeology of Us*, edited by R. Gould and M. Schiffer, pp. 269–282. New York: Academic Press.

Gould, Richard A., Dorothy A. Koster, and Ann H. L. Sontz
  1971   The Lithic Assemblage of the Western Desert Aborigines of Australia. *American Antiquity* 36(2):149–169.

Gould, Stephen Jay
  1982   The Importance of Trifles. *Natural History* 91(4):16–23.

Gowlett, John
  1984   *Ascent to Civilization: The Archaeology of Early Man*. New York: Alfred A. Knopf.

Gowlett, John A. J.
  1984   Mental Abilities of Early Man: A Look at Some Hard Evidence. In *Hominid Evolution and Community Ecology: Prehistoric Human Adaptation in Biological Perspective*, edited by Robert Foley, pp. 167–172. London: Academic Press.

Green, F. E.
  1963   The Clovis Blades: An Important Addition to the Llano Complex. *American Antiquity* 29:145–165.

Green, H. Stephen
  1980   *The Flint Arrowheads of the British Isles*. British Archaeological Reports, British Series 75(i). Oxford: B.A.R.

Green, James P.
  1975   McKean and Little Lake Technology: A Problem in Projectile Point Typology in the Great Basin of North America. In *Lithic Technology: Making and Using Stone Tools*, edited by Earl Swanson, pp. 159–171. The Hague: Mouton.

Griffiths, D. R., C. A. Bergman, C. J. Clayton, K. Ohnuma, G. V. Robins, and N. J. Seeley
  1987   Experimental Investigation of the Heat Treatment of Flint. In *The Human Uses of Flint and Chert*, edited by G. Sieveking and M. Newcomer, pp. 43–52. Cambridge: Cambridge University Press.

Griffiths, D., and P. C. Woodman
  1987   Cretaceous Chert Sourcing in North East Ireland: Preliminary Results. In *The Human Uses of Flint and Chert*, edited by G. Sieveking and M. Newcomer, pp. 249–252. Cambridge: Cambridge University Press.

Gryba, Eugene M.
  1988   A Stone Age Pressure Method of Folsom Fluting. *Plains Anthropologist* 33(119):53–66.

Guernsey, Samuel J., and Alfred V. Kidder
    1921   *Basket-maker Caves of Northeastern Arizona. Papers of the Pea-
    body Museum of American Archaeology and Ethnology* 8(2). Cambridge:
    Harvard University Press.
Gunn, Joel
    1975   Idiosyncratic Behavior in Chipping Style: Some Hypotheses and Pre-
    liminary Analysis. In *Lithic Technology: Making and Using Stone Tools,*
    edited by E. Swanson, pp. 35–61. The Hague: Mouton.
    1977   Idiosyncratic Chipping Style as a Demographic Indicator: A Pro-
    posed Application to the South Hills Region of Idaho and Utah. In *The
    Individual in Prehistory,* edited by J. Hill and J. Gunn, pp. 166–204. New
    York: Academic Press.
Gurfinkel, D. M., and U. M. Franklin
    1988   A Study of the Feasibility of Detecting Blood Residue on Artifacts.
    Journal of Archaeological Science 15:83–97.
Hambly, Wilfrid D.
    1931   Types of "Tronattas" or Stone Implements Used by the Aborigines
    of Tasmania. *American Anthropologist* 33:88–91.
Hamilton, T. M.
    1972   *Native American Bows.* York: George Shumway Publishers.
Hammond, Norman
    1976   Maya Obsidian Trade in Southern Belize. In *Maya Lithic Studies,*
    edited by T. R. Hester and N. Hammond, pp. 71–82. Special Report no. 4.
    San Antonio: Center for Archaeological Research, University of Texas at
    San Antonio.
Harbottle, G.
    1982   Chemical Characterization in Archaeology. In *Contexts for Prehis-
    toric Exchange,* edited by J. E. Ericson and T. K. Earle, pp. 13–51. New
    York: Academic Press.
Harkness, Barbara M.
    1986   Results on the Experimental Replication of the Turner Earthworks
    Pit-and-Tunnel Systems. *Lithic Technology* 15(2):78–80.
Hardaker, Chris
    1979   Dynamics of the Bi-Polar Technique. *Flintknappers' Exchange*
    2(1):13–16.
Hardin, Margaret Ann
    1977   Individual Style in San José Pottery Painting: The Role of Deliberate
    Choice. In *The Individual in Prehistory,* edited by J. Hill and J. Gunn,
    pp. 109–136. New York: Academic Press.
Harry, Karen G.
    1989   The Obsidian Assemblage from Homol'ovi III: Social and Economic
    Implications. *Kiva* 54(3):285–296.
Harwood, Ray H.
    1986   California Points. *Ancient Man Information Exchange* 2:1–32.
Hayden, Brian
    1981   *Palaeolithic Reflections—Lithic Technology and Ethnographic Ex-
    cavation among Australian Aborigines.* Canberra: Australian Institute of
    Aboriginal Studies.
Hayden, Brian (editor)
    1979   *Lithic Use-Wear Analysis.* New York: Academic Press.
Heizer, Robert F. (editor)
    1976   *A Collection of Ethnographical Articles on the California Indians.*
    Ramona: Ballena Press.

Heizer, Robert F., and Thomas R. Hester
    1978   *Great Basin Projectile Points: Forms and Chronology.* Ballena Press
        Publications in Archaeology, Ethnology, and History, no. 10. Socorro: Bal-
        lena Press.
Heizer, Robert F., and Adan E. Treganza
    1944   Mines and Quarries of the Indians of California. *California Journal
        of Mines and Geology* 40(3):291–359.
Hellweg, Paul
    1984   *Flintknapping: The Art of Making Stone Tools.* Canoga Park: Can-
        yon Publishing Co.
Henderson, Julian (editor)
    1989   *Scientific Analysis in Archaeology and Its Interpretation.* Los Ange-
        les: UCLA Institute of Archaeology.
Hester, Thomas R.
    1972   Ethnographic Evidence for the Thermal Alteration of Siliceous
        Stone. *Tebiwa* 15:63–65.
    1974   Archaeological Materials from Site NV-WA-197, Western Nevada:
        Atlatl and Animal Skin Pouches. *Contributions of the University of Cali-
        fornia Archaeological Research Facility,* no. 21, pp. 1–43. Berkeley: Uni-
        versity of California.
    1989   Perspectives on the Material Culture of the Mission Indians of the
        Texas-Northeastern Mexico Borderlands. In *Columbian Consequences:
        Archaeological and Historical Perspectives on the Spanish Borderlands
        West,* edited by David H. Thomas, pp. 213–229. Washington, D.C.:
        Smithsonian Institution Press.
Hester, Thomas R. (editor)
    1978   *Archaeological Studies of Mesoamerican Obsidian.* Socorro: Bal-
        lena Press.
Hester, Thomas R., and Robert E. Heizer
    1973   *Bibliography of Archaeology I: Experiments, Lithic Technology, and
        Petrography.* Addison-Wesley Module 29. Reading: Addison-Wesley.
Hester, Thomas R., Robert F. Heizer, and R. N. Jack
    1971   Technology and Geological Sources of Obsidian from Cerro de las
        Mesas, Veracruz, Mexico, with Observations on Olmec Trade. In *Papers
        on Olmec and Maya Archaeology,* pp. 133–142. *Contributions of the
        University of California Archaeological Research Facility,* no. 13. Berke-
        ley: University of California.
Hester, Thomas R., and Harry J. Shafer
    1987   Observations on Ancient Maya Core Technology at Colha, Belize. In
        The Organization of Core Technology, edited by J. K. Johnson and C. A.
        Morrow, pp. 239–258. Boulder: Westview Press.
Hester, T. R., H. J. Shafer, J. D. Eaton, R. E. W. Adams, and G. Ligabue
    1983   Colha's Stone Tool Industry. *Archaeology* 36:45–52.
Hill, James N.
    1970   *Broken K Pueblo: Prehistoric Social Organization in the American
        Southwest.* Anthropological Papers of the University of Arizona, no. 18.
        Tucson: University of Arizona Press.
    1977   Individual Variability in Ceramics and the Study of Prehistoric So-
        cial Organization. In *The Individual in Prehistory,* edited by J. Hill and
        J. Gunn, pp. 55–108. New York: Academic Press.
Hill, J. N., and R. K. Evans
    1972   A Model for Classification and Typology. In *Models in Archaeology,*
        edited by David L. Clarke, pp. 231–273. London: Methuen.

Hill, James, and Joel Gunn (editors)
1977   *The Individual in Prehistory.* New York: Academic Press.
Hill, Willard Williams
1982   *An Ethnography of Santa Clara Pueblo, New Mexico.* Albuquerque: University of New Mexico Press.
Hodder, Ian
1982   *Symbols in Action: Ethnoarchaeological Studies of Material Culture.* Cambridge: Cambridge University Press.
Hodder, Ian (editor)
1987   *The Archaeology of Contextual Meanings.* Cambridge: Cambridge University Press.
1989   *The Meanings of Things: Material Culture and Symbolic Expression.* London: Unwin Hyman.
Hoffman, Michael Allen
1979   *Egypt before the Pharaohs: The Prehistoric Foundations of Egyptian Civilization.* New York: Dorset Press.
1987   Late Gerzean Ripple Flaked Knife. Cast EG-2. Lithic Casting Lab Catalogue no. 2. Troy: Lithic Casting Lab.
Hofman, Jack L.
1987   Hopewell Blades from Twenhafel: Distinguishing Local and Foreign Core Technology. In *The Organization of Core Technology,* edited by J. K. Johnson and C. A. Morrow, pp. 87–118. Boulder: Westview Press.
Holdaway, Simon
1989   Were There Hafted Projectile Points in the Mousterian? *Journal of Field Archaeology* 16(1):79–86.
Holland, John D.
1988   Some Dover Billets. *20th Century Lithics* 1:93–96.
Holland, William R., and Robert J. Weitlaner
1960   Modern Cuicatec Use of Prehistoric Sacrificial Knives. *American Antiquity* 25(3):392–399.
Holmer, Richard N., and Dennis G. Weder
1980   Common Post-Archaic Projectile Points of the Fremont Area. *State of Utah Antiquities Section Selected Papers* 7(16):55–68.
Holmes, W. H.
1890   A Quarry Workshop of the Flaked-Stone Implement Makers in the District of Columbia. *American Anthropologist,* o.s. 3(1):1–26.
1891   Manufacture of Stone Arrow-points. *American Anthropologist,* o.s. 4: 49–58.
1900   The Obsidian Mines of Hidalgo, Mexico. *American Anthropologist* 2(3):405–416.
1919   *Handbook of Aboriginal American Antiquities. Part 1: Introductory and the Lithic Industries.* Bureau of American Ethnology Bulletin 60. Washington, D.C.: Government Printing Office.
Honea, Kenneth
1983   *Lithic Technology: An International Annotated Bibliography 1725–1980.* Lithic Technology Special Publication no. 2. San Antonio: Center for Archaeological Research, University of Texas at San Antonio.
Howard, Calvin D.
1974   The Atlatl: Function and Performance. *American Antiquity* 39(1): 102–104.
1976   Atlatl Function: A Reply to Butler. *Plains Anthropologist* 21(74): 313–314.

1990   The Clovis Point: Characteristics and Type Description. *Plains Anthropologist* 35(129):255–262.

Howell, F. Clark
1965   *Early Man*. New York: Time-Life Books.

Huckell, Bruce B.
1979   Of Chipped Stone Tools, Elephants, and the Clovis Hunters: An Experiment. *Plains Anthropologist* 24(85):177–189.
1982   The Denver Elephant Project: A Report on Experimentation with Thrusting Spears. *Plains Anthropologist* 27(97):217–224.

Hughes, Richard E.
1986   *Diachronic Variability in Obsidian Procurement Patterns in Northeastern California and South Central Oregon*. Los Angeles: University of California Press.

Hunter, Wryley
1992   Reconstructing a Generic Basketmaker Atlatl. *Bulletin of Primitive Technology* 1(4):57–61.

Hyland, David C., and Thomas R. Anderson
1990   Blood Residue Analysis of the Lithic Assemblage from the Mitchell Locality, Blackwater Draw, New Mexico. *Plains Anthropologist* 35(130): 105–110.

Hyland, D. C., J. M. Tersak, J. M. Adovasio, and M. I. Siegel
1990   Identification of the Species of Origin of Residual Blood on Lithic Material. *American Antiquity* 55(1):104–111.

Iannone, Gyles John
1992   Ancient Maya Eccentric Lithics: A Contextual Analysis. M.A. thesis, Trent University, Peterborough, Ontario.

Ibarra, Raouel, and John Wellman
1988   Folsom Fluting: An Aboriginal Approach. *20th Century Lithics* 1:29–36.

Imel, Ivan
1988   Heat Treating West Texas Materials. *20th Century Lithics* 1:78–79.

Ives, David J.
1975   *The Crescent Hills Prehistoric Quarrying Area*. Museum Briefs, no. 22. Columbia: University of Missouri, Museum of Anthropology.

Jack, R. N.
1976   Prehistoric Obsidian in California: Geochemical Aspects. In *Advances in Obsidian Glass Studies*, edited by R. E. Taylor, pp. 183–217. Park Ridge: Noyes Press.

James, Steven R.
1989   Hominid Use of Fire in the Lower and Middle Pleistocene: A Review of the Evidence. *Current Anthropology* 30(1):1–26.

Jelinek, Arthur J.
1965   Lithic Technology Conference, Les Eyzies, France. *American Antiquity* 31:277–278.
1976   Form, Function, and Style in Lithic Analysis. In *Cultural Change and Continuity: Essays in Honor of James B. Griffin*, edited by C. E. Cleland, pp. 19–33. New York: Academic Press.
1982   Obituary: François Bordes, 1919–1981. *American Antiquity* 47(4):785–792.

Johnson, Jay K.
1976   Long Distance Obsidian Trade: New Data from the Western Maya Periphery. In *Maya Lithic Studies*, edited by T. R. Hester and N. Ham-

mond, pp. 83–90. Special Report no. 4. San Antonio: Center for Archeology Research, University of Texas at San Antonio.

Johnson, L. Lewis
1978   A History of Flint-Knapping Experimentation, 1838–1976. *Current Anthropology* 19(2):337–372.

Jolly, Clifford, and Fred Plog
1979   *Physical Anthropology and Archeology.* 2d ed. New York: Alfred A. Knopf.

Jolly, Fletcher, III
1970   Fluted Points Reworked by Later Peoples. *Tennessee Archaeologist* 26(2):30–44.

Jones, Rhys
1990   Hunters of the Dreaming: Some Ideational, Economic and Ecological Parameters of the Australian Aboriginal Productive System. In *Pacific Production Systems: Approaches to Economic Prehistory,* edited by D. Yen and J. Mummery, pp. 25–52. Canberra: Australian National University.

Jones, Rhys, and N. White
1988   Point Blank: Stone Tool Manufacture at the Ngilipitji Quarry, Arnhem Land 1981. In *Archaeology with Ethnography: An Australian Perspective,* edited by B. Meehan and R. Jones, pp. 51–87. Canberra: Highland Press.

Joyce, Daniel J.
1985   Heat Treatment of Alibates Chalcedony. *Lithic Technology* 14(1):36–40.

Jurmain, Robert, Harry Nelson, and William A. Turnbaugh
1984   *Understanding Physical Anthropology and Archeology.* 2d ed. St. Paul: West Publishing Company.

Justice, Noel D.
1987   *Stone Age Spear and Arrow Points of the Midcontinental and Eastern United States.* Bloomington: Indiana University Press.

Kalin, Jeffrey
1981   Flint Knapping and Silicosis. *Flintknappers' Exchange* 4(2):2–9.

Kamp, Kathryn A., and John C. Whittaker
1986   Unproductive Lithic Resources at Lake Mead. *American Antiquity* 51(2):383–388.
1990   Lizard Man Village: A Small Site Perspective on Northern Sinagua Social Organization. *Kiva* 55(22):99–125.

Keeley, Lawrence H.
1977   The Functions of Paleolithic Flint Tools. *Scientific American* 237:108–126. Reprinted in *Human Ancestors: Readings from* Scientific American, edited by G. Isaac and R. Leakey, pp. 102–109. San Francisco: W. H. Freeman, 1979.
1980   *Experimental Determination of Stone Tool Uses: A Microwear Analysis.* Chicago: University of Chicago Press.

Kelterborn, Peter
1981   The Livre de Beurre Method. *Flintknappers' Exchange* 4(3):12–20.
1984   Towards Replicating Egyptian Predynastic Flint Knives. *Journal of Archaeological Science* 11:433–453.

Keyser, James D., and John L. Fagan
1987   ESP: Procurement and Processing of Tongue River Silicified Sediment. *Plains Anthropologist* 32(117):233–256.

Knudson, Ruthann
  1982 Obituary, Don E. Crabtree, 1912–1980. *American Antiquity*
     47(2):336–343.
Kobayashi, Hiroaki
  1975 The Experimental Study of Bipolar Flakes. In *Lithic Technology:
     Making and Using Stone Tools,* edited by E. Swanson, pp. 115–127. The
     Hague: Mouton.
Krieger, A. D.
  1944 The Typological Concept. *American Antiquity* 9:271–288.
Kroeber, A. L.
  1905 Notes on "The Obsidian Blades of California" by H. N. Rust. *Ameri-
     can Anthropologist* 7:689–695.
  1925 Yurok Law and Custom. *Handbook of Indians of California.* Bureau
     of American Ethnology Bulletin 78. Reprinted in *The California Indians:
     A Source Book,* edited by R. F. Heizer and M. A. Whipple, pp. 336–368.
     Berkeley: University of California Press, 1951.
Kroeber, Theodora
  1961 *Ishi in Two Worlds.* Berkeley: University of California Press.
Laubin, Reginald, and Gladys Laubin
  1980 *American Indian Archery.* Norman: University of Oklahoma Press.
Laville, Henri, Jean-Philippe Rigaud, and James Sackett
  1980 *Rock Shelters of the Perigord: Geological Stratigraphy and Ar-
     chaeological Succession.* New York: Academic Press.
Leakey, Mary D.
  1971 *Olduvai Gorge. Vol. 3: Excavations in Beds I and II, 1960–1963.*
     Cambridge: Cambridge University Press.
Lewenstein, Suzanne M.
  1987 *Stone Tool Use at Cerros.* Austin: University of Texas Press.
Lewin, Roger
  1981 Ethiopian Stone Tools Are the World's Oldest. *Science* 211(4484):
     806–807.
  1988 *In the Age of Mankind.* Washington, D.C.: Smithsonian Books.
Lomberg, Ebbe
  1973 *Die Flintdolche Dänemarks: Studien über Chronologie und Kultar-
     beziehungen des Südskandinavischen Spätneolithikums.* Copenhagen:
     H. J. Lynge and Son.
Longacre, William A.
  1970 *Archaeology as Anthropology: A Case Study.* Anthropological Pa-
     pers of the University of Arizona, no. 17. Tucson: University of Arizona
     Press.
Luchterhand, Kubet,
  1970 *Early Archaic Projectile Points and Hunting Patterns in the Lower
     Illinois Valley.* Illinois State Museum Reports of Investigations, no. 19.
     Evanston: Illinois State Museum.
Luedtke, Barbara
  1978 Chert Sources and Trace-Element Analysis. *American Antiquity*
     43(3):413–423.
  1979 The Identification of Sources of Chert Artifacts. *American Antiq-
     uity* 44(4):744–756.
  1992 *An Archaeologist's Guide to Chert and Flint.* Los Angeles: Univer-
     sity of California Press.

Lyon, Caleb
    1859   How the Indians Made Stone Arrow Heads. *Historical Magazine*
        3:214.
Magne, Martin, and David Pokotylo
    1981   A Pilot Study in Bifacial Lithic Reduction Sequences. *Lithic Tech-
        nology* 10(2–3):34–47.
Magnusson, Magnus, and Hermann Palsson (translators)
    1965   *The Vinland Sagas: The Norse Discovery of America—Graen-
        lendinga Saga and Eirik's Saga.* Harmondsworth: Penguin Books.
Mandeville, M. D.
    1973   A Consideration of the Thermal Pretreatment of Chert. *Plains An-
        thropologist* 18(61):177–202.
Mandeville, M. D., and J. Jeffrey Flenniken
    1974   A Comparison of the Flaking Qualities of Nehawka Chert before and
        after Thermal Pretreatment. *Plains Anthropologist* 19(64):146–148.
Marsden, Barry M.
    1983   *Pioneers of Prehistory: Leaders and Landmarks in English Archae-
        ology (1500–1900).* Omskirk: G. W. and A. Hesketh.
Martin, Paul S., and Richard G. Klein (editors)
    1984   *Quaternary Extinctions: A Prehistoric Revolution.* Tucson: Univer-
        sity of Arizona Press.
McDonald, Mary M. A.
    1991   Systematic Reworking of Lithics from Earlier Cultures in the Early
        Holocene of Dakhleh Oasis, Egypt. *Journal of Field Archaeology* 18(2):
        269–273.
McGuire, Joseph D.
    1896   Classification and Development of Primitive Implements. *American
        Anthropologist,* o.s. 9:227–236.
McGuire, Randall H., John Whittaker, Michael McCarthy, and Rebecca
McSwain
    1982   A Consideration of Observational Error in Lithic Use-Wear Analysis.
        Lithic Technology 11(3):59–63.
McIlrath, Sharon
    1984   Obsidian Blades: Tomorrow's Surgical Tools? *American Medical
        News,* Nov. 2, 1984, pp. 29–30.
McPherson, John
    1987   *The Primitive Bow and Arrow.* Randolph: Prairie Wolf.
McPherson, John, and Geri McPherson
    1991   *Primitive Tools: Making and Using Them.* Randolph: Prairie Wolf.
McSwain, Rebecca
    1991   A Comparative Evaluation of the Producer-Consumer Model for
        Lithic Exchange in Northern Belize, Central America. *Latin American
        Antiquity* 2(4):337–351.
Mercer, R. J., and A. Saville
    1981   *Grimes Graves, Norfolk: Excavations 1971–1972.* Vol. 2. London:
        Her Majesty's Stationery Office.
Mewhinney, H.
    1957   *A Manual for Neanderthals.* Austin: University of Texas Press.
Michels, Joseph W., and Ignatius S. T. Tsong
    1980   Obsidian Hydration Dating: A Coming of Age. In *Advances in Ar-
        chaeological Method and Theory,* edited by M. B. Schiffer, 3:405–443.
        New York: Academic Press.

Midant-Reynes, Béatrix
1984 La Taille des Couteaux de Silex du Type Gebel-el-Arak et la Dénomination du Silex en Égyptien. In *Origin and Early Development of Food-Producing Cultures in North-Eastern Africa,* edited by L. Krzyzaniak and M. Kobnsiewicz, pp. 261–264. Poznan: Polish Academy of Sciences.

Moctezuma, Eduardo Matos
1988 *The Great Temple of the Aztecs: Treasures of Tenochtitlan.* London: Thames and Hudson.

Moffat, Charles R.
1981 The Mechanical Basis of Stone Flaking: Problems and Prospects. *Plains Anthropologist* 26(93):195–212.

Moholy-Nagy, Hattula, and Fred W. Nelson
1987 More Source Analyses of Obsidian from Tikal, Guatemala. *Lithic Technology* 16(1):13–21.

Moir, J. Reid
1917 The Position of Prehistoric Research in England. *Proceedings of the Prehistoric Society of East Anglia 2:* 381–391.
1919 *Pre-Paleolithic Man.* London: Privately published.

Monastersky, Richard
1990 Reopening Old Wounds. *Science News* 137(3):40–42.

Montelius, Oscar
1888 *The Civilization of Sweden in Heathen Times.* Reprint. New York: Haskell House Publishers, 1969.

Moratto, Michael J.
1972 *A Study of Prehistory in the Southern Sierra Nevada Foothills, California.* Ph.D. diss., Department of Anthropology, University of Oregon.
1984 *California Archaeology.* New York: Academic Press.

Morley, Sylvanus G.
1946 *The Ancient Maya.* Stanford: Stanford University Press.

Morrow, Carol A.
1987 Blades and Cobden Chert: A Technological Argument for Their Role as Markers of Regional Identification during the Hopewell Period in Illinois. In *The Organization of Core Technology,* edited by J. K. Johnson and C. A. Morrow, pp. 119–150. Boulder: Westview Press.

Morrow, Toby
1984 *Iowa Projectile Points.* Iowa City: University of Iowa.

Movius, Hallam L.
1968 Note on the History of the Discovery and Recognition of the Function of Burins as Tools. In *La Préhistoire: Problèmes et Tendances,* edited by F. Bordes and D. de Sonneville-Bordes, pp. 311–318. Paris: Centre Nationale de la Récherche Scientifique.

Muller, Jon
1977 Individual Variation in Art Styles. In *The Individual in Prehistory,* edited by J. Hill and J. Gunn, pp. 23–29. New York: Academic Press.

Müller, Sophus
1902 Flintdolkene i den Nordiske Stenalder. *Nordiske Fortidsminder* 1(5):125–180, Plates 23–28.

Muto, Guy R., Peter J. Mehringer, Jr., and Claude N. Warren
1976 A Technological Analysis of Projectile Points from a Burial, Amargosa Desert, Nevada. *Kiva* 41(3–4):267–276.

Nagle, Ed
    1914   Arrow-chipping by Means of Fire and Water. *American Anthropologist* 16:140.
Nations, James D.
    1989   The Lacandon Maya Bow and Arrow: An Ethnoarchaeological Example of Postclassic Lowland Maya Weapon Manufacture. In *La Obsidiana en Mesoamerica*, edited by M. Gaxiola and J. E. Clark,
    pp. 449–457. Mexico City: Instituto Nacional de Antropologia e Historia.
Nations, James D., and John E. Clark
    1983   The Bows and Arrows of the Lacandon Maya. *Archaeology* 36(1):36–43.
Needler, Winifred
    1984   *Predynastic and Archaic Egypt in the Brooklyn Museum*. New York: Brooklyn Museum.
Neill, Wilfred T.
    1952   The Manufacture of Fluted Points. *Florida Anthropologist* 5(1–2): 9–16.
Nelson, F. W., K. K. Nielson, N. F. Mangelson, M. W. Hill, and R. T. Matheny
    1977   Preliminary Studies of the Trace Element Composition of Obsidian Artifacts from Northern Campeche, Mexico. *American Antiquity* 42:209–225.
Nelson, Nels C.
    1916   Flint Working by Ishi. In *William Henry Holmes Anniversary Volume*, edited by Frederick W. Hodge, pp. 397–402. Washington, D.C.: J. W. Bryan Press. Reprint. New York: AMS Press, 1976.
Newcomer, M. H.
    1971   Some Quantitative Experiments in Handaxe Manufacture. *World Archaeology* 3(1):85–93.
    1975   "Punch Technique" and Upper Paleolithic Blades. In *Lithic Technology: Making and Using Stone Tools*, edited by E. Swanson, pp. 97–102. The Hague: Mouton.
Newcomer, Mark, R. Grace, and R. Unger-Hamilton
    1986   Investigating Microwear Polishes with Blind Tests. *Journal of Archaeological Science* 13:203–217.
    1987   Microwear Polishes, Blind Tests, and Texture Analysis. In *The Human Uses of Flint and Chert*, edited by G. Sieveking and M. Newcomer, pp. 253–263. Cambridge: Cambridge University Press.
Oakley, Kenneth P.
    1964   *Man the Tool-maker*. Chicago: University of Chicago Press.
Oakley, Kenneth P., Peter Andrews, Lawrence H. Keeley, and J. Desmond Clark
    1977   A Reappraisal of the Clacton Spearpoint. *Proceedings of the Prehistoric Society* 43:13–30.
O'Connell, James F.
    1967   *Elko Eared/Elko Corner-notched Projectile Points as Time Markers in the Great Basin*. University of California Archaeological Survey Reports 70. Berkeley: University of California, Berkeley.
Odell, George H., and Frank Cowan
    1986   Experiments with Spears and Arrows on Animal Targets. *Journal of Field Archaeology* 13(2):195–212.

Ohnuma, Katsuhiko, and Christopher Bergman
    1982   Experimental Studies in the Determination of Flaking Mode. *Bulletin of the Institute of Archaeology* 19:161–170.
Olsen, Larry D.
    1990   *Outdoor Survival Skills*. 5th ed. Chicago: Chicago Review Press.
Olsen, Sandra L.
    1979   A Study of Bone Artifacts from Grasshopper Pueblo AZ P:14:1. *Kiva* 44(4):341–373.
    1980   Bone Artifacts from Kinishba Ruin: Their Manufacture and Use. *Kiva*: 46(1–2):39–67.
Oxford University Press
    1971   *The Compact Edition of the Oxford English Dictionary*. Oxford: Oxford University Press.
Parkes, Penelope A.
    1987   *Current Scientific Techniques in Archaeology*. New York: St. Martin's Press.
Pasztory, Esther
    1983   *Aztec Art*. New York: Harry N. Abrams.
Patten, Bob
    1978   The Denver Series, Point #13: Eden. *Flintknappers' Exchange* 1(1):18–20.
    1979a   The Denver Series, #5, Folsom Point from Folsom, New Mexico. *Flintknappers' Exchange* 2(3):16.
    1979b   The Denver Series, Point #34: Blackwater Draw Clovis, New Mexico. *Flintknappers' Exchange* 2(2):5–6.
    1980   Folsom Staging: A Speculative Approach. *Flintknappers' Exchange* 3(2):7–10.
Patten, Bob, J. B. Sollberger, and L. W. Patterson
    1978   The Staging Problem. *Flintknappers' Exchange* 1(3):25–27.
Patterson, L. W.
    1978   Practical Heat Treating of Flint. *Flintknappers' Exchange* 1(3):7–8.
    1979a   Comments on Abrasion of Striking Platform Edges. *Flintknappers' Exchange* 2(3):7.
    1979b   Quantitative Characteristics of Debitage from Heat Treated Chert. *Plains Anthropologist* 24(85):255–259.
    1981a   Fracture Force Changes from Heat Treating and Edge Grinding. *Flintknappers' Exchange* 4(3):6–9.
    1981b   Stone Pressure Flaking Tools. *Flintknappers' Exchange* 4(3):10–11.
Patterson, Patience E.
    1977   A Lithic Reduction Sequence: A Test Case in the North Fork Reservoir Area, Williamson County, Texas. *Bulletin of the Texas Archaeological Society* 48:53–82.
Payen, Louis A.
    1982   Artifacts or Geofacts at Calico: Application of the Barnes Test. In *Peopling of the New World*, edited by J. E. Ericson, R. E. Taylor, and R. Berger, pp. 193–201. Los Altos: Ballena Press.
Peets, Orville
    1960   Experiments in the Use of Atlatl Weights. *American Antiquity* 26(1):108–110.
Pelegrin, Jacques
    1981   Experiments in Bifacial Work: About "Laurel Leaves." *Flintknappers' Exchange* 4(1):4–7.

Perrot, J.
    1968   *La Préhistoire Palestinienne: Extrait du Supplément au Diction-naire de la Bible.* Paris: Letouzey and Ané.
Pfeiffer, John E.
    1985   *The Emergence of Humankind.* 4th ed. New York: Harper and Row.
Pires-Ferreira, Jane
    1976   Obsidian Exchange in Formative Mesoamerica. In *The Early Meso-american Village,* edited by K. V. Flannery, pp. 292–306. New York: Academic Press.
Pond, Alonzo W.
    1930   Primitive Methods of Working Stone: Based on Experiments of Halvor L. Skavlem. *Logan Museum Bulletin* 2(1):1–143.
Pope, Saxton T.
    1918   Yahi Archery. *University of California Publications in Archaeology and Ethnology* 13(3):103–152.
    1923   *A Study of Bows and Arrows.* Berkeley: University of California Press.
    1974   Hunting with Ishi—The Last Yana Indian. *Journal of California Anthropology* 1(2):151–173. Reprinted from *Hunting with the Bow and Arrow.* San Francisco: J. H. Barry Co., 1923.
Purdy, Barbara Ann
    1974   Investigations Concerning the Thermal Alteration of Silica Minerals: An Archaeological Approach. *Tebiwa* 17(1):37–66.
Raftery, Joseph
    1951   *Prehistoric Ireland.* London: B. T. Batsford.
Ray, P. H.
    1886   Manufacture of Bows and Arrows among the Natano (Hupa) and Kenuck (Klamath) Indians. *American Naturalist* 20:832–833. Reprinted in *A Collection of Ethnographical Articles on the California Indians,* edited by R. F. Heizer, pp. 1–2. Ramona: Ballena Press, 1976.
Raymond, Anan
    1986   Experiments in the Function and Performance of the Weighted At-latl. *World Archaeology* 18(2):153–177.
Redding, B. B.
    1879   How Our Ancestors in the Stone Age Made Their Implements. *American Naturalist* 13(11):667–674.
    1880   Prehistoric Treasures. *Californian* 1:125–128. Reprinted in *A Collection of Ethnographical Articles on the California Indians,* edited by R. F. Heizer, pp. 18–22. Ramona: Ballena Press, 1976.
Reid, J. J., and Stephanie Whittlesey
    1990   The Complicated and the Complex: Observations on the Archaeological Record of Large Pueblos. In *Perspectives on Southwestern Prehistory,* edited by P. Minnis and C. Redman, pp. 184–195. Boulder: Westview Press.
Renfrew, Colin
    1977   Alternative Models for Exchange and Spatial Distribution. In *Exchange Systems in Prehistory,* edited by J. K. Earle and J. E. Ericson, pp. 71–90. New York: Academic Press.
Renfrew, Colin, and Paul Bahn
    1991   *Archaeology: Theories, Methods, and Practice.* New York: Thames and Hudson.

Renfrew, Colin, J. R. Cann, and J. E. Dixon
   1968   Further Analysis of Near Eastern Obsidian. *Proceedings of the Prehistoric Society* 34:319–331.
Ritchie, William A.
   1961   *A Typology and Nomenclature for New York Projectile Points.* New York State Museum and Science Service Bulletin 384. Albany: University of the State of New York, State Education Department.
   1969   *The Archaeology of New York State.* Garden City: Natural History Press.
Robicsek, Francis, and Donald M. Hales
   1984   Maya Heart Sacrifice: Cultural Perspective and Surgical Technique. In *Ritual Human Sacrifice in Mesoamerica,* edited by E. H. Boone, pp. 49–90. Washington, D.C.: Dumbarton Oaks.
Rolland, Nicolas, and Harold L. Dibble
   1990   A New Synthesis of Middle Paleolithic Variability. *American Antiquity* 55(3):480–499.
Romano, Tony, and Gene Altiere
   1992   If They Had It, They Used It. *The Platform* 4(4):7–8.
Rouse, Irving
   1960   The Classification of Artifacts in Archaeology. *American Antiquity* 25:313–323.
Rudebeck, Elisabeth
   1987   Flintmining in Sweden during the Neolithic Period: New Evidence from the Kuarnby-S. Sullerup Area. In *The Human Uses of Flint and Chert,* edited by G. Sieveking and M. Newcomer, pp. 151–158. Cambridge: Cambridge University Press.
Rust, Horatio N.
   1905   The Obsidian Blades of California. *American Anthropologist* 7:688–695.
Sackett, James R.
   1973   Style, Function, and Artifact Variability in Paleolithic Assemblages. In *The Explanation of Culture Change,* edited by C. Renfrew, pp. 317–325. London: Duckworth.
   1977   The Meaning of Style in Archaeology: A General Model. *American Antiquity* 42:369–380.
   1982   Approaches to Style in Lithic Archaeology. *Journal of Anthropological Archaeology* 1(1):59–112.
Schild, Romauld
   1987   The Exploitation of Chocolate Flint in Central Poland. In *The Human Uses of Flint and Chert,* edited by G. Sieveking and M. Newcomer, pp. 137–150. Cambridge: Cambridge University Press.
Schreiber, J. P., and W. J. Breed
   1971   Obsidian Localities in the San Francisco Volcanic Field, Arizona. *Plateau* 43(3):115–119.
Schumacher, Paul
   1877   *Stone-flaking of the Klamath River Yurok.* U.S. Geographical and Geological Survey, vol. 3, Bulletin 3(1877), Art. 17, pp. 547–549. Reprinted in *The California Indians: A Source Book,* edited by R. F. Heizer and M. A. Whipple, pp. 305–307. Berkeley: University of California Press, 1951.
Sellers, George Ercol
   1886   Observations on Stone-chipping. *Smithsonian Institution Annual*

Report for 1885, pp. 871–891. Washington, D.C.: Government Printing Office.

Semenov, S. A.
1973   *Prehistoric Technology: An Experimental Study of the Oldest Tools and Artifacts from Traces of Manufacture and Wear.* Bath: Adams and Dart.

Seton, Ernest T.
1903   *Two Little Savages.* New York: Doubleday Page and Company. Reprint. New York: Dover Publications, 1962.

Shafer, Harry J.
1985   A Technological Study of Two Maya Lithic Workshops at Colha, Belize. In *Stone Tool Analysis: Essays in Honor of Don E. Crabtree*, edited by M. Plew, J. Woods, and M. Pavesic, pp. 277–315. Albuquerque: University of New Mexico Press.
1991   Late Preclassic Formal Stone Tool Production at Colha, Belize. In *Maya Stone Tools*, edited by T. R. Hester and H. J. Shafer, pp. 31–44. Madison: Prehistory Press.

Shafer, Harry J., and Thomas R. Hester
1983   Ancient Maya Chert Workshops in Northern Belize, Central America. *American Antiquity* 48(3):519–543.
1986   Maya Stone-Tool Craft Specialization and Production at Colha, Belize: Reply to Mallory. *American Antiquity* 51(1):158–166.
1991   Lithic Craft Specialization and Product Distribution at the Maya site of Colha, Belize. *World Archaeology* 23(1):79–97.

Sharp, Lauriston
1952   Steel Axes for Stone Age Australians. *Human Organization* 11(2):17–22. Reprinted in *Conformity and Conflict: Readings in Cultural Anthropology*, 6th ed., edited by J. Spradley and D. McCurdy, pp. 389–403. Boston: Little, Brown and Company, 1987.

Shea, John J.
1988   Spear Points from the Middle Paleolithic of the Levant. *Journal of Field Archaeology* 15(4):441–450.
1992   Lithic Microwear Analysis in Archeology. *Evolutionary Anthropology* 1(4):143–150.

Sheets, Payson, Kenneth Firth, Fred Lange, Fred Stross, Frank Asaro, and Helen Michel
1990   Obsidian Sources and Elemental Analyses of Artifacts in Southern Mesoamerica and the Northern Intermediate Area. *American Antiquity* 55(1):144–158.

Sheets, Payson D., and Guy R. Muto
1972   Pressure Blades and Total Cutting Edge: An Experiment in Lithic Technology. *Science* 175: 632–634.

Shelford, P., F. Hodson, M. E. Cosgrove, S. E. Warren, and C. Renfrew
1982   The Obsidian Trade: The Sources and Characterization of Melian Obsidian. In *An Island Polity: The Archaeology of Exploitation on Melos*, edited by C. Renfrew and J. M. Wagstaff, pp. 182–192. Cambridge: Cambridge University Press.

Shepherd, Walter
1972   *Flint: Its Origins, Properties, and Uses.* London: Faber and Faber.

Shippee, J. M.
1963   Was Flint Annealed before Flaking? *Plains Anthropologist* 8(22):271–272.

Simpson, Ruth D.
   1982   The Calico Mountains Archaeological Project: A Progress Report.
      In *Peopling of the New World*, edited by J. E. Ericson, R. E. Taylor, and
      R. Berger, pp. 181–192. Los Altos: Ballena Press.
Singer, Clay, and Jonathon E. Ericson
   1977   Quarry Analysis at Bodie Hills, Mono County, California: A Case
      Study. In *Exchange Systems in Prehistory*, edited by Timothy Earle and
      Jonathon Ericson, pp. 171–188. New York: Academic Press.
Skertchly, Sydney B. J.
   1879   *On the Manufacture of Gun-Flints, the Methods of Excavating for
      Flint, the Age of Paleolithic Man, and the Connection between Neolithic
      Art and the Gun-Flint Trade*. Memoirs of the Geological Survey of En-
      gland and Wales. London: Geological Survey.
Smith, John
   1624   *The Generall Historie of Virginia, New England, and the Summer
      Isles*. London: Michael Sparkes. Reprint. New York: Macmillan, 1907.
Solecki, Ralph S.
   1971   *Shanidar: The First Flower People*. New York: Alfred Knopf.
Sollberger, J. B.
   1968   A Partial Report on Research Work Concerning Lithic Typology and
      Technology. *Bulletin of the Texas Archaeological Society* 39:95–109.
   1969   The Basic Tool Kit Required to Make and Notch Shafts for Stone
      Points. *Bulletin of the Texas Archaeological Society* 40:231–240.
   1976   Bifacing Patterns on Prismatic Flakes. *Bulletin of the Texas Ar-
      chaeological Society* 47:261–267.
   1977a   Fracture Theory, Applied to Flaking Forces and Lithic Analysis. Pa-
      per presented at Conference on Lithic Use-Wear, Simon Fraser Univer-
      sity, March 1977.
   1977b   On Fluting Folsom: Notes on Recent Experiments. *Bulletin of the
      Texas Archaeological Society* 48:47–52.
   1978   Lever Flaking as a Credible Alternative to Hand-Held Pressure Flak-
      ing. *Flintknappers' Exchange* 1(1):6–7.
   1979   Solly's Tip Sheet: Hand Anvils. *Flintknappers' Exchange* 2(1):9–10.
   1985   A Technique for Folsom Fluting. *Lithic Technology* 14(1):41–50.
   1986   Lithic Fracture Analysis: A Better Way. *Lithic Technology* 15(3):
      101–105.
Sollberger, J., and L. W. Patterson
   1976a   The Myth of Bipolar Flaking Industries. *Newsletter of Lithic Tech-
      nology* 5(3):40–41.
   1976b   Prismatic Blade Replication. *American Antiquity* 41(4):518–531.
   1980   Attributes of Experimental Folsom Points and Channel Flakes. *Bul-
      letin of the Texas Archaeological Society* 51:289–299.
   1986   Comments on Folsom Fluting Experiments by Boldurian et al. *Plains
      Anthropologist* 31(113):241–244.
Spaulding, A. C.
   1953   Statistical Techniques for the Discovery of Artifact Types. *Ameri-
      can Antiquity* 18:305–313.
   1954   Reply to Ford. *American Antiquity* 19:391–393.
Spence, Michael W.
   1967   The Obsidian Industry of Teotihuacan. *American Antiquity*
      32:507–514.
   1981   Obsidian Production and the State in Teotihuacan. *American An-
      tiquity* 46(4):769–788.

Spencer, Lee
   1974   Replicative Experiments in the Manufacture and Use of a Great Basin Atlatl. In *Great Basin Atlatl Studies*, edited by R. F. Heizer, pp. 37–60, Figures 13–19. Ramona: Ballena Press.
Speth, John D.
   1972   Mechanical Basis of Percussion Flaking. *American Antiquity* 37(1):34–60.
   1974   Experimental Investigations of Hard-Hammer Percussion Flaking. *Tebiwa* 17(1):7–36.
   1975   Miscellaneous Studies in Hard-Hammer Percussion Flaking: The Effects of Oblique Impact. *American Antiquity* 40(2):203–207.
   1981   The Role of Platform Angle and Core Size in Hard-Hammer Percussion Flaking. *Lithic Technology* 10(1):16–21.
Spurrell, F. C. J.
   1892   Notes on Early Sickles. *Archaeological Journal* 49:53–69.
Stafford, Barbara
   1980   Prehistoric Manufacture and Utilization of Lithics from Corduroy Creek. In *Studies in the Prehistory of the Forestdale Region, Arizona*, edited by C. R. Stafford and G. E. Rice, pp. 251–297. Anthro Field Studies, no. 1. Tempe: Arizona State University.
Stark, Barbara L., Lynette Heller, Michael D. Glascock, J. Michael Elam, and Hector Neff
   1992   Obsidian-Artifact Source Analysis for the Mixtequilla Region, South Central Veracruz, Mexico. *Latin American Antiquity* 3(3):221–239.
Steensberg, Axel
   1943   *Ancient Harvesting Implements: A Study in Archaeology and Human Geography*. Nationalmuseets Skrifter, Arckaeologisk-Historisk Raekke, vol. 1. Copenhagen: Nordisk Forlaq.
Stevenson, Christopher M., and Maria Klimkiewicz
   1990   X-Ray Fluorescence Analysis of Obsidian Sources in Arizona and New Mexico. *Kiva* 55(3):235–243.
Stiles, Daniel
   1979   Paleolithic Culture and Culture Change: Experiment in Theory and Method. *Current Anthropology* 20(1):1–21.
Straus, Lawrence G.
   1989   On Early Hominid Use of Fire. *Current Anthropology* 30(4):488–491.
Stuart, George E.
   1989   Copan, City of Kings and Commoners. *National Geographic* 176(4):488–505.
Suhm, D. A., and E. Jelks
   1962   *Handbook of Texas Archaeology: Type Descriptions*. Special Publication 1. Abilene: Texas Archaeological Society.
Swartz, B. K.
   1967   A Logical Sequence of Archaeological Objectives. *American Antiquity* 32:487–497.
Taçon, Paul S. C.
   1991   The Power of Stone: Symbolic Aspects of Stone Use and Tool Development in Western Arnhem Land, Australia. *Antiquity* 65:192–207.
Taylor, R. E. (editor)
   1976   *Advances in Obsidian Glass Studies*. Park Ridge: Noyes Press.
Thomas, David Hurst
   1970   Archaeology's Operational Imperative: Great Basin Projectile Points

as a Test Case. *University of California Archaeological Survey Annual Reports* 12:27–60. Los Angeles: University of California.

1976   A Diegueño Shaman's Wand: An Object Lesson Illustrating the "Heirloom Hypothesis." *Journal of California Anthropology* 3(1): 128–132.

1981   How to Classify the Projectile Points from Monitor Valley, Nevada. *Journal of California and Great Basin Anthropology* 3(1):7–43.

1983   *The Archaeology of Monitor Valley: 2. Gatecliff Shelter.* Anthropological Papers of the American Museum of Natural History Volume 59(1). New York: American Museum of Natural History.

1986   Points on Points: A Reply to Flenniken and Raymond. *American Antiquity* 51(3):619–627.

1989   *Archaeology.* 2d ed. Ft. Worth: Holt, Rinehart and Winston.

Tindale, Norman B.

1985   Australian Aboriginal Techniques of Pressure-Flaking Stone Implements: Some Personal Observations. In *Stone Tool Analysis: Essays in Honor of Don E. Crabtree,* edited by M. G. Plew, J. C. Woods, and M. G. Pavesic, pp. 1–33. Albuquerque: University of New Mexico Press.

Titmus, Gene

1980   Large Obsidian Boulder Reduction. *Flintknappers' Exchange* 3(3):21–22.

1985   Some Aspects of Stone Tool Notching. In *Stone Tool Analysis: Essays in Honor of Don E. Crabtree,* edited by M. G. Plew, J. C. Woods, and M. G. Pavesic, pp. 243–264. Albuquerque: University of New Mexico Press.

Titmus, Gene, and James C. Woods

1986   An Experimental Study of Projectile Point Fracture Patterns. *Journal of California and Great Basin Anthropology* 8(1):37–49.

1991   Fluted Points from the Snake River Plain. In *Clovis Origins and Adaptation,* edited by R. Bonnichsen and K. L. Turnmire, pp. 119–132. Corvallis: Center for the Study of the First Americans.

Tixier, J.

1974   *Glossary for the Description of Stone Tools, with Special Reference to the Epipalaeolithic of the Maghreb.* Translated by M. H. Newcomer. Newsletter of Lithic Technology Special Publication, no. 1.

Tobey, M. H.

1986   *Trace Element Analysis of Maya Chert from Belize.* Papers of the Colha Project, no. 1. San Antonio: Center for Archaeological Research, University of Texas at San Antonio.

Torrence, Robin

1986   *Production and Exchange of Stone Tools: Prehistoric Obsidian in the Aegean.* Cambridge: Cambridge University Press.

Tozzer, Alfred M.

1941   *Landa's Relación de las Cosas de Yucatán. Papers of the Peabody Museum of American Archaeology and Ethnography* 18. Cambridge: Harvard University Press.

Tringham, Ruth

1971   *Hunters, Fishers, and Farmers of Eastern Europe 6000–3000 B.C.* London: Hutchinson and Co.

Tringham, R., G. Cooper, G. Odell, B. Voytek, and A. Whitman

1974   Experimentation in the Formation of Edge Damage: A New Approach to Lithic Analysis. *Journal of Field Archaeology* 1:171–196.

Trinkhaus, Erik, and William W. Howells
1979   The Neanderthals. *Scientific American* 241(6):118–133.
Tsirk, Are
1979   Regarding Fracture Initiations. In *Lithic Use-Wear Analysis*, edited by Brian Hayden, pp. 83–96. New York: Academic Press.
Turner, Ellen Sue, and Thomas R. Hester
1985   *A Field Guide to Stone Artifacts of Texas Indians.* Austin: Texas Monthly Press.
Unger-Hamilton, Romana
1989   The Epi-Paleolithic Southern Levant and the Origins of Cultivation. *Current Anthropology* 30(1):88–103.
Upham, Steadman
1982   *Politics and Power: An Economic and Political History of the Western Pueblo.* New York: Academic Press.
Van Peer, Philip
1992   *The Levallois Reduction Strategy.* Madison: Prehistory Press.
Vaughan, Patrick
1985   *Use-Wear Analysis of Flaked Stone Tools.* Tucson: University of Arizona Press.
Waite, E. G.
1874   The First Trade. *Overland Monthly* 7:185–186.
Waldorf, D. C.
1984   *The Art of Flint Knapping.* 3d ed. Branson: Mound Builder Arts and Trading Co.
1988   The Flint Daggers of Denmark. *20th Century Lithics* 1:48–58.
Waldorf, D. C., and Valerie Waldorf
1985   *The Art of Making Primitive Bows and Arrows.* Branson: Mound Builder Books.
Waldorf, Valerie, and D. C. Waldorf
1987   *Story in Stone: Flint Types of the Central and Southern U.S.* Branson: Mound Builder Books.
Walker, Phillip L.
1978   Butchering and Stone Tool Function. *American Antiquity* 43(4):710–715.
Warren, S. Hazzledine
1914   The Experimental Investigation of Flint Fracture and Its Application to Problems of Human Implements. *Journal of the Royal Anthropological Institute* 44:412–450.
Watson, William, and G. de G. Sieveking
1968   *Flint Implements: An Account of Stone Age Techniques and Cultures.* London: British Museum Publications.
Weigand, Phil C.
1970   Huichol Ceremonial Reuse of a Fluted Point. *American Antiquity* 35:365–367.
1989   Notes Concerning the Use and Reuse of Lithic Materials among the Huicholes of Jalisco. In *La Obsidiana en Mesoamérica*, edited by M. Gaxiola and J. E. Clark, pp. 465–466. Mexico City: Instituto National de Antropologia e Historia.
Weisgerber, G.
1987   The Ancient Chert Mines at Wadi el-Sheikh (Egypt). In *The Human Uses of Flint and Chert*, edited by G. Sieveking and M. Newcomer, pp. 165–172. Cambridge: Cambridge University Press.

Weissner, Polly
  1983   Style and Social Information in Kalahari San Projectile Points. *American Antiquity* 48(2):253–276.
White, J. Peter
  1968   Ston Naip Bilong Tumbuna: The Living Stone Age in New Guinea. In *La Préhistoire: Problemes et Tendances*, edited by F. Bordes and D. de Sonneville-Bordes, pp. 511–517. Paris: Centre National de la Récherche Scientifique.
Whittaker, John C.
  1981   *Archeology in Yosemite National Park: The Wawona Testing Project*. Western Archeological and Conservation Center Publications in Anthropology, no. 18. Tucson: National Park Service, WACC. (Also available from the National Technical Information Service.)
  1984   Arrowheads and Artisans: Stone Tool Manufacture and Individual Variation at Grasshopper Pueblo. Ph.D. diss., University of Arizona.
  1987a   Individual Variation as an Approach to Economic Organization: Projectile Points at Grasshopper Pueblo, Arizona. *Journal of Field Archaeology* 14(4):465–480.
  1987b   Making Arrowpoints in a Prehistoric Pueblo. *Lithic Technology* 16(1):1–12.
Whittaker, John, Alan Ferg, and John Speth
  1988   Arizona Bifaces of Wyoming Chert. *Kiva* 53(4):321–334.
Whittaker, John C., and Harold Dibble
  1979   Systematic Aspects of Percussion Flaking: Evidence from Controlled Experiment. Paper presented at annual meeting of the Society for American Archaeology, Vancouver.
Whittaker, John C., and Lee Fratt
  1984   Continuity and Change in Stone Tools at Mission Tumacacori, Arizona. *Lithic Technology*. 13(1):11–19.
Whittaker, John C., and Kathryn A. Kamp
  1985   Drained Lakes and Small Sites: Rock Creek Lake. *Journal of the Iowa Archaeological Society* 32:91–102.
Whittlesey, Stephanie M.
  1978   Status and Death at Grasshopper Pueblo: Experiments toward an Archaeological Theory of Correlates. Ph.D. diss., University of Arizona.
Willey, Gordon R.
  1972   *The Artifacts of Altar de Sacrificios*. Papers of the Peabody Museum of American Archaeology and Ethnology 64(1). Cambridge: Harvard University Press.
Willey, Gordon R., and Jeremy A. Sabloff
  1974   *A History of American Archaeology*. San Francisco: W. H. Freeman.
Willig, Judith A.
  1991   Clovis Technology and Adaptation in Far Western North America: Regional Pattern and Environmental Context. In *Clovis: Origins and Adaptations*, edited by Robson Bonnichsen and Karen L. Turnmire, pp. 91–118. Corvallis: Center for the Study of the First Americans.
Witthoft, John
  1966   A History of Gunflints. *Pennsylvania Archaeologist* 36(1–2):12–49.
Wobst, H. Martin
  1977   Stylistic Behavior and Information Exchange. In *Papers for the Director: Research Essays in Honor of James B. Griffin*, edited by C. Cleland, pp. 317–342. New York: Academic Press.

Woods, James C.
  1987   Manufacturing and Use Damage on Pressure-Flaked Stone Tools.
  M.A. thesis, Idaho State University.
Wynn, Thomas
  1985   Piaget, Stone Tools, and the Evolution of Human Intelligence. *World
  Archaeology* 17(1):32–43.
Young, David E., and Robson Bonnichsen
  1984   *Understanding Stone Tools: A Cognitive Approach.* Orono: University of Maine.

INDEX

Acheulean industry, 27, Fig. 3.3. *See also* Handaxes
Africa, ethnographic, 51
Agate, 71, Fig. 4.1
Amateurs, 60–61, 62–63
Amorphous, 13, 65, 66
Analogy, archaeological use of, 280–281
Antler, 129, 131, 149, 180–181, Fig. 8.4, 221, 226, 246
Archaic: cultures, 43, 45; points, 44, Fig. 3.17, Fig. 11.1, 203, 262–268
Arrow points. *See* Points: arrow
Assemblages, definition, 25
Atlatls, 44–45, Fig. 3.18, 49, 248, 251, 256, 265
Australia: glass, 67; stone tools, 51, 85, 130, 289
Australopithecines, 23–25
Aztecs, 49, 177, Fig. 8.1

Basalt, 66, 69–70, 180, 270
Batons, 178, 180
Beginners: advice for, 1–2, 5, 7, 61–63, 74, 79, 85, 98–99, 117, 129, 133, 153, 206; problems of, 95, 98, 134, 140, 146–147, 166, 193
Bending fractures. *See* Fractures: bending
Beveling, 137, 141, 145, 237
Bifaces, 177–217; California, 178, 276–280; definition, 178; fracture, 212–217, 246; Grasshopper Pueblo, Fig. 8.22, 212–216; manufacture, 207–212; Solutrean, Fig. 3.8, Fig. 8.15, 190, 194; use, 246, 251, 253. *See also* Handaxes
Biface thinning flakes, 185–187, 276
Bifacial, definition, 19, Fig. 2.6
Bifacing, 136, 137
Billets, 178–180
Binfords, Lewis and Sally, 268–269
Bipolar flaking, 113–115, Fig. 6.32, Fig. 6.33
Bird points, 159

Blades: Bronze Age, 223–224, Fig. 9.4; crested, 221, 232, Fig. 9.13; definition, 33, 178, 219; gunflint, Fig. 3.22; manufacture, Fig. 3.27, 105, 219–233; Mesoamerican, Fig. 3.19, 49, 50, 221–223, 298; Upper Paleolithic, 33, Fig. 3.6, Fig. 3.7; uses, 219, Fig. 9.1
Blanks, 153–155, 201–202, 213, 277
Blood analysis, 285
Blow: angle of, 91, Fig. 6.6, 95–97, 98, Fig. 6.13, 109, 116, 188, 191, 198, 241–242; as arc, 107, 191, 193; force of, 91, 97–98, 106, 109, 116, 185, 187, 192–193, 227; soft-hammer, 191–193
Bonnichsen, Rob, Fig. 1.5
Bordes, François: 4, 58–60, Fig. 3.25, Fig. 3.27, 179, 225, 268–269, 290
Bow and arrow: 161, 250; experiments, 56, 256; Lacandon, 51, Fig. 3.21; origins, 49
Buffeting, 103, 141
Bulb of percussion: definition, 14; diffuse, 185, 189; large, 126, 224; negative, 15, 102, Fig. 6.21, 141, 145, 171, 173; use of, 101
Burins, 33, Fig. 3.7, 246; manufacture, 118–121; spall, 118
Butchering, 244–246, 257

California: bifaces, 178, 276–280; points, 55, Fig. 3.4, Fig. 11.5, 276–277, Fig. 11.6
Callahan, Errett, Fig. 1.6, 61, 66, 171, Fig. 7.50, 301
Centerplane, 133, 141, Fig. 7.12, 146, 156, 191, 196–197, 206, 207
Chalcedony, Fig. 4.1, 71
Chalcolithic, 40
Chase, Phillip, Fig. 6.3, Fig. 6.4, 244–248, 269
Chert: characteristics, 66, 67, 70–71, 274; heat-treatment, 74; sources, 70–71, 273, 296

Chest crutch, 221, Fig. 9.3, 235
Chopper, 25, Fig. 3.2
Clark, John, 223
Clovis: culture, 41–42; points, Fig. 3.14, 262
Colha, 49
Conchoidal fracture: definition, 12; principles, 14–15, 106–107
Cone: angle principle, 97, Fig. 6.14; Hertzian, 12, Fig. 2.1, 97; incipient, 17, 95, 115; split, 115
Context, 280–282
Copper knapping tools, 130, 175, 179, 180, 182, 199, 206, 221
Cores, Fig. 6.28, Fig. 6.29; amorphous, 113; bipolar, 113–115; blade, Fig. 3.19, 220–223, 225, 227–233; definition, 13, Fig. 2.2; hard-hammer, 113–116, Fig. 6.34; Levallois, 121–125; multidirectional, 113; starting, 113–115, Fig. 6.31, Fig. 6.34
Cortex: 70, 276; definition, 17
Crabtree, Don: 4, Fig. 1.5, 58–60, Fig. 3.25, Fig. 3.26, 61, 147, 219, 221–223, 232, 235; surgery, 19, 243
Cryptocrystalline, 65; definition, 13; silicates, 71–72. *See also* Chert; Flint
Cushing, Frank H., 1, 129

Danish daggers, 167, Fig. 7.45
Debitage: 20–21, 261, 291; analysis, 78, 212, 276–280; definition, 20; disposal of, 76–77, 83
Delta, 173, 175
Denticulates, 30, 268
Dibble, Harold, 4, 79, 80, 269, Fig. 11.16
Distal, 14
Doney, Carl, Fig. 7.20
Dust, 82–83

Eccentrics, Fig. 3.20, 177
Edge-bite, 189–190, 194
Edge damage. *See* Use-wear
Edge-ground cobble technique, 228
Egypt, 170, 173–176
Eklund, George, Fig. 8.22
Elf stones, 54
Ellis, Holmes, 57, 59
Eoliths, 17, 55
EPA, 91
Equipment. *See* Tools, knapping; Safety
Erraillures, definition, 15

Ethics, 75–76, 77, 83
Experiment, limitations of, 234, 267, 282–283

Facetting, 101, 104, Fig. 6.16, 224
Fakes, 77, 55
Feather termination, definition, 17
Flakes: curvature, 113; definition, 14, Fig. 2.2, Fig. 2.3; natural, 17; size, 91, 93, Fig. 6.8, 99; terminations, 17–19, Fig. 6.7, Fig. 6.13, 99, 106–111; variables, 91, Fig. 6.6. *See also* Biface thinning flake; Debitage
Flake scars, 15–16; as evidence, 15, 73, 126, 292–293; parasitic, 15; as ridges, 105, 221, 231, 232
Flenniken, Jeff, Fig. 1.5
Flint: characteristics, 66, 67, 70; sources, 70–71, 273
Flint Jack, 55, 127
Flintknapping, definition, 11–12
Fluted points, Fig. 3.14, Fig. 3.15, 41, Figs. 9.17–9.21. *See also* Clovis; Folsom
Flutes: functions of, 234–235; impact, 165; manufacture of, 236–242
Folsom points, 42, Fig. 3.15, 221, 241, 262
Foreshaft, Fig. 3.18, 248–256
Fracture: bending, 109, 134, Fig. 7.39, Fig. 7.40, 150, 151, 161, 163–165, 166, 189, Fig. 8.12, 213, 215–216, 246; of bifaces, 212–217; crenelated, Fig. 7.38; heat, 73, Fig. 7.38; impact, Fig. 7.38, 165; initiation of, 146, 188, 193, 194, 232; perverse, 165, Fig. 7.38, 213, Fig. 8.33; plunging, 165, 166, Fig. 7.38; points, 161–166. *See also* Conchoidal fracture
Function, analysis of, 270, 280–288

Gatecliff Shelter, 262–263, 267, Fig. 11.4
Gender roles, 294, 295, 297–298
Gerzian. *See* Egypt
Glass, Fig. 4.1, 67–68, 81, 85, 131, 133
Glue, 180, 251, 255
Grade scale, lithic, 66, Fig. 4.1
Grasshopper Pueblo: bifaces, Fig. 8.22, 212–216; points, 152, 159–163, 166, Fig. 7.43, Fig. 7.44, 212, 290, 291–297
Grimes Graves, 71
Grinding of surfaces, 167, 170, 175
Groove-and-snap, 251, 254

Ground stone, 39, Fig. 3.11
Gunflints, 11, 52, Fig. 3.22, Fig. 3.23, 55, 82, 88, 221

Hafting, 31, 234–235, 245, 246, 248–256
Hammerstones, 85–87, Fig. 6.1, Fig. 6.2, 93, 98, Fig. 7.1, 131, 135, 182, 187, 199, 228
Hand anvil, 151, 241
Handaxes, 27, Fig. 3.2, Fig. 3.3, 30, 121, 180, 185, 202, 261; discovery of, 54; functions of, 27, 282–283; manufacture of, 120–121
Handles. See Hafting
Hard-hammer percussion. See Percussion, hard-hammer
Heat-treatment, 72–74
Hinge termination: causes of, 107–109, 147, 166, 197; definition, 17
Holmes, W. H., 199
Homo erectus, 25–29, 121
Homogeneous, 12
Homo habilis, 24–25
Homo sapiens, 30, 40
Hopper, Jim, Fig. 1.6
Huckell, Bruce, Fig. 11.16
Hunt, Bob, Fig. 8.22, 302

Illustration, conventions of, 14, 15, 62
Index fossil, 261, 268
Indirect percussion. See Percussion, indirect
Industry: definition, 25
Injuries, 3, 69, 79–80. See also Safety
Ishi, 56, Fig. 3.24, 79, 81, 130–131, 140, 150, 256

Jasper, Fig. 4.1, 71

Knap-ins, 63, 74, 302–303
Knappers, illustrated. See Bonnichsen; Bordes; Callahan; Crabtree; Dibble; Doney; Eklund; Flenniken; Hopper; Huckell; Hunt; Ishi; McCartney; Ortega Vidal; Silsby; Solberger; Titmus; Whittaker; Wickham-Jones
Knives, sacrificial, 177, Fig. 8.1, Fig. 8.2

Lacandon, 51, Fig. 3.21
Lame à crête. See Blade, crested
Lanceolate points, 42
Laurel leaf. See Solutrean

Levallois technique, 30–31, Fig. 3.5, 121–125, Figs. 6.41–6.47
Levers, for fluting, 236–237
Limestone, 17, Fig. 4.1, 68, 70, 71, 180
Lips, 161, 185–187, 189, 215
Literature: how-to, 61; newsletters, 61–62
Lizard Man Village, Fig. 6.1, Fig. 6.2, Fig. 6.33, Fig. 11.1, 270
Lower Paleolithic, Fig. 3.1, 268. See *also* Acheulean; Oldowan

McCartney, Peter, Fig. 11.16
Materials: 65–78; analysis, 271–274; chemical composition, 13, 67, 271–274; collecting, 74–76; properties of, 12–14, 65–66, 73. See *also* Agate; Basalt; Chalcedony; Chert; Flint; Glass; Heat treatment; Jasper; Novaculite; Obsidian; Opal; Porcelain; Quarries; Quartz; Quartzite; Rhyolite; Slag
Maya, Fig. 3.20, 49, 177, Fig. 8.2, 199, 257
Meaning. See Symbolic meaning
Mechanical fracturing, 55, 87–90, 97
Megafauna, 32
Mesoamerica: cultures, 49; ethnographic, 51, Fig. 3.21, 126; obsidian, 50, Fig. 3.19, 48, 69, 177, 221–223, 273
Mesolithic, 37, Fig. 3.9, Fig. 3.10, Fig. 11.2
Metal: compared to stone, 19–20, 243; replacing stone, 50–54
Metamorphic rocks, 72
Microblades, manufacture of, Fig. 3.26, 232–234
Microflaking. See Use-wear
Microlith, 37, Fig. 3.9, Fig. 3.10
Midden, 275
Middle Paleolithic, Fig. 3.21, 268. See *also* Mousterian industry; Neanderthals
Mines. See Quarries
Missions, Spanish, 50
Mousterian industry, 30–31, Fig. 3.4, Fig. 3.5, 121, Fig. 6.41, 245, 268–270

Neanderthal, 30–31, 124, 269. See *lso* Mousterian industry
Neolithic, 39, Figs. 3.11–3.13, 70, 261; daggers, 167, Fig. 7.45. See *also* Points: Neolithic

Notching, 148–150
Novaculite, 72

Obsidian, 69, 81, 237, 270; Aegean, 272–273; blades, 49, Fig. 3.19, 50, 243; California, 273; exchange, 49, 271–273, 280; hydration, 273–274; knives, 177; scrapers, 51; sharpness, 19; sources, 69, 271–273, 276–277; Southwestern, 273. *See also* Meso-america: obsidian
Olduwan industry, 25, Fig. 3.2
Opal, 67
Ortega Vidal, Amado, Fig. 6.48
Outrepassé. See Overshoot
Overshoot: in blades, 229; definition, 19, Fig. 2.4; in points, 163

Paleo-Indian: cultures, 42; points, 41, Figs. 3.14–3.16, Fig. 7.46, 234–235, 262, Fig. 9.21. *See also* Clovis, Folsom
Patination, 70
Percussion: hard compared to soft, 185, 187; hard-hammer, 27, 85–126; in-direct, 33, 179, 221, 229–231, 237–239; soft-hammer, 27, 177–217
Percussors, 178
Petrified wood, Fig. 4.1, 71
Plateaus, 109, Fig. 6.28, 166, 213, 215, Fig. 8.34
Platforms: angle of, 91, 93, Fig. 6.6, 97, 98, 99, 101, Fig. 6.8, Fig. 6.16, 116, 133, 136, 152, 191, 223; definition of, 14; depth, 91, Fig. 6.12; flat biface, 197–198; for fluting, 237, Fig. 9.17, 242; isolation of, 104, Fig. 6.23, 146, Fig. 7.19, 194, 237; Levallois, Fig. 6.41, 123; normal biface, 196–197, 206; preparation of, 98–104, 140–147, 194–199, 223–224; soft-hammer, 185–187, 189, 191, steep biface, 198–199
Point of percussion, 14
Points: Archaic, 44, Fig. 3.17, Fig. 11.1, 203, 262–268; arrow, 152, 280–281, 282, 291, 294; British, 262, Fig. 11.2, Fig. 11.3; Bronze Age, Fig. 11.3, Fig. 11.8; California, Fig. 11.5, 276–277, Fig. 11.6; Cottonwood Triangu-lar, Fig. 11.4, Fig. 11.5, 276; Desert Side-notched, Fig. 11.4, Fig. 11.5, 276–277; Elko, 265, 267–268, Fig. 11.4; experiments with, 165,

256, 265, 267; fracture, 161–166; function, 159, 161, 165, 281, 283, Fig. 11.9, 291; Grasshopper, 152, 159–163, 166, Fig. 7.43, Fig. 7.44, 212, 291–297; Great Basin, Fig. 11.4, 262–263, 276; Ishi, Fig. 3.24; La-candon, Fig. 3.21, 51; manufacture, 152–161; Mesolithic, Fig. 3.10, Fig. 11.2; Mousterian, Fig. 3.5, 31; Neolithic, 127, Fig. 9.1, Fig. 11.2, Fig. 11.3, Fig. 11.8; Paleo-Indian, 41, 42, Fig. 3.14–3.16, Fig. 7.46, 171, Fig. 9.21; Sinagua, Fig. 11.1, Fig. 11.8; types, 262–268; Upper Paleolithic, 33, Fig. 3.7. *See also* Clovis; Folsom
Polish. *See* Use-wear
Porcelain, Fig. 4.1, 68, 85
Potlids, 73, Fig. 7.38
Preform, 153, 156–157, 202
Pressure flaking, 127–176; definition, 33; patterned, 166–176
Projectile points. *See* Points
Proximal, 14
Punches, 221, 224, 226–229, 230, 238–239

Quarries, 76, 176, 202, 277, Fig. 11.7; Aegean, 272; Great Basin, 276–277; Grimes Graves, 71
Quartz, Fig. 4.1, 66, 67, 69
Quartzite, Fig. 4.1, 66, 72, 180

Radial fissures, definition, 15
Replication, definition, 12, 235
Resharpening, 283, Fig. 11.9, 290
Residues. *See* Use-wear
Retouch, 20; definition, 19
Reworking, 264, 265, 267
Rhyolite, 33, Fig. 4.1, 67, 69–70
Ridges, 105–106, Fig. 6.24, 147, Fig. 8.14, 221, 231, 237
Ring crack, 14
Ripples, 14
Rubbing, 102–104

Safety, 79–83, 85, 93, 131, 183, 251. *See also* Injury
Scrapers: definition, Fig. 2.5, 27; manu-facture, 116–118; Mousterian, 30, Fig. 3.4, Fig. 3.5, 268–269; use, 246, Fig. 10.5, 254, Fig. 11.12, Fig. 11.13
Shaft smoother, 254
Shatter: definition, 21

Shearing, 141
Sickles, Fig. 3.9, Fig. 3.12, Fig. 3.13, 40, 223, 285, Fig. 11.12, Fig. 11.14
Signing work, Fig. 2.6, 77–78
Silica, 67, 70, 72. *See also* Materials: chemical composition
Silicosis, 82
Silsby, Scott, 170, Fig. 7.47
Sinew, 235, 255
Skertchly, Sidney, 55
Slabbing, 77
Slag, 68, 79
Soft-hammer percussion. *See* Percussion, soft-hammer
Sollberger, J. B., Fig. 1.4
Solutrean, 33, Fig. 3.6–3.8, Fig. 8.15, 190, 194
Sous le pied, 225
South America, 51
Specialists, prehistoric, 49, 176, 296–297, 298
Stacks, 109
Staging, 152–153, 199–201
Step fracture: causes of, 107–109, 147, 193, 215, 227; definition, 17, Fig. 2.4
Stratigraphy, 262, 263–264, 268–269
Style, 263, 270–271, 289–291
Support, 92, 115, 134, 151, Fig. 7.39, 183–185, 216, 217, 236, 238, 242
Symbolic meaning, 51, 54, 176, 177–178, 264, 282, 289, 294–295

Teotihuacan, 49
Terminations. *See* Feather termination; Flake termination; Hinge termination; Overshoot; Step fracture
Thinning by pressure, 147–148
Tines. *See* Antler
Titmus, Gene, Fig. 1.4

Tixier, Jacques, 59, 225
Tools, knapping: Fig. 4.1, 85–87, Fig. 6.1, Fig. 6.2, 129–131, 149, 150–151, 175, 178–183, 221–223, 226–229, 236–237
Trace-element analysis, 271–272, 273
Trimming, 101–104, Fig. 6.18, Fig. 6.19, 223–224
Turning the edge, 136, 137, Fig. 7.10, 154, 201
Typology: dating, 261–268; theory, 260–261; type names, 27, 262, 280

Unifacial, 19, Fig. 2.5
Upper Paleolithic, 31–33, Fig. 3.6–3.8, 41
Use-wear, 243; analysis, 257, 283–288; on hammerstones, 87, Fig. 6.2

Vices, 221, 225–226, 232, 236

Waldorf, D. C., 61, 301
Wawona, 274–280
Weathering, 70
Whittaker, John: Fig. 1.1–1.3, Fig. 2.5–2.7, Fig. 6.24, Fig. 6.29, 6.34–6.40, Fig. 6.42–6.47, Fig. 7.20, Fig. 7.26–7.33, Fig. 7.46, Fig. 8.23–8.30, Fig. 9.7–9.15, Fig. 9.17, Fig. 9.19, Fig. 9.20, Fig. 11.6, Fig. 11.8, Fig. 11.16
Wickham-Jones, Caroline, Fig. 11.16
Women. *See* Gender roles
Wood: working with stone, 27, 246, 251–254, 256, 257; knapping tools, Fig. 4.1, 130, 180–181

Yosemite. *See* Wawona